SURGEON TO WASHINGTON

DR. JOHN COCHRAN

1730–1807

☙

DR. JOHN COCHRAN

Director General of Military Hospitals etc.

SURGEON TO WASHINGTON

DR. JOHN COCHRAN ❧ 1730–1807

MORRIS H. SAFFRON

1977

NEW YORK

COLUMBIA UNIVERSITY PRESS

LIBRARY OF CONGRESS CATALOGING IN PUBLICATION DATA

Saffron, Morris Harold.
Surgeon to Washington, Dr. John Cochran (1730–1807)

Bibliography: p.
Includes index.
1. Cochran, John, 1730–1807. 2. Physicians—United States—Biography. 3. United States—History—Revolution, 1775–1783—Medical and sanitary affairs. I. Title.
R154.C43S23 616.9'8023'0924 [B] 77-2675
ISBN 0-231-04186-1

Columbia University Press
New York Guildford, Surrey
 Printed in the United States of America

IN MEMORIAM

A ❧ B ❧ C

FOREWORD

Historians of the American Revolution have often commented on the apparent scarcity of authentic source material on which to base a sound judgment of the quality of medical care during the years of struggle. It is true that our early physician-historians were content to sing the praises of such heroes as Joseph Warren and Hugh Mercer while pointing with solemn pride to the fact that the war cost the lives of more surgeons than generals. Naturally these latter-day hagiographers were quick to brush aside disconcerting rumors connecting key figures in the Medical Department with such practices as nepotism, speculation in commodities, and political maneuvering for sinecures.

Today, fortunately, a clearer picture is developing as qualified social historians find renewed interest in the development of medicine during the late colonial and Revolutionary decades. It is our hope that the publication of the war correspondence of Surgeon General John Cochran will give added insight into such vexing problems as departmental morale, threats of resignation, chronic shortages and frequent misuse of supplies, antagonism between regimental and hospitals surgeons, and the uncertain relationship between medical officers and the line.

As for Cochran himself, only one who has studied his remarkable record of activities during the war years is in a position to contrast his motivation and energy with the relative indolence of William Shippen, his immediate predecessor. Held in high esteem by Washington, Lafayette, and other members of the commander in chief's official family, Cochran remained on excellent terms with James Craik, William Burnet, David Oliphant, and other leaders of the medical establishment. While John Morgan, Shippen, and Benjamin Rush were amusing and eventually offending the general public with the charges and countercharges of their poison-pen newspaper war, Cochran, "happily divorced from the internecine bickerings of the Philadelphia medicos," continued to work faithfully and unswervingly for his country and the cause of independence. Even Congress, disaffected by the Shippen regime to the point of incredible parsimony with regard to the Medical Department, was gradually won over by Cochran's obvious sincerity. Those who read the letters will agree that no single person could have worked more conscientiously for the officers under his command and for the sick and wounded who were their joint responsibility.

Although no one would deny the importance to American medical education of the overly publicized triumvirate of Philadelphia professors, the time has come to recognize the stark truth that as leaders of the medical services during our Revolution, they were all, for one reason or another, considered by their contemporaries to be failures. Only one man retired from the office of Surgeon General with the universal admiration of his co-workers and an unsullied reputation, and it is this man, John Cochran, who deserves a more universal recognition from his countrymen than he has hitherto been accorded.

MORRIS H. SAFFRON, M.D., PH.D.

New York City
February 1977

ACKNOWLEDGMENTS

During the years spent on this work I have accumulated a multitude of obligations. First I should like to thank Mrs. Franklin B. Manierre, a lineal descendant of John Cochran, who kindly gave me permission to publish the Letter-Book of her famous ancestor and loaned interesting material relating to the family. I owe an especial debt of gratitude to Miss Gertrude Annan, Librarian Emeritus of the New York Academy of Medicine and a friend of many years. It was Miss Annan who, when I was still unaware of its location, produced the manuscript from the Rare Book Room and loaned me the typescript and notes she had prepared for a projected edition. I am also grateful to Mrs. George W. Jacobs and Mrs. John Pelehaut, local historians of Cochranville, Pennsylvania; Mr. W. S. Roberts of Philadelphia; Mr. James P. Mitchell of Atlanta, Georgia; Mr. Hamilton Cochran of Wallingford, Pennsylvania; Mr. Edward Pinkowski of the Philadelphia Historical Commission; and to Professors E. James Ferguson and John Catanzariti, co-editors of *The Papers of Robert Morris.*

Others who gave encouragement to my efforts include Dr. William J. McGill, President of Columbia University; Dr. Stanley S. Bergen, Jr., President of the College of Medicine and Dentistry of New Jersey; and three friendly medical historians, Drs. William B. Ober, Fred B. Rogers, and William B. Stark. I should also like to acknowledge my gratitude to Mr. Richard Steins of Columbia University Press, who managed to make a difficult manuscript ready for the printer. I am happy to acknowledge that publication of this book was assured by a generous grant from the Josiah Macy, Jr. Foundation, Dr. John Z. Bowers, President.

Among institutions my primary obligation is to the library staff of The New-York Historical Society, and especially to Sue A. Gilles, Thomas J. Dunnings, Jr., and Roger Mohovich, who displayed unending patience in answering my innumerable requests. Other institutions and individuals to whom I am indebted include:

American Antiquarian Society (Marcus A. McCorison)
American Philosophical Society Library (Whitford J. Bell, Jr.)

Bard College (Margrit Libbin)

Boston Public Library (James Lawton)

Chester County Historical Society (Jeffrey Winant, Rosemary B. Philips)

Columbia University Libraries (Kenneth A. Lohf, Bernard R. Crystal)

The Library of Congress (Roy P. Basler)

Connecticut State Library (Linda S. Winters)

Daughters of the American Revolution (Sarah M. King)

Delaware Hall of Records (Elizabeth Moyne)

Duke University Medical Center Library (G. S. T. Cavanagh)

Harvard University—The Houghton Library (Marte Shaw)

Historical Society of Pennsylvania (Peter J. Parker, Robert Greene)

Henry E. Huntington Library (Daniel H. Woodward)

Lancaster County Historical Society (Laura G. Lundgren)

Massachusetts Historical Society (Stephen T. Riley)

Morristown National Park Library (Bruce Stewart)

National Archives and Record Service (Elmer O. Parker)

Newark Public Library (Charles F. Cummings, Miriam V. Studley)

The New Jersey Historical Society (Robert C. Morris, Don C. Skemer, E. Richard McKinstry)

The New Jersey State Library (David C. Munn, Rebecca B. Colesar)

The New York Academy of Medicine (Alice B. Weaver, Sali Morgenstern, Elliott D. Zak)

The New York Public Library (Paul R. Rugen, Jean R. McNeice)

The New York State Library (Peter Christoph, Lee Stanton)

The Oneida Historical Society (Elizabeth Kroll)

The Presbyterian Historical Society (Sheila Hallowell)

The Rhode Island Historical Society (Nathaniel N. Shipton)

Rutgers University Library (Donald A. Sinclair, Clark L. Beck, Jr.)

Syracuse University—The George Arents Research Library (Sara B. McCain)

The University of Michigan—William L. Clements Library (William S. Ewing)

Valley Forge Historical Society (John F. Reed)

Yale University Library (Judith A. Schiff)

Yale University Library—The Beinecke Rare Book and Manuscript Library (Herman W. Liebert, Christina M. Hanson)

CONTENTS

LIST OF ILLUSTRATIONS

Abbreviations

GW	George Washington
JC	John Cochran
PS	Philip Schuyler
WL	Walter Livingston

CUL	Columbia University Libraries, New York
HSP	Historical Society of Pennsylvania Library, Philadelphia
LC	Library of Congress, Washington, D.C.
NA	National Archives, Washington, D.C.
NJHS	New Jersey Historical Society Library, Newark, New Jersey
NYHS	New-York Historical Society Library, New York
NYPL	New York Public Library, New York

LIFE

Family and Youth

The return of Mary Stuart to Scotland in 1561 raised at once the spectre of a new religious war and again placed dissenters in a tenuous position. Although Mary was forced to abdicate in 1567 and the Protestant Establishment was reaffirmed, the country remained in a state of political and economic turmoil. As a consequence a few hardy souls in search of freedom and fortune decided to venture across the narrow Irish Sea to Ulster, many years before the "Great Plantation" of James I (1609) brought waves of Scottish Presbyterians to northern Ireland.

Among these self-uprooted Scotsmen was one John Cochran (or Cochrane) who, according to tradition, left the family seat at Fernois, a small locality near Paisley, as early as 1570. He owed allegiance to the Lairds of Dundonald, claiming direct kinship with the head of that powerful Renfrewshire house which was later to be elevated to an earldom.[1]

Patriarch John was evidently a man of vigor and determination. After settling in the Lough Foyle region of County Derry, he and his three sons became progenitors of a large number of descendants, many of whom seem to have successfully survived the civil war of 1641 which claimed the lives of 15,000 settlers. For a century and a half the Cochrans continued to oversee salmon fisheries or cultivate the low plains of their adopted land in a modest way, either as yeomen or members of the lesser gentry.[2]

During this interval nearby Londonderry had become the center of a flourishing textile industry, thus bringing added prosperity to the entire region. But such a potential rival to their own industry could not long be tolerated by the English manufacturers. Britain, consequently, "in her industrial madness," began to press restrictive legislation on the commerce and navigation of the Ulster Scots similar to

1. An early 15th-century John Cochrane is the first member of the family identified in *Burke's Peerage* (1956 ed., p. 170). See also Wickes, p. 210.

2. For the earliest records of this branch of the Cochrans, see "A Genealogical Account of the Cochran Family in Ireland and America" (MS, Presbyterian Historical Society, Philadelphia). See also Walter Biddle (a great-grandson of Cochran), pp. 241–42, and Scharf, 2: 999–1000.

that which was later to alienate the American colonies. As land leases expired, rent-racking by absentee English owners reduced formerly prosperous farmers to abject poverty. Added to these economic woes, which affected both artisan and farmer alike, were the civil indignities imposed on all those who, like the Cochrans, did not adhere to the Anglican church. The fierce anti-British animus, which to a man motivated the Scotch-Irish émigrés to go to America and later made them "hot for rebellion," was certainly based on valid grounds.

Their exodus to the colonies, which began early in the eighteenth century, is a phenomenon of undisputed importance in our pre-Revolutionary history. True to their frontier tradition, the majority refused to settle in the towns but headed for Pennsylvania, where land hunger could easily be satisfied and religious freedom was assured. James Logan, secretary to the Penns, wrote: "It looks as if Ireland is to send all its inhabitants hither for last week six ships arrived, and every day two or three arrive also." [3]

It is not clear exactly when our own James Cochran (1698–1766) and his relatives, Stephen and David, arrived in Pennsylvania. One local authority, H. F. C. Heagey, has them landing in New Castle before 1720 and migrating northward along the trail of the Indian traders into Lancaster County, having been "pushed out by the Penns" into the dangerous frontier along the Susquehanna River. Concerned with the growing threat of Indian massacres, the Cochrans withdrew to the relative safety of Chester County, where they settled on unoccupied land bordering the Octorara, the "rippling current" which was later (1729) to become the boundary between Chester and Lancaster counties.[4]

The aggressive Scotch-Irish settlers, being prone to seize vacant land on which they paid no taxes and from which few had the temerity to evict them, made the Quakers uneasy. James Cochran was

3. Orth (pp. 10–12) speaks of the Scotch-Irish migration as the most important and influential influx of non-English stock into the colonies.

4. Heagey's opinion cannot be reconciled with the data in the "Genealogical Account," where the emigrants are called cousins rather than brothers (p. 5), and is at variance with that of another local historian, Harry K. Wilson, who believes that our Cochrans arrived in Chester County after 1720, the year of the founding of the Upper Octorara church. The largely unpublished writings of these two men, preserved at the Chester County Historical Society, West Chester, Pa., form the basis for much that follows.

certainly among this unruly lot. In May 1723 he married Isabella, a Cochran cousin, and by 1724 his name appears for the first time on the assessment rolls of Fallowfield Township as the owner of a house facing the Limestone Road, which was then being laid down. This road made the entire area more accessible to New Castle and its shipping, and the astute James quickly foresaw the importance of a triangular piece of land near the junction of the Gap and Newport Turnpike, the Limestone Road, and a Shawnee trail leading from Maryland to Berks County. At this crossroads he later laid the foundation of the original Cochran tavern which, with its successor, was to serve as a community center for nearly a century.[5] In 1725, James was named an executor of the will of another settler of Scotch-Irish stock, one Cornelius Rowan, a man of considerable substance who had fled from Ireland to "preserve his wealth and life." Rowan, who seems to have assisted the Cochrans financially, owned a corn-grinding mill as well as a desirable tract in Fallowfield Township. When Rowan died in 1725, James, with dubious propriety, immediately took possession of this contiguous property, resisting all attempts of the rightful Irish heirs to evict him. He finally gained full possession some twenty years later by paying them the insignificant quit fee of forty-five pounds.[6]

John Cochran was born within the confines of what is now Cochranville, West Fallowfield Township, Chester County, Pennsylvania on September 1, 1730. The two local historians differ as to the exact site of his birthplace, one opting for the family farmhouse, the foundation of which can still be identified about one mile southeast of the village center, the other insisting that John's birth took place in his father's tavern at the crossroads.[7]

By the time this fourth child and third son was born, James

5. The Cochrans divided the tract of Sarah Fallowfield, after whose family the township took its name. The triangular tract formed by the intersection of the Limestone Road (present Route 10), the Gap and Newport Turnpike (present Old Route 41), and a Shawnee trail, became the center of the 100-acre tract forming the site of present-day Cochranville. James eventually held 430 acres, some of which were not patented until 1745.

6. Will Book I, p. 173 (Chester County Court House, Chester, Pa.); the Rowan tract was surveyed May 27, 1732.

7. It seems reasonable to agree with Wilson that John was born in the farmhouse rather than in the primitive tavern of 1730, then hardly capable of housing a family of six. The birthplace has traditionally been given as Sadsbury, although Fallowfield (now

Cochran was rapidly becoming a leader in the growing community. Its atmosphere was not unlike that of a midwestern border town. If the church followed more closely than usual on the home, the distillery was never far behind. The veneer of religion lay particularly thick at James's home. An ardent Whitefield revivalist of the "spare no man" variety, he had joined the Upper Octorara church shortly after coming to the area. In the very year of John's birth he helped to found Fagg's Manor church at New Londonderry, which still remains a landmark in that region. Nine years later he was the leader of the ruling elders who prevailed on the already famous preacher, Samuel Blair, to join the congregation. The aura of respectability enjoyed by the family is underscored by the fact that two of John's sisters later married ministers.[8]

Yet Blair found community morals very lax, with "religion as it were dying, and ready to expire its last breath." Even allowing for exaggeration, it would seem that young John could easily have familiarized himself with all the passions and vices of humanity. Emotional repenters in church, the Scotch-Irish were callous and undisciplined in dealing with their fellowmen. The religious court heard accusations of general contentiousness, trading with Indians on the Sabbath, unbecoming speech, "great scandalous excess in strong drink" often ending in blows, as well as the universal crimes of fornication and bastardy. Among the sanctimonious youngsters who were encouraged to testify against their elders in two trivial cases were a Mary and brother Robert Cochran.[9]

Much more serious from a legal standpoint was the Cochrans' persistent ruthlessness, which led them to encroach on land to which they had no right whatsoever. James coveted a tract which had been set apart by the Penns as a Nanticoke Indian reservation and began to

---

West Fallowfield) had been officially separated from Sadsbury in 1728. See Futhey and Cope, p. 203, and a letter of Gilbert Cope to Heagey, October 22, 1895, placing James in Sadsbury in 1726 and in Fallowfield in 1729 (Chester County Historical Society).

8. The seven children of James and Isabella are listed in the "Genealogical Account," p. 11. The date September 16 attached to John's name must refer to the baptism. See also Houghton, 2: 79.

9. For the community life of John's childhood, see Webster, pp. 427–28; Keith, 2: 628; and Turner, "Records," pp. 345–52.

trespass on it. The Land Commissioners repeatedly denied him the right to survey because of the reluctance of some members of the Board of Property to condone such high-handed measures. But his persistence slowly wore down the opposition, and eventually he did obtain possession of this most desirable property.[10]

With a growing family of seven children, James Cochran was naturally concerned with the lack of good schools in the vicinity. In 1739, Samuel Blair, himself a product of William Tennent's famous Log Cabin College, had opened at Fagg's Manor an academy, or classical school, which may be regarded as a worthy successor to that pioneer institution. James actively supported the new school; yet, because it was intended primarily to prepare young men for the ministry, there is no evidence that he sent any of his sons there. Instead, as luck would have it, when John was thirteen the Reverend Francis Alison opened a school in nearby New London. This famous educator, praised by President Ezra Stiles of Yale as the greatest Greek scholar in America, remained at New London only until 1752. Later he was associated with schools which became precursors of the University of Delaware and the University of Pennsylvania. Alison's classical studies had imbued him with a passionate love of freedom which in turn he inculcated into John, among other admiring pupils. This early hotbed of independence produced three signers of the Declaration of Independence—Thomas McKean, George Reed, and Charles Thomson—as well as a score of others destined to play prominent parts during the Revolution.[11]

John must have matured rapidly in the stimulating atmosphere of this great school, and he probably never forgot the impression made by the generous but irascible and unusually demanding Alison. Here he acquired the modicum of Latinity which he displays on occasion in

10. James Logan to Adam Boyd, June 29, 1731/32 (Egle, p. 106). The fact that the Cochrans did not reach a formal agreement with the Penns until 1739 would seem to indicate that they had been squatters for some 15 years. See also Taylor Papers, 11: 2217 (HSP) and the Letter Book of James Steele (1730/31), p. 65 (HSP).

11. For Alison and his school, see the article by Thomas Moody in *Dictionary of American Biography*, s.v. "Alison, Francis"; and Coleman, pp. 16–23, 244–46. Other medical revolutionaries who came from this school were Francis Alison, Jr., and Hugh Williamson. Alison's medically trained successor, the Reverend Alexander McDowell, had David Ramsay and Matthew Wilson as pupils.

his legible and well-composed letters. His subsequent avid interest in quality instruction for his own children, as well as in the character of their teachers, clearly stems from this youthful experience.

John apparently excelled to such an extent in his preparatory studies that his ambitious and prosperous father was encouraged to apprentice the willing lad to an eminent "practitioner of physick" in Lancaster, Pennsylvania. John, then in his late teens, arrived to begin his studies under Dr. Robert Thompson, his preceptor, one of the early settlers in the recently incorporated borough, and already regarded as a man of considerable importance. Land speculator, justice of the peace, and coroner, Thompson presided over what must have been a busy office on Orange Street. Here injuries from construction, Conestoga River traffic, and hostile Indians provided the necessary raw material for any willing apprentice; and here John received the hard, practical training that invariably characterized colonial medical instruction. Aside from learning to bleed and cup, he was taught to prepare and dispense drugs, to set bones, to treat arrow and gunshot wounds, to reduce hernias and, possibly, to inoculate against the ever-present smallpox. Although the ancient distinction between physician and surgeon was practically nonexistent under these primitive, backwoods conditions, young Cochran undoubtedly found himself becoming more than a "bit of a surgeon" before his apprenticeship came to an end.[12]

Only a few doors from Dr. Thompson lived the eminent settler Edward Shippen, at whose home John might well have met his future military associate, William Shippen, Jr. Thompson also had as a medical colleague the European-trained Dr. Adam S. Kuhn, father of the more famous Adam Kuhn who later taught at the Philadelphia College. In the small community John Cochran probably made the acquaintance of both father and son.[13]

12. For Thompson, first clearly identified here, see *Historical Papers and Addresses* 13 (1909): 269; 27 (1923): 31 (Lancaster County Historical Society). His will, prepared by Edward Shippen (Lancaster County Court House C-1-94), is dated May 12, 1764, and probated September 24, 1764.

13. Edward Shippen had settled permanently in Lancaster by 1752. For Thompson's association with the elder Kuhn, see *Historical Papers and Addresses* 23 (1919): 133–34 (Lancaster County Historical Society).

The French and Indian War

While the twenty-five-year-old Cochran was completing his apprenticeship, the long-smoldering rivalry between France and England for the control of the Ohio Valley was growing in intensity. Consequently, the Indians of western Pennsylvania, incited by the French, had become more daring in their depredations. The Scotch-Irish had already formed a cordon around the noncombatant Quakers, and as early as 1747, James Cochran was listed as an officer in the militia organized to protect Lancaster and Chester counties.[14] The defeat of Braddock in 1755 made the danger to all the colonies more apparent. However, it posed a special menace to Pennsylvania, where the Quakers, about to lose their domination of the legislature, now began belatedly to make provisions for the defense of the province by encouraging their warlike Scotch-Irish neighbors to enroll for service.

From time immemorial the battlefield has been considered an ideal training ground for aspiring surgeons. For Cochran, who had no American medical school to which he could turn for further study, it seemed a natural step to enlist as a regimental surgeon's mate. He later stated that he had served in the French and Indian War from 1755 to 1760; but other firm facts about his army career and posts are scanty. We do know that John was originally assigned to South Carolina independent companies, and he may well have had his initial baptism under fire while serving under Sir William Johnson at the battle of Lake George in 1756.[15] In the same year, when the French recaptured Fort Oswego, the young surgeon almost lost his life when a cannonball from an enemy vessel tore through the room of the ship on which he was serving, destroying table and instruments just as Cochran was preparing to perform an operation.[16] John is known to

14. Futhey and Cope, p. 50; John's brother Stephen commanded a company of the Pennsylvania militia in 1779 (Houghton, 2: 79).

15. Thacher, *Medical Biography*, 1: 226–27.

16. Oswego fell to the French on August 14, 1756. The incident is related by Wickes (p. 207), who must have heard it from John Cochran's grandson, Brigadier General John Cochrane, who had a summer home in Brookside, Morris Co., N.J.

have had a long and pleasant association with Dr. George Monro, a relative of the famous trio of Edinburgh anatomists, who served as commander of the British medical forces in North America from 1756 to 1760. An army surgeon since 1740, Monro brought to his assignment in America the most advanced knowledge of military medicine then available, and under his tutelage Cochran must have progressed rapidly, not only in surgical skill but also in the field of medical administration.[17] Monro is known to have had his principal hospital at Fort Edward; at nearby Fort William Henry Cochran may well have received an early impression of the unfavorable conditions he would have to face during the Revolutionary War. He undoubtedly learned a great deal about smallpox, "flux," and the "venereal." One writer states: "The Fort stinks enough to cause an Infection, their Camp nastier than anything I could conceive, their Necessary houses, kitchens, Graves and Slaughtering Cattle, all mix through their Encampment. . . ." [18]

John may also have assisted in caring for the sick and wounded who managed to flee from the Indian massacre at Fort William Henry on August 9, 1757. It is probably no coincidence that his efforts were recognized by his superiors at this very time, for on August 31, 1757, he was commissioned a hospital mate.[19] He remained at Fort Edward until the following summer while the British concentrated a large force of ten thousand men for an attack on Ticonderoga.

Cochran appears somewhat dramatically on the stage of history on July 8, 1758, when General James Abercromby's attack on Fort Ticonderoga was repulsed by Montcalm with great loss of life. The ancestral Schuyler home on the Flatts near Albany had been hastily con-

17. For references to George Monro, see Thacher, *Medical Biography*, 1: 227, and Ray, pp. 23, 59. European surgeons, including Donald Monro, who later served in Germany, learned much from the experiences of the "Physical Gentlemen employed in the American Service." Similar problems arose in both armies (Wright-St. Clair, pp. 66, 251, 320). Fort Edward, located at the "carrying place on the Hudson," and Fort William Henry, at the foot of Lake George, were both built in 1755. Both Philip Schuyler and Dr. John Jones were known to have been at the battle of Lake George; Schuyler was also at Oswego (Gordon, p. 166; Hamilton, p. 127). Cochran may possibly have met these men at this early period.

18. Lieutenant Burton to the Earl of Loudoun, August 27, 1756 (*Canadian Archives* Colonial Office, part 5, vol. 47, pp. 409–14). For the hospital at Fort Edward, see Hill, p. 226; a smallpox hospital is also mentioned (p. 229). Cochran must have had ample experience with the disease and some knowledge of variolation, which was again becoming popular in the 1750s (Duffy, pp. 35–36).

19. Peterkin and Johnston, 1: 27.

verted into an emergency hospital, and as the injured were transferred from the bateaux to the improvised operating table in the dining room, the young surgeon worked heroically with the assistance of the Schuyler and Cuyler women as nurses. It was here that John learned to admire the charm and efficiency of his future wife, Gertrude Schuyler, Philip's recently widowed older sister and the mother of two children. Among Cochran's patients on that hectic occasion was Captain (later Major General) Charles Lee, as insolent as ever, who kept uttering a constant volley of oaths, although wounded seriously—some thought mortally—by a musket shot which had shattered two ribs and passed through his body.[20]

When Colonel John Bradstreet arrived in Albany the following day as a replacement for Abercromby, he immediately began preparing his troops for an expedition against Fort Frontenac. He dispatched Schuyler, Cochran, and a corps of carpenters to the Oneida "carrying place," where they found General John Stanwix building a fort on the site near the present city of Rome. Hurrying on to Oswego, Schuyler and Cochran supervised the construction within three weeks of the schooner *Mohawk*, which later took part in the successful attack on Frontenac.[21] John must have been kept busy when Bradstreet's men came down with a "very extraordinary illness . . . probably owing to the bad quality of the waters." But these waters could not be made more potable even by the copious addition of rum, which was in good supply.[22] Bradstreet's troops later joined those under the command of Major General Jeffrey Amherst. Cochran was present at the capture of the forts at Ticonderoga and Crown Point, which were demolished by the retreating French in July of 1759.[23] He is known to have spent

20. Desmond, p. 10; Grant, 2: 82. For Lee's injury, see Alden, p. 10; his subsequent shameful treatment of another surgeon (Lee, *Lee Papers*, 4: 353) gives insight into the generally inferior position of the medical man in the British army.

21. Lossing, *Schuyler*, 1: 156–57.

22. For the water-borne epidemic at Frontenac (possibly typhoid), see Bradstreet, pp. 15–16; see also the alarming report of General Stanwix to General Abernethy of "a thousand dead or dying daily" (Preston and Lamontagne, p. 267). Ray (p. 52) later reports on the "Dysentery, scurvy and Slow Putrid Nervous Fever" at Ticonderoga.

23. The New Jersey Blues fought at Oswego and Frontenac, and Cochran undoubtedly became friendly with the officers of this famous regiment. Among these was the hero Colonel Peter Schuyler (d. 1762) of Essex County, who was captured at Oswego and exchanged after the fall of Frontenac. The Middlesex men may well have encouraged Cochran to consider New Brunswick as a likely place in which to settle down and practice.

his final, relatively peaceful year of active duty at the latter post, which was being rapidly rebuilt as the active phase of this protracted contest gradually drew to a close.[24]

In 1760, after five years of military service, Cochran returned to civilian life as a mature, competent, and self-reliant surgeon. He had undoubtedly benefited much from his association with well-trained British medical men. But Cochran had also gained a healthy respect for his own abilities, as well as an equally hearty dislike for the sprigs of British nobility, frequently inefficient as line officers, who regarded all surgeons, and especially colonials, with a thinly disguised contempt. Cochran's later efforts to secure proper respect for the physicians and surgeons of the Continental Army must have stemmed from these early experiences.

On March 12, 1760, his mother died, and in all probability the thought of returning to Chester County now held even less attraction for a man whose horizon had been broadened immeasurably by years of travel and new friendships.[25] John's ready acceptance by the Schuylers seems to have been decisive. His fondness for the pleasant and susceptible Gertrude had deepened into an intimacy which produced the customary effect on the thirty-year-old bachelor. On December 4, 1760, they were married at the Flatts by Dominie Elardus Westerlo, and although Gertrude was John's senior by six years, the marriage proved to be a long and happy one.[26] As a result of this union, the engaging son of an immigrant farmer soon found himself caught up in the tight circle of the wealthy and influential grandees of the Hudson Valley and New York City. Gertrude's mother, Cornelia, was a Van Cortlandt and her sister-in-law a Van Rensselaer; her daughter would marry a Livingston of the Manor. Schuyler relatives in New York and New Jersey had alliances with the Beekmans, DeLanceys, and other socially prominent colonial families. For the sake

24. JC to PS, August 6, 1788 (Schuyler Papers, NYPL). Although fully garrisoned, Fort Amherst at Crown Point was never completed. Cochran undoubtedly had to contend with smallpox and measles, which raged epidemically at nearby Ticonderoga and at Saratoga. George Monro also served in this region (Wilson, *Orderly Book*, p. 171).

25. Futhey, p. 162. James Cochran lived until 1766, but his will (Chester County Court House) was not probated until 1769. He left John, among other children, one shilling, "as he has heretofore received what I think his share of my estate." See unpaginated addendum to the "Genealogical Account" by Margaret S. Ward.

26. Westerlo had just succeeded Peter Frelinghuysen as pastor of the Reformed Protestant Dutch church (Weise, p. 332). The ceremony is recorded in the church register.

of his wife, who had attachments to home and family, Cochran made an effort to build up a practice in Albany, then a dull, fur-trading border town.[27]

New Brunswick

Cochran remained in Albany for two years after his marriage, but gradually found himself growing restless and disenchanted. The overpowering sense of Schuyler domination, Gertrude's unconcealed adulation of her brother, the latter's moodiness, hauteur, and unusually close association with his protégé and personal physician, Dr. Samuel Stringer, were all factors in bringing Cochran to a decision to move south, well beyond the Schuyler orbit. The death late in 1762 of Cochran's mother-in-law dissolved still another tie with Albany and made the transition somewhat less traumatic for Gertrude. With respect to Cornelia's estate, Philip, now chief heir according to the Dutch tradition of primogeniture, proceeded with the same generosity he had already shown in dividing up the Saratoga estate upon reaching his majority: he insisted on sharing the 7,000-acre Van Cortlandt property equally with his sister and two brothers.[28] Gertrude was also left some valuable property in New York City, including a "water-lott," the disposal of which was to cause Cochran no little aggravation over the years.[29]

27. The latest evidence of Cochran's presence in Albany is a bill for medicine received from a Mr. Windale (Wendell), presumably an importer of drugs, dated November 10, 1762 (NYHS). But by mid-winter 1762–63, we can place Cochran at Newark, New Jersey, where with Jacob Ford, Thomas Kinney, and John Ogden, all of Morris County, he is being inducted into the Masonic fraternity (McGregor, p. 39).

28. Cornelia's will was probated November 24, 1762 (*Abstracts of Wills* [1760–66] pp. 204–6); Gerlach (pp. 63–64) comments on the amicable division of the estate but denies any unusual munificence on the part of Philip.

29. The two houses on Queen Street (now 258–260 Pearl Street) were sold to Jasper Drake on November 12, 1764 (*Collections of the New-York Historical Society for the Year 1897*, pp. 205–6). For the "water-lott" at Beekman's Slip, see JC to PS, August 13, 1763, and January 12, 1764 (Schuyler Papers, NYPL). See also [New York City] *Minutes of the Common Council*, 8: 370–71, 385. The matter dragged on for years and was finally settled in a manner unsatisfactory to the Cochrans (JC to PS, August 6, 1785 [American Physician's Case 7, box 27, HSP]).

By May of 1763 we find John and Gertrude Cochran living in the East Jersey town of New Brunswick. They were expecting their first child while working feverishly on renovating and redecorating their house, which was located in the fashionable quarter of the town at the corner of Water and Somerset Streets.[30] Just why John had selected the bustling Middlesex County seat on the Raritan as his future home is not entirely clear. During the recent war he may well have visited or even been stationed in the handsome barracks, constructed there in 1758, which were later to be used as the courthouse and jail. The presence of Schuylers and even of Cochrans in the town, the wealth of the successful Dutch farmers who supplied fruit and vegetables to New York City across the bay, and the attractiveness of the growing community of 150 houses, which was already vying with Elizabeth as the principal stopping-off place between New York and Philadelphia, were undoubtedly contributing factors.[31]

Cochran, with his pleasing personality and professional competence, soon found himself with an active practice. In his extensive correspondence with Philip Schuyler we catch glimpses of the difficulties besetting the new country practitioner: he "is awaiting a curricle built for me in Boston"; the horses sent from Albany are "good only for draught, stumble intolerably, and I have had so many falls I am resolved never to cross either one of them again. I am obliged to borrow of my friends as often as I ride which I do almost every day for my business increases in such a manner that I have scarcely a moment to myself." [32] Another chronic problem was the shortage of cash caused by the postwar slump in farm prices, with the result "that we

30. Benedict (p. 252) locates the Cochran residence. Philip and Catherine Schuyler were sponsors at the baptism of their niece, Isabella, on October 17, 1763. Another daughter was baptized on March 16, 1766, but the two daughters died in infancy. The three sons, John, James, and Walter Livingston were baptized on September 13, 1767, May 15, 1769, and May 31, 1773, respectively. Only the two latter grew to maturity ("New Brunswick First Reformed Church, Baptisms, 1717–1820," *Proceedings of the New Jersey Historical Society* 12 [1927]: 83, 226, 228, 229, 232).

31. An Albany Street in New Brunswick bears witness to the influx of Dutch settlers from upper New York. Benedict (pp. 35–36) lists Cochrans and Schuylers among the residents of New Brunswick. The sale of "that noted house, and lot of ground" in Newark by a John Cochran on June 26, 1775 (*New Jersey Archives*, 31 (1923): 147), raises the possibility that he may have at one time considered settling there.

32. Cochran may have been one of the first American physicians to make his rounds in a carriage. Much later, in postbellum New York, Cochran's associate, Charles McKnight, attracted attention by this method of transportation (Batchelder, p. 509).

are obliged to trust our employers for one year" before demanding payment. Other letters are concerned with the usual family matters—births, deaths, wills, exchange of gifts and visits. In one letter he gently reproaches Philip for detaining Gertrude too long in Albany because he misses her so. Cochran naturally had to depend on his brother-in-law to protect his northern interests, and there is every reason to believe that the latter, a noted expert in all matters relating to land development, carefully carried out his obligations to his sister. But Schuyler, whose star was very much in the ascendancy, had many social, political, and financial obligations, and although he visited New York City not infrequently, he seldom found time to cross over to New Jersey. As time went on a perceptible coolness developed in the relationship between the warm, outgoing Cochran and his austere brother-in-law. At one point Schuyler's failure to respond at once to a letter delivered to him by hand so annoyed John that "it put him on the verge of troubling [Schuyler] no more." But the misunderstanding must have been temporary, and in general the two men seem to have remained on very friendly terms.[33]

Cochran carried out his obligations to Gertrude's two adolescent children with kindness and tact. Young Cornelia proved to be no problem, making a handsome marriage in 1767 with Walter Livingston, a scion of the Upper Manor. However, her brother Peter, "a promising lad," proved to be something of a cross to bear. Orphaned as a youth and undisciplined, he neglected his preparatory studies for the College of New Jersey, causing Cochran to consult President Samuel Finley on at least two occasions to determine whether the boy had any "genius" for the law. Receiving a favorable opinion, he sent Peter for a trial to the office of an outstanding New York lawyer, William Smith (later the Loyalist historian of the Revolution), "for he thought it extremely wrong to bring up a boy to a profession he was not calculated for and might be the means of making him unhappy for

33. JC to PS, May 26, 1773 (Schuyler Papers, NYPL). The seventy-nine letters from Cochran to Philip Schuyler dating from May 21, 1763 to August 10, 1791, in the New York Public Library afford a mine of information about family life and customs in 18th-century America, and deserve separate publication. The salutary influence of Philip Schuyler on his brother-in-law persisted throughout Cochran's active career, and there is ample evidence that the latter was proud of Schuyler and grateful for his advice and assistance.

life." Again Cochran strongly approved of keeping Peter at "Mathematical Studies, knowing that it must be useful to him, to the last degree in whatever character he may assume." In the end the willful young man disappointed his relatives by eloping with an Albany girl and remaining something of a problem to the family.[34]

By virtue of his obvious sincerity, Cochran soon found himself a central figure in New Brunswick's civic and professional life. Like his own father, he recognized the importance of a good secondary school for his children. As early as 1767 he joined with the son of New Brunswick's former mayor and other leading citizens in the establishment of such a school, thus preparing for the eventual admission of students to the recently chartered Queens College some four years later. The sponsors spoke of the "pure, wholesome air, and its concomitant health" and somewhat later added glowingly that "the diligence of the tutor [Caleb Cooper of Princeton], as well as the uncommon progress which the pupils have made in learning in the last six months gives a pleasant prospect of its increase." [35]

As a preceptor of would-be surgeons, Cochran seems to have treasured his own professional library, preserving it later from the hands of the British, requesting its return at the earliest safe moment, and even attempting to expand it during the war years, when imported books were virtually unobtainable.[36]

As a citizen whose personal integrity was beyond reproach, Cochran's name appears several times as witness to wills and once as guardian of a minor.[37] His name is also associated with at least three public lotteries. With New Brunswick an important center of the "New Light" Presbyterianism, it is not surprising that two of the lotteries were for the benefit of churches of that denomination; the third, which involved the sale of lands belonging to the perpetually finan-

34. The letters relating to stepson Peter are dated July 10, 1764, July 3, August 6, 1766, January 31, June 9, 1767 (Schuyler Papers, NYPL). Peter later served as major in the Continental Army.

35. For the New Brunswick school, see *The New York Mercury*, February 1, 1768; *The Pennsylvania Chronicle*, March 21, 1768; and *New Jersey Archives*, series 1, vol. 26 (1909): 29–30.

36. See JC to his brother-in-law, Alexander Mitchell, April 26, 1777 (Ely Autograph Collection, MG14, NJHS), where Cochran lists the medical books in his library ("Additional Letters," *infra* pp. 217–18); see also *infra* n. 128.

37. *New Jersey Archives*, series 1, vol. 33 (1928): 248, 255; *ibid.*, vol. 34 (1929): 209, 281.

cially embarrassed Lord Stirling, associated Cochran with some of the most prominent citizens of East Jersey, including James Parker, Elias Boudinot, Isaac Ogden, and James Hude of New Brunswick.[38]

In general, Cochran, like many physicians, does not appear to have been a particularly astute man of business, depending almost invariably on Schuyler's sound advice in matters relating to the lease or sale of family-owned lands in Saratoga, Fort Edwards, Cortland Manor, and Glens Purchase. On one occasion he bemoans the fact that "New England men were cutting down and destroying timber on some of my lots, I beg you will do something about it and not let anything of the kind to go unpunished." [39] Yet, in connection with a loan which had been overdue for many years, he seems reluctant to carry matters to the full extent of the law: "I do not want to injure the man but cannot afford to lose so much money, every shilling of which I advanced for his son. . . . I don't want to put him in gaol—he hasn't a friend to take him out. . . . I have pushed the son very hard, but don't want to injure the young man's credit." In respect to a medical fee owed by Richard Peters "in a case for which I never received any satisfaction," he sets no figure, but adds, "I never took any particular account of the services rendered him, therefore, must leave the matter with you." [40]

Only occasionally does he show real business acumen and offer Schuyler a constructive suggestion. In December 1765, for example, he writes: "Lord Stirling last summer erected a mill to clean Flax which answers the purpose very well, would [one] of near the same construction answer for hemp and save much labour and expense?" Actually, Schuyler must have taken this idea seriously; for he is usually considered to have been among the first in the colonies to erect such a mill, and in 1767 received a medal for his contribution in this direction.[41]

38. For the church lotteries, see *The New-York Journal, or General Advertiser*, February 6, 1772; and *The New-York Gazette, or Weekly Post-Boy*, June 19, 1772. The Stirling sale was advertised in *The New-York Gazette, and Weekly Mercury*, April 12, 1773.

39. JC to PS, July 14, 1769, quoted in Gerlach, p. 64.

40. For the loan to Peter Graham, see *New Jersey Archives*, series 1, vol. 34 (1929): 209; JC to PS, December 5, 1770, February 19, November 18, 1782 (Schuyler Papers, NYPL); for the Peters bill, see "Additional Letters," *infra* p. 211. Cochran's easy approach to the matter of collecting money gives an insight into the kindly spirit of the man.

41. JC to PS, December 16, 1765 (Schuyler Papers, NYPL). For the prize given by the Society for the Promotion of Agriculture, Arts, and Manufacture in New York, see Lossing, *Schuyler*, 2: 258.

Cochran's neighborliness and desire to lend a helping hand is reflected in much of his correspondence. He sends a note to Schuyler with Dr. William Mercer of "Belle-View," a New Brunswick neighbor who wished to "try the Springs near Albany for a disorder he has long laboured under, and as he is much of an invalid may perhaps stand in need of some Friendly assistance." When another acquaintance, Dr. Joseph Sackett, Jr., contemplated settling near the "thriving neighborhood" of Saratoga, New York, John again asks his brother-in-law to give advice and encouragement, for "he has a Family, but I fear not much beforehand in the world." Cochran even shows sympathy with innocent victims of the impending Revolutionary War and pleads with Thomas McKean, an old friend and fellow alumnus of Alison's school, in favor of a paroled British officer, then residing peacefully in New Brunswick with his wife and large family.[42]

In 1766, only three years after his arrival in New Brunswick, Cochran became one of the prime movers in a project which alone should qualify him for the lasting respect of the medical profession. This was nothing less than an attempt to encourage all the medical men of East Jersey to unite in a society to "enlarge the stock of knowledge and experience of the pursuit of this science." The historian of the Medical Society of New Jersey believes that Cochran, who missed the five years of "friendship and consulting privileges with eminent English physicians attached to British regiments," was the one who wrote and paid for the original newspaper announcement of the organization meeting, which was held in New Brunswick on July 23, 1766. At this meeting Cochran was named treasurer and immediately ordered to head a committee to draw up a "table of fees and rates." In November 1768 he was chosen president to succeed his friend William Burnet, and retained this position for the next two years, a token of the high regard in which he was held. During his final term in office he delivered a paper, "On Putrefaction, its Causes, Effects and Remedies," which was obviously based on his army experiences. Unfortunately the paper does not seem to have survived. At an earlier meeting Cochran had been authorized to draw up a petition to the

42. Mercer, JC to PS, July 26, 1767; Sackett, JC to PS, February 2, 1772 (Schuyler Papers, NYPL); JC to McKean, July 7, 1776 (Force, 5th series, vol. 1, col. 104); see also "Additional Letters," *infra* p. 213.

legislature of the colony for a code providing for the examination and licensing of all those who wished to practice medicine in East Jersey. This move was naturally opposed by quacks and those who profited from the status quo, and it was not until 1772, and then only with the assistance of Cochran's friend, Lord Stirling, that this progressive legislation was finally pushed through the Assembly. Cochran and his colleague, Moses Bloomfield, received a vote of gratitude for their efforts in "obtaining a Law for the Regulation of the Practice of Physic and Surgery in this Province." [43] Much more stringent in its requirements than any previous attempts at control, this pioneer effort has received just praise from all students of health legislation in America.[44]

By the end of 1771, Cochran had become increasingly discouraged by the crushing load of professional work and a persistent shortage of ready money. He complains to Schuyler:

> Besides I find that the fatigues of my profession are so hurtful to my health, that it will be impossible for me to support it very long. I would, therefore, chuse as soon as I can to procure a small place in the country and quit a profession from which there is little to be made on account of our bad pay and scarcity of cash in this part of the Country.[45]

In an attempt to build up a less taxing type of practice Cochran turned at this time to the growing specialty of inoculation. During his French and Indian War service he had had ample opportunity to study the classical symptoms of smallpox, which at times assumed epidemic proportions in the British posts, and to familiarize himself with

43. Fred B. Rogers (Rogers and Sayre, pp. 18–20) rightly credits Cochran with a pivotal role in the pre-Revolutionary history of the Society. It was unfortunate for medical progress in New Jersey that he did not return to that state after the war. In the 1875 printed version of *The Rise, Minutes* (original MS, NJHS) Cochran appears as treasurer (pp. 8, 17, 22), and as president from November 1, 1768, to November 13, 1770 (pp. 23, 28). After acknowledging a defeat in the 1770 General Assembly (p. 29), he received the thanks of the Society two years later (p. 33). In 1774 and 1775, Cochran was a member of the committee appointed to petition Governor William Franklin for a charter of incorporation (pp. 37–38).

44. For the significance of the New Jersey legislation, see Shryock, pp. 17–18.

45. JC to PS, March 25, 1772 (Schuyler Papers, NYPL). A personal loan of £20 from a Thomas Riche of Philadelphia, dated March 6, 1770 (Stauffer Papers, HSP) had not been repaid as late as June 25, 1784 (Henry E. Huntington Library, San Marino, Cal.). On the other hand, see the £200 owed to Cochran by Loyalist Beverley Robinson from February 1777 to 1788 (JC to Nicholas Low [possession of W. S. Roberts, Philadelphia, Pa.]).

the latest methods of preparing the patient for variolation. When he came to East Jersey he undoubtedly learned much from the technique of Dr. William Barnet of Elizabeth, whose fame as an inoculator had brought him invitations from Boston and Philadelphia to explain his method.[46] The decision by Virginia and other colonies to outlaw the hazardous procedure encouraged Cochran to open a smallpox hospital, probably in the Bound Brook area.[47] From 1771 to 1775 a series of notices similar in content to the following appeared in the newspapers of Virginia, New York, Connecticut, and Rhode Island:

INOCULATION

The Subscriber begs Leave to inform the Public, that he has opened a very convenient House in a remote tho' pleasant Situation, within three miles of New Brunswick for the Reception of such Persons as propose taking the Small-pox by Inoculation. The best Attendance will be given, and every Thing for their Accomodation shall be furnished, at a very low and easy Rate.

Many are deterred from being inoculated, on Account of sore Arms, Boils and large Abscesses, often attending the common Method of treating the Disease; but more particularly from the ill Effects of the too free and indiscriminate Use of Mercury, by which many (tho' they recover the Smallpox, yet the Constitution being Injured), soon fall Victims to some other Malady.

All these Inconveniences are avoided by a particular Method of preparing the Patient, the most efficacious and least detrimental to the Constitution, by the Manner of conveying the Infection, and by the subsequent Treatment of the Disease without the least Confinement; the Advantages of which have been fully and clearly demonstrated in upwards of 400 Persons under the Subscribers Care in the space of a few Month's last Winter and Spring, without the Misfortune of losing any; nor has there died more than one of that Number since, which plainly shows the singular Advantages of this Method.

A sufficient Number to make it worth his While, in any Part of the

46. According to Ruston (pp. 6–9), the revival of interest in inoculation came primarily from American colonial physicians. William Barnet (1723–90) of Elizabethtown, N.J., was one of the most successful of these early colonial inoculators. In 1759 he was invited to Philadelphia to demonstrate his method (Wickes, p. 136); in February 1764 he came to Boston at the request of the faculty to establish an inoculation hospital (Gordon, p. 236; Guerra, *passim*).

47. For laws against inoculation, see Duffy, pp. 38–41. Virginia outlawed the practice on June 27, 1770 (Blanton, p. 285). Since Cochran was a member of the Bound Brook Inferior Medical Society (Medical Society of New Jersey, *Minutes*, p. 14), it seems logical to assume that his smallpox hospital was in this general area.

Country not contiguous to a Person properly qualified. (I don't mean authorized) shall be waited on, at a short Notice by the Publick's

Most obedient humble servant,

JOHN COCHRAN

New Brunswick December 12, 1771 [48]

Two months later he writes: "I have just inoculated my two little boys for the smallpox. They are happily over it." [49] That this move toward specialization must have been eminently successful becomes evident in the following excerpt from a letter written to Schuyler two years later in an entirely different vein:

> I know not whence came the report of my going to live at the Manor of Livingston could arise for I assure you that I have not had the most distant thought of it. I had thought of removing southward, where I might stand a chance of making something considerable by my profession, but could not pitch on a place to my mind. I am very well settled in a good house, and in a good neighborhood, and can from my Business make out to live tolerably decent and believe I can bring up my children very well as we have a most excellent school at this place. All this is by no means adequate to my services yet I do not think I shall mend the matter by removing to the manor where I can have none but country practice, the most fatiguing on Earth.

Again, on the eve of Gertrude's journey to Albany in April 1775, Cochran regrets that he will not accompany her, "For I cannot be for so long absent from Business without manifest injury." [50]

Although we can thus speak with some degree of confidence about Cochran's medical activities in the decade before the Revolution, we know relatively less about his changing political views during that period. As early as 1765—the year of the Stamp Act—he notes, somewhat gloomily, that "the affairs of the Country seem to be in a Strange condition at Present." [51] But as the intensity of anti-British

48. *The New-York Journal, and General Advertiser.* For similar advertisements in Virginia, Connecticut, and Rhode Island papers, see Guerra, pp. 490, 556, 564, 566, 579, 581, 677. The last advertisement gives $9 as the cost of inoculation and board. In 1775, Cochran proudly asserts that "his method of treatment has been the saving of thousands within these three years in New Jersey" (McLenahan, p. 368).

49. JC to PS, February 19, 1772 (Schuyler Papers, NYPL).

50. JC to PS, December 19, 1773, April 30, 1775 (Schuyler Papers, NYPL).

51. JC to PS, September 5, 1765 (Schuyler Papers, NYPL).

agitation increased, Cochran, with his ancestral bias, soon found himself firmly on the side of those working for independence. In 1774 he shows marked approval of Schuyler's decision to serve as a delegate to the first Continental Congress in Philadelphia, and hopes for a visit. But it was not until June 24, 1775, when Washington (accompanied by Schuyler on the road from Trenton to Newark) stopped off at Brunswick that Cochran must have had his first introduction to the man who was destined to exert so great an influence on his future career.[52] In July, Walter Livingston, Cochran's stepson, was appointed Commissary of Stores, and thus found himself concerned with the problems of hospital food and supplies. It seems certain that he turned to both Cochran and Schuyler for advice, thus bringing the former into closer contact with current military affairs.[53] Cochran must also have noted with interest the appointment on October 19, 1775, of John Morgan, rather than Washington's choice, William Shippen, Jr., to the post left vacant by the arrest of the first Director General of the Medical Department, Benjamin Church.[54] By the beginning of the year 1776 he notes with satisfaction the house arrest of the Loyalist Governor William Franklin at Amboy, and adds, prophetically:

> I believe nothing (however base) will be left unattempted by Administration seconded by our pious monarch to reduce our Western world to the most abject slavery and that we must maintain our Freedom and Liberty

52. PS to Peter van Brugh Livingston (Force, series 4, vol. 2, col. 1078); Benedict, p. 348. Although the Middlesex County Committee of Correspondence met in New Brunswick on July 15, 1774, Cochran's name does not appear.

53. See Samuel Chase to PS, July 18, 1775, and the correspondence of WL to PS (Schuyler Paper, NYPL). Washington was favorably inclined toward Schuyler's nephew-in-law and would have retained him as deputy commissary general (Elbridge Gerry to Joseph Trumbull [Burnett, 1: 472]). However, as a "Yorker" and Schuyler relative, he was accused by the New England clique of "not paying attention to his orders" and was forced to resign on September 7, 1766 (Burnett, 2: 84). Throughout the war Walter and his brothers engaged in a brisk trade with the Army, supplying such commodities as rum, beef, and drugs. Although there is no evidence that Cochran profited from these sales, there is no doubt that he was called upon for information and advice. See, *inter alia*, WL to JC, June 6, August 12, November 14, 20, 1777, November 20, 21, 25, 1778; and WL to brother Robert, January 19, 1782 (Livingston Family Papers, NYHS).

54. It was not until July 27, 1775, that the Continental Congress deferred to Washington's request and established a hospital for an army of 20,000 men, appointing Benjamin Church as director. The unmodified term "hospital" was often used interchangeably with "medical department." Shippen later claimed (Gibson, p. 272) that it was he who recommended John Morgan to replace Church.

through a Field of Blood, and if God only continues to smile on our Endeavors, we have nothing to dread. Unanimity in our Councils, firmness and Resolution in the execution of our Plans will go a great way towards crowning us with success. . . . Nothing can save us on the other side of the water but the people. To them we must appeal for Virtue, Honor and Justice seem to have taken their departure from every Branch of Legislature.[55]

Lord Stirling, Cochran's companion at arms in the French and Indian War, was one of the first to raise a regiment in New Jersey. By January 1776, William Barnet, Jr., had already been appointed to the "surgeoncy" of the first New Jersey battalion, but Cochran was called upon to aid in the treatment of several officers.[56] He sponsored, successfully, the appointment of his former apprentice, Lewis Dunham, to become a brigade surgeon, but had less success with another youthful apprentice, Benjamin Thomson of Somerset County, who insisted on joining the Royal Army.[57] In February 1776 he speaks of "this day of Public calamity when our all and that of our Posterity is at stake and calls for the most vigorous exertion of every Person in our common Defense." [58] Schuyler's own position was too neutralist to suit the New Englanders. Indeed, at one point there was some real danger of his being seized as a Tory until Washington, disturbed at rumors of an impending attack on Schuyler's person and property, came to his defense.[59]

When Cochran's friend, Colonel John Neilson, read the Declaration of Independence in New Brunswick on July 7, it was apparent to all that the die had finally been cast. The good people of New Jersey were "earnestly desired to send their donations [of old sheets and

55. JC to PS, January 9, 1776; see also JC to PS, February 22, 1776 (Schuyler Papers, NYPL).

56. Wickes, p. 138; for Cochran's assistance to Captains John Polhemus and Nathaniel Ramsay, see Stryker Collection, 2271 (New Jersey State Library, Trenton, N.J.)

57. Cochran's standing in the medical community is indicated by the fact that he had at least two apprentices, and there may well have been others. Dunham applied in February 1776 for an appointment as battalion surgeon; his certificate, signed by Cochran, is in the New Jersey Historical Society. Having served with distinction during the war, Dunham later became President of the Medical Society of New Jersey (Wickes, p. 239). For Thomson, see Jones, "Loyalists," p. 26.

58. JC to PS, February 22, 1776 (Schuyler Papers, NYPL).

59. Force, series 4, vol. 6, col. 744–45; GW to PS, May 21, 1776 (Fitzpatrick, 5: 65–66n).

other linen] to Dr. Cochran in New Brunswick," and he may well have made a start in accumulating a stock of medicines.[60] He was now quick to denounce all Loyalists, including former friends such as "cousin" Cortlandt Skinner. Cochran is known to have had a quarrel with Judge Richard Stockton of Princeton, whose attachment to the rebel cause was questioned by some, even though he had been one of the signers of the Declaration of Independence.[61] As early as mid-July, Middlesex County had a foretaste of things to come when rumors became rife that New Jersey Loyalists and British troops were planning a foray into the area of Amboy and Woodbridge. Although the alarm proved false, ardent revolutionaries began to think seriously about the protection of their loved ones.[62]

The Revolution

The disastrous defeat on Long Island, in which the Jersey contingent under Lord Stirling fought a gallant delaying action, the resultant loss of New York City, and the retreat of Washington across the Jerseys, soon brought the hazards of war directly to Cochran's doorstep.[63] By the last week of November it was clear that the decimated

60. *Pennsylvania Journal and Weekly Advertiser*, July 17, 1776. Military matters must now have increasingly occupied his attention. On November 10, 1776 (Stryker Collection) he signed a certificate of disability for a militiaman.

61. John Witherspoon to David Witherspoon, March 17, 1777, cautiously refers to "Dr. Cochran's known quarrel" with Judge Richard Stockton (Burnett, 2: 243n). Stockton was captured by the British in December 1776 and was suspected of having gone to General Howe to seek protection. Fuel was added to the argument by Mrs. Cochran, who had entered the enemy's lines under a flag of truce and returned with information adverse to the Judge's own statement. The truth has never been clearly established.

62. Dalley, p. 242.

63. As early as 1775, William Burnet had opened a small hospital in Newark (Clark, p. 15) and was thus able to assist John Morgan, who had managed to move most of the sick and wounded and his precious stores out of the city (Wickes, p. 68). Washington later commended him as "being among the last who stayed" (Fitzpatrick, 13: 482). Two general hospitals were established at Newark and Hackensack, each capable of accommodating almost 1,000 men (Duncan, *Medical Men*, pp. 138–46). In addition, the stone barracks built during the French and Indian War were prepared for hospital service; capable of sleeping several hundred men, these barracks, located at Elizabethtown, Amboy, Brunswick, Bordentown, and Trenton, served both armies on occasion. On Novem-

and bedraggled rebel army could offer no effective resistance to Cornwallis on the eastern side of the Delaware. Long before the British crossed the Raritan, Cochran had sent his wife, three sons, and most cherished possessions, including his library, to the relative safety of Tinecum, near Philadelphia. There his brother-in-law, the Reverend Alexander Mitchell, served as minister, and the family was to remain with him for over a month before Gertrude thought it safe to leave for Cornelia's home at Teviotdale, Livingston Manor.[64]

When the British finally entered New Brunswick on December 1, 1776, the house of Dr. Cochran, the well-known rebel, was one of the first of many structures earmarked for destruction.[65] Joining his friend John Neilson, the now homeless but resolute Cochran cheerfully attached himself to Washington's army in the "flight thro' Brunswick." He must have remained at Trenton to assist in the evacuation of the hospital, for by December 8, when the Jersey sick and wounded arrived in Bethlehem, Pennsylvania, Cochran was also there.[66] It was on that date that William Shippen, Jr., already anticipating his ap-

---

ber 4, Morgan was still hampered by the absence without leave of many regimental surgeons (Warren, pp. 113–14), and when he arrived in New Jersey to take command he found that his authority had been cleverly undermined by an arch rival, William Shippen, Jr., who as surgeon general of the flying or mobile field hospital now claimed complete autonomy. On October 9, Congress had divided the command in a manner so artificial and politically motivated that neither man could assert full authority. Although Washington continued for a while to support Morgan's position, Shippen's criticism of conditions at Hackensack, of men "lying on straw in cold barns," had the desired effect on Congress, which on November 28 gave Shippen complete control in New Jersey (Lee, *Memoir*, 2: 171; Owen, p. 52).

64. JC to Alexander Mitchell, April 26, 1777 ("Additional Letters," *infra* pp. 217–18). Mitchell, Cochran's brother-in-law and a graduate of Princeton (class of 1768), later served at Faggs Manor church; his wife Jane was one of the principal heirs of the James Cochran estate (*Historical Papers,* 23 (1919): 89 [Lancaster County Historical Society]). Teviotdale was one of the several estates on Livingston Manor, lying on the east side of the Hudson.

65. Despite the assertion of the two local historians (Wall, p. 231; Benedict, p. 258), there is good reason to believe that the house was not burned. See JC to John Neilson, May 4, 1784 ("Additional Letters," *infra* pp. 252–53) and his complaint to PS on February 24, 1785, about his inability to sell the house. Smith (1: 292) uses the expression "Flight thro' Brunswick."

66. When Morgan arrived in New Jersey about November 12, he ordered the Newark hospital moved to Morristown, where it might well have remained. But Shippen, as his first official act under the new ruling of Congress, ordered the Morristown hospital to Bethlehem on December 3, thus consigning many men, unprotected as they were from the cold and often unfed, to certain death in the lumbering wagon trains (Gibson, pp. 198–99).

pointment as Director General of the Hospitals, wrote to Washington for permission to use John Morgan's precious stores, and then added:

> As it is possible an action will happen between you and General Howe's army, I have thought it necessary that some gentlemen of eminence should be near your Excellency and the army, in case of extraordinary accidents, for which purpose I know of no one more proper than the bearer Dr. Cochran, who will wait your Excellency's commands in this department.[67]

Cochran must have remained with Shippen at Bethlehem or Buckingham at least until December 12, awaiting the return from Philadelphia of John Warren, who bore orders from Morgan.[68] It was during this period that Shippen, already confident of his forthcoming advancement, may well have discussed with the older and more experienced Cochran the current confused state of Army medical affairs and the urgent need of a new plan for the reorganization of the department, specifically, one that would provide for a more unified command. It seems more than a coincidence that Shippen suddenly produced just such a plan shortly after meeting with Cochran. He sent a preliminary draft to his brother-in-law, Richard Henry Lee, then in Baltimore with Congress. Lee, however, suggested that it be transmitted to Washington, who had just then been granted the supreme command of the Continental Army, with wide powers of appointment.[69]

With Shippen's letter of introduction in hand, Cochran left Bethlehem in search of General Washington, who had crossed over into

67. Shippen to GW, December 8, 1776 (Force, series 5, vol. 3, col. 1119).

68. Warren's orders were to conduct the surgeons and mates then in Philadelphia to some convenient point in Bucks County to consult with Cochran about establishing a flying hospital (Warren, p. 137). Both Cochran and Shippen were at Buckingham on December 12 (Shippen to GW [George Washington Papers, LC]).

69. Shippen to R. H. Lee, December 17, 1776 (Lee, *Memoir*, 2: incorrectly paginated 170–72, 168–69). Written while Morgan and Stringer were still in office, this vicious letter, which Shippen was perfectly willing to have circulated among the delegates of Congress, calls Morgan "a damned rogue," accuses him of speculation in stores and other offenses, and discusses a deal with the New Englanders providing for their favorites Isaac Foster and John Warren. No one who reads this revealing letter can have the slightest doubt that Shippen did everything in his power to destroy Morgan. Writing to Shippen on January 1, 1777, Lee discusses the powers granted to Washington and suggests that he lay the plan before him. "As for Morgan the very air teems with Complaints against him. If all charged against him be true I would not have my conscience so burthened for Mountains of Gold" (Ballagh, 1: 166–67).

Bucks County on December 8. Here began a close association destined to last through war and peace. The physician and the commander in chief had for each other a mutual respect which on Cochran's part bordered on hero-worship. Shippen remained safely in Bethlehem while John saw his first action at Trenton, having crossed the Delaware with Washington on the momentous night of December 25. He writes later to Schuyler with customary optimism:

> You will have heard of the favorable turn our Affairs have taken since the 25th of December. I had the Pleasure to see the Garrison of Trenton lay down their Arms and submit Prisoners of War. Never were a set of beings so panic struck since the Creation as the whole Garrisons on the Delaware when they heard of the fate of Trenton.[70]

He must have recrossed the Delaware briefly after the rout, though we soon find him back in Jersey. On the night of January 1, 1777, Cochran was in the company of Colonel Clement Biddle and three line officers—General Arthur St. Clair, General Hugh Mercer, and young James Wilkinson—all of whom had received some medical training.[71] Benjamin Rush was also present at the second battle of Trenton; indeed, it is from his pen that we have a vivid account of the events on the night of January 2, when Washington made his almost successful end-run around the forces of Cornwallis:

> In the evening all the wounded, about twenty in number, were brought to the hospital and treated by Dr. Cochran, myself, and several young surgeons who acted under our direction. We all lay down in the same room as our wounded patients. . . . About 4 o'clock Dr. Cochran went up to Trenton in inquire for our army. He returned in haste and said they were not to be found. We now produced waggons and after putting patients in them directed that they should follow us to Bordentown to which place we supposed our army had retired.[72]

This neglect on the part of Washington to provide protection for Cochran, Rush, and their charges irked Rush so much that it may

70. JC to PS, January 21, 1777 ("Additional Letters," *infra* pp. 213–14).

71. Cochran and Warren were at both battles of Trenton, while Rush and Morgan were at the second only (January 2). Rush had been with the Mercer-Biddle party the previous afternoon (Corner, *Benjamin Rush*, p. 120; Wilkinson, 1: 146). Shippen was not present at either battle, much to the distress of Washington and the frustration of Morgan, who was present on observer status only (Duncan, *Medical Men*, p. 176).

72. Corner, *Benjamin Rush*, pp. 128–29.

have triggered the animosity he was later to display towards the commander in chief during the Conway cabal. But the more disciplined Cochran took this potentially dangerous situation with the coolness of a veteran.[73]

At Bordentown the two men heard the firing at Princeton, but they could hardly have arrived at the scene of battle before the following day or even later. Rush is known to have stayed on until January 12 to treat General Hugh Mercer, and Cochran must also have worked with the wounded of both armies before pushing on to rejoin Washington, then already en route via Somerset Courthouse and Pluckemin to Morristown.[74] This quiet agricultural village of about one hundred houses had recently been occupied by patients evacuated from the Newark military hospital. Morristown now became the center of the war effort and was destined to be the scene of Cochran's medical activities during the entire winter and spring of 1777.[75] As a volunteer he still had no official status, but Washington seems to have quickly recognized his merits. Moreover, Cochran's relationship to General Schuyler, Washington's good friend, was not apt to be overlooked.[76]

The move to replace John Morgan, the second Director General, had actually begun in Congress when the territory to be supervised by Morgan and Shippen had been sharply defined by the Hudson River. With neither man given supreme authority, conflicts between the two naturally continued to mount, but it was not until January 9, 1777, that Congress bowed to popular clamor and the efforts of the Lee-Adams "family compact" by abruptly voting the dismissal of Morgan and Samuel Stringer from the service.[77] Stringer, who had earlier op-

73. See Butterfield, 2: 1198, for Rush's reaction to Washington's neglect in notifying the surgeons of his plans. Warren also felt that the surgeons had been needlessly exposed to capture (Warren, p. 140; Thacher, *Medical Biography*, 2: 257).

74. Butterfield (1: 124–25n) thinks that Rush, and presumably Cochran, could not have reached Princeton until January 5, well after the battle had ended.

75. When Washington arrived at Morristown on January 6, smallpox had already been introduced into the town, probably by the sick who were there at the general hospital during November.

76. "I hope you will pay General Washington a visit" (JC to PS, January 21, 1777 [Schuyler Papers, NYPL]).

77. Owen, pp. 49, 52, 55. Samuel Adams, writing to John, approved of the move (Burnett, 2: 211–12). R. H. Lee, one of two Shippen brothers-in-law in Congress, later shifted the entire blame for Morgan's dismissal on Samuel Chase and the Maryland delegates. Although they may have spearheaded the attack (Bell, *John Morgan*, p. 201), the

posed the concept of a Director General for the whole continent, was to be replaced by young Jonathan Potts, already on active duty in the Northern Department.[78] On January 14, 1777, Potts was ordered "to repair to Ticonderoga without delay; that Doctor Stringer be directed to deliver to Dr. Potts such medicines and other medical stores as may be in his hand belonging to the Continent." [79] On the same day Rush, who seems to have been preparing his own plan "based on a perfect knowledge of the methods of taking care of the sick in the British military hospitals," wrote that he could point out "several worthy characters who could immediately be placed on the medical staff in our army. Dr. Cochran of Brunswick is one of them. He possesses humanity as well as skill, and is dear to all who know him." [80]

Shippen's ill-concealed delight on learning of the action of Congress dispels any doubt that he had worked actively for Morgan's dismissal, or that he wanted desperately to supersede him. Apparently assured of eventual success, he had been working since mid-December, as we have already seen, on a plan to reorganize the Medical Department. The following excerpts from a letter to a friend of the Lee family exudes an air of smug confidence, implying that the whole matter is a fait accompli: "Your displacing of Dr. M-n and S-r gives general satisfaction. Some new plan respecting the whole should be adopted. I don't know of a better than [the one] I have sent to Col. Lee and yourself." Continuing with supreme egotism he suggests that John Jones be made head of the Northern Department in place of Potts, who already held this position, and then adds: "If you appoint my subs or

---

true culprits were the Lees, who were out to get Morgan, and the pro-Gates New Englanders anxious to humiliate Schuyler through the dismissal of his favorite. These two factions worked together behind the scene (see n. 170 *infra*).

78. Samuel Stringer had served in the French and Indian War as an apothecary's mate (1758) and later settled in Albany, where he became Schuyler's personal physician and confidant. Appointed by Congress on September 14, 1775, to head all medical services for the Northern Department (Duncan, *Medical Men*, p. 104), he resisted the concept of an overall director and refused to cooperate with John Morgan, whose appointment (October 17) postdated his own. The appointment of Jonathan Potts (June 6, 1776) to serve with the "Canada department" added another element of confusion. See Morgan to Samuel Adams, June 25, 1776 (Force, series 4, vol. 6, col. 1069–70); Stringer to PS, July 31, 1776 (Schuyler Papers, NYPL). For the best account of the Morgan-Stringer-Gates affair, see Gibson, pp. 104–14.

79. Owen, p. 55.

80. Rush to R. H. Lee, January 14, 1777 (Lee, *Memoir*, 2: 166).

Assistants I should be glad Cochran and Potts may be two of them and T. Bond, Jr. another, and I will make Way one of my first surgeons. I write in confidence and in a great hurry."[81]

In fact Shippen's qualifications for this important assignment were virtually nil. Unlike John Morgan, who had served in the French and Indian War, Shippen had had no previous military experience and knew little or nothing of camp life or hospital sanitation. Moreover, his special delight in teaching anatomy to successive classes of admiring students for more than a decade had alienated him almost completely from the normal exigencies of general practice. His proper milieu was the dissecting room rather than the hospital ward. Scion of a Loyalist family whose true feelings were thinly veiled throughout the war, Shippen was motivated only by an overweening vanity and a passionate desire to humiliate John Morgan. With Joseph W. Shippen serving as Paymaster of the Pennsylvania troops and with two Lee brothers-in-law serving in the Continental Congress, William Shippen, Jr., could await without much concern the final decision on his appointment.[82]

News must have traveled slowly over the snow-packed wintry roads. On January 21, 1777, Cochran writes Schuyler: "Both Morgan and Stringer are dismissed the service and one Potts appointed in Stringer['s] room. Morgan's Place not yet filled up." Apparently Stringer did not receive notice of his dismissal for almost three weeks after the

81. Shippen to Elbridge Gerry, January 17, 1777 (in possession of W. S. Roberts, Philadelphia, Pa.). An earlier letter of January 14 to R. H. Lee is even more emphatic, speaking of the "general joy" over the dismissals. Shippen's determination to have Cochran as his adviser becomes clear from the fact that Cochran is the only name that he mentions in all three letters as a future assistant director (Lee, *Memoir*, 2: 170–72; *supra* n. 67).

82. After having originally declined the appointment as Director General in favor of John Morgan, Shippen soon realized that he could not remain indefinitely on the sidelines (Gibson, pp. 117, 272). Although General Hugh Mercer would have preferred William Brown of Virginia to serve as Hospital Director of the Flying Camp, Shippen managed to get himself appointed (Force, series 5, vol. 1, col. 371). On October 9 he became Director of Hospitals in the Middle Department, superseding Isaac Foster; by November 28 he had become Director of the Medical Department on the west side of the Hudson River, and thus completely divorced from Morgan's direction. Although ostensibly a Quaker, William Shippen, Jr., appeared to contemporaries as much of a sybarite; William Brown to John Morgan, in Middleton, "Shippen," p. 544, calls him a person "easily captivated by the prospect of pleasure." See also his concern about the loss of his "old wine" (Lee, *Memoir*, 2, p. 167). On October 17, 1777, Lee sends Shippen payment for 25 gallons of the precious fluid (Ballagh, 1: 333–34).

action of Congress, for on January 30 he still titles himself "Director of General Hospitals" in a letter to Schuyler concerning the shortage of women nurses.[83] The abrupt dismissal of the overly ambitious Stringer seems to have aroused the ire of Philip Schuyler, who considered this act against his friend and personal physician as a direct affront. Schuyler's overly spirited defense of his protégé in a letter of February 4 was considered insulting by Congress, which in turn reacted violently, ordering Schuyler to be more guarded of his language in the future.[84] The anti-Schuyler bias of the New Englanders was already making itself felt, and Jonathan Potts, the youthful successor to Stringer, seems now to have shared in this sentiment. In a letter dated March 30, a good four months before his own dismissal, Schuyler accuses Potts of spreading the rumor that Congress "certainly intends to supersede me and that General Gates was to take command." His correspondent, Richard Varick, replies that although Potts and Morgan Lewis both deny this story, he does not believe they are telling the truth; for the doctor is known to be prejudiced in Gates' favor, being "violently attached to him." [85]

When the troops finally settled down in Morristown, Cochran's reputation as a successful inoculator made him especially welcome. Washington's own pock-marked face kept him constantly concerned with "this greatest of all calamities," then spreading havoc among the civilians of the town and countryside as well as in camp. Washington originally had a healthy fear of the dangers of inoculation, but Morgan's success with the troops at Cambridge had helped remove these qualms. The general was now eager to cooperate with the Medical Committee, which on February 12 agreed to recommend a mass attack on smallpox.[86] Cochran, although still a volunteer, was asked to

83. JC to PS, January 21, 1777 ("Additional Letters," *infra* pp. 213–15). Stringer to PS, Jan. 30, 1777 (Schuyler Papers, NYPL).

84. For the resolve of Congress, March 15, 1777, see Owen, p. 63.

85. Anxious to supersede Stringer, whom he had first found agreeable (Neill, "Potts," p. 27), the ambitious young Potts fell readily into the anti-Schuyler, anti-Stringer conspiracy (Potts to Varick, October 14, 1776 [Force, series 5, vol. 2, col. 1040]; Varick to PS, April 2, 1777 [Schuyler Papers, NYPL]). For Washington's support of Schuyler, see Force, series 4, vol. 6, col. 744–45, and GW to the president of Congress (Force, series 4, vol. 6, col. 767).

86. Morgan's enthusiasm for inoculation at Boston helped to allay the fears of Washington, who later became a strong advocate of the practice. For his concern over smallpox at Morristown, see the Shippen correspondence (Gibson, pp. 131–34; see also Sher-

supervise the campaign, in which he was ably assisted by Nathaniel Bond. For a short time the disease was so severe that the Baptist and Presbyterian churches were turned into closely guarded hospitals for the reception of those unfortunates in whom the smallpox had already made its appearance "in the natural way" before they could be inoculated.[87] We have already seen that Cochran had devised his own routine procedure for those under inoculation, and one source, Ashbel Green, insists that the method used was extremely successful. According to Green, the strict "regimen was, by far, the most objectionable part of the whole concern; the whole army had the desease so lightly, that I really believe that there was not a day while they were under inoculation, in which they might not have, with a few exceptions, marched against the enemy, and would actually have done so if necessity had required it." Apparently Cochran was so certain of success under his regimen that he refused to tolerate "gold-bricking" on the part of those under inoculation. When he caught the Green brothers playing sick one morning he ordered "the young rogues to get up immediately. . . . I would rather see them up to the waistband of their breeches in a snow bank, than that they should be lying in bed at this time of the day." [88]

---

man, p. 68). On February 12 the Medical Committee gave its approval to a large-scale inoculation (Owen, p. 57). Despite the fear of smallpox, promiscuous inoculation by the unqualified was frowned upon (Burnett, 2: 143, 459). Washington urged secrecy at the Peekskill inoculation center, fearing an attack on the weakened troops (Fitzpatrick, 7: 64, 129).

87. Whitehead, p. 22. As late as 1778 the Presbyterians had to demand that the Army relinquish their building (Sherman, p. 261).

88. The plan of JC excluded antimony: vegetable diet exclusively, salt and spices forbidden, calomel and nitre powders every other day for five or six doses, cathartics one week after inoculation and at the period when pocks are expected, patient to keep cool and avoid violent exercise (Ashbel Green, p. 90–91). Green later became president of the College of New Jersey. Cochran had complete confidence in the effectiveness of his regimen. He avoided extremely hot weather for inoculation and insisted on single bunks with a plentiful supply of straw to promote cleanliness in the huts (Hughes to JC, April 10, 1782; D. Townsend to Hughes, April 18, 1782 [Hughes, Letter-Book, Ely Autograph Collection, EN 172, NJHS). The administration of molasses was considered beneficial in making the bland diet more attractive, or as a mild laxative. The successful result of the large-scale inoculation is noted by Peter van Brugh Livingston in a letter to Gerard Bancker on March 3, 1777 (*Proceedings of the New Jersey Historical Society*, 13 [1928]: 268), in which he reports: "800 inoculated at Hanover last week." Yet, Dr. Eneas Munson, reminiscing in his old age (Lossing, *Field-Book*, 1: 308) insisted that there was only a partial inoculation at the Morristown area encampment.

So impressed was Washington with Cochran's competence in the matter of smallpox prevention and control that as early as January 21 he sent him into Bucks County, Pennsylvania, with instructions "to use every possible means in [his] power to prevent that disease from spreading in the Army and among the inhabitants, which may otherwise prove fatal to the Service." At Newtown, the Army supply center, Cochran "was necessarily detained for four days, removing smallpox patients, procuring a house" to be used as a hospital, and instructing the medical men in his own method of patient preparation which he considered so vital to success.[89]

Aside from the matter of smallpox control, Washington was understandably concerned with the broader problem of reforming the Medical Department and preventing the controversies which had plagued the Morgan administration.[90] This brings us logically to a discussion of the so-called Shippen-Cochran plan, which, with minor modifications, was to govern the activities of this department for more than three years.

Although Shippen's own version of a medical plan was not formally submitted to Washington until the last week in January 1777, the latter may already have heard rumors of its existence. But as weeks of growing intimacy rolled by, Washington had become increasingly impressed with the record of Cochran's military experience and his familiarity with problems of medical administration. Determined to obtain the best possible plan for the Medical Department, he sent for Cochran on the night of January 20. According to Cochran, Washington "desired I should draw up an arrangement for the Hospital for the ensuing Campaign which I have done and expect to set out today for Philadelphia to assist Dr. Shippen in completing the Plan and having everything on the best footing." [91] Washington's official orders read as follows:

89. JC to PS, January 21, 1777 ("Additional Letters," *infra* pp. 213–14). He probably arrived at Newtown on January 22 and remained there until January 26, arriving at Philadelphia the next day. He spent the next four days conferring with Shippen (Shippen to GW, January 31, 1777 [George Washington Papers, LC]).

90. Although Washington was annoyed at the nonappearance of William Shippen at the second battle of Trenton, he seems to have taken it for granted that Shippen would eventually succeed Morgan, and immediately treated him as Director General. From his letter to Cochran of January 20, it is obvious that he already anticipated the arrival of the new plan. See also Jordan, p. 151.

91. JC to PS, January 21, 1777 ("Additional Letters," *infra* p. 214).

> You will then proceed [from Newtown] to Philadelphia and consult Doctor Shippen the Director, about forming an Hospital for the ensuing Campaign, in such manner, as that the Sick and Wounded may be taken the best care of, and the inconveniences in that Department, so much complain'd of, the last Campaign, may be remedied in future. You will also, in conjunction with Doctor Shippen, point out to me, in writing, such Officers and Stores, as you may think necessary for the arrangement of an Hospital, in every branch of the Department, as well to constitute one for an Army in the field, which may be stiled a flying Hospital; as also, fixed Hospitals in such parts of the Country, as the nature of the service, from time to time may require. Let your standard be for 10,000 Men for one Campaign, and so in proportion for a greater or less number, as you may hereafter be ordered.[92]

While Cochran was still at Newtown an undated letter from Shippen, enclosing a copy of the plan, arrived at Morristown. Now Washington showed his complete confidence in Cochran by refusing to forward the text to Congress until Cochran had scrutinized and approved it. On January 27 he wrote to Shippen, obviously referring to Cochran:

> Those who have already distinguished themselves by their assiduity will not be forgotten. . . . By not dating your Letter, I am not able to determine whether Doctor Cochran had reached Philadelphia, when you wrote; but as I conclude he had not, I shall defer sending your plan to Congress till you have seen him, as I sent him down purposely to consult with you upon the Subject perhaps he may think some alterations necessary.[93]

The original draft of the plan in Shippen's handwriting remains in the George Washington Papers at the Library of Congress. Here also is Shippen's letter of January 31, co-signed by Cochran:

92. GW to JC, January 20, 1777 (Fitzpatrick, 7: 45).

93. Shippen to GW, undated, but probably January 25 (George Washington Papers, LC, with plan enclosed); GW to Shippen, January 27, 1777 (Fitzpatrick, 7: 71–72). Shippen's letter is important for an insight into his thoughts. He has already submitted the plan to Congress, but sends it now to Washington, who has "the full power to adopt any plan." He mentions every name but his own as a possible replacement for Morgan, and would exclude the Southern Department from the control of the Director General—an obvious concession to the southern bloc; he emphasizes the importance of the role of the Director of the Flying Hospital, the man who would relieve Shippen of any responsibility for combat duty. With his usual interest in finances half of this revealing letter is devoted to the matter of a pay scale.

> When I wrote you concerning Military Hospitals I had not been favor'd by Dr. Cochran's advice, but am happy to find that his ideas on the subject square with mine exactly. We are fully of opinion there should be a supervisory power in some one person over the whole, the necessity of which we feel now . . . The Flying Hospital is a matter of great consequence, and we think should consist of a Director who on occasions must act as Surgeon and Physician, and attend on the Commander-in-Chief.[94]

The final plan "drawn up by Dr. Shippen in concert with Dr. Cochran" was forwarded to Congress by Washington in a letter of February 14. It has rightly been considered by all historians as embodying many basic recommendations of John Cochran. It is also safe to assume that Shippen would have preferred claiming the entire credit for himself, while Cochran, still uncertain of his future status in the service, might have been reluctant to challenge the ideas of his superior had Washington not taken so firm a stand in the matter.[95]

By the beginning of March, with the worst of winter over and inoculation almost completed, Cochran writes quite cheerfully:

> Our army is in fine spirits and pretty healthy unless that the smallpox is and has been troublesome. We have now under inoculation about 300 and as one set gets out we take in another and so on till we inoculate the whole of our regular Troops.

He seems equally sanguine about his own future, intimating that he had turned down an offer of the directorship of the Northern Army:

> There is nothing yet fixed respecting myself. A new general arrangement for the whole Continental Hospital is expected to take place very shortly.

94. Shippen to GW, January 31, 1777, countersigned by Cochran (George Washington Papers, 4th series, vol. 40, LC). I believe that Shippen could speak so easily of unanimity with Cochran because the two had already discussed a general outline of a plan some six weeks earlier.

95. GW to Congress (Fitzpatrick, 7: 149–51). The plan had several glaring deficiencies. First, having catered to the Lee-Adams group in order to insure his promotion, Shippen was left with virtually no control over the Southern and Eastern Departments and was thus unable to move men freely from one department to another as needed. Second, it provided for a superfluity of politically appointed superior officers who later saw little or no action. Third, the absence of an Inspector General and a Purveyor-General was to leave Shippen without any competent check on his activities. Finally, the plan would result in the practical elimination of the regimental hospitals in favor of large general hospitals. This measure appealed to Shippen's grandiose ideas, but it proved impractical and dangerous and was soon disregarded by the more pragmatic and experienced Cochran.

The General only waits for the approbation of Congress before he carries the plan into Execution. The arrangement was given him by Doctor Shippen and myself for which purpose I was sent by the General to Philadelphia. I expect to hold some Place worth my while. I even had an aversion for a Directorship for many Reasons but should have no Objection to a Rank which would intitle me to the same Emoluments. Should I go to the northward, in all probability I would be farther from my Family than being with General Washington. I know little of Doctor Potts, but sure I am that such a Trust would require a man of Temper and Skill in his Profession. The moment any thing is settled for me I shall not fail to acquaint you therewith.[96]

Early in March, Washington suffered a severe attack of quinsy, the same ailment which was to plague him periodically for the rest of his life. Apprehensive of recovery and made unusually short-tempered by the severe pain and high fever, Washington tried in vain to keep the seriousness of his condition from all but his designated successor, General Nathanael Greene, and other close associates. It was probably Cochran who saw him through this trying episode and inspired the confidence Washington was to show later when he ordered Cochran to the bedside of the critically ill Lafayette.[97]

Martha Washington reached camp on March 15 in time to hasten her husband's recovery, but Cochran's wife was not so fortunate. As late as mid-May the roads from Teviot to Morristown were so unsafe that Gertrude, despondent though she was at the prolonged separation from her husband, was forced to turn back. She became so discouraged that she is said to have urged John "to leave Mr. Washington's army". Eventually she did arrive at camp in late summer to spend a few weeks, remaining astounded at the highly inflated prices of food.[98]

96. JC to PS, January 21, 1777 (Schuyler Papers, NYPL); see also "Additional Letters," *infra* p. 214.

97. Sherman, pp. 218–19. As is well known, Washington was subject to severe attacks of sore throat, and probably insisted on using Martha's favorite prescription for this disorder, namely, a mixture of onions in molasses, which he later recommended to a fellow sufferer (Wells, p. 67). Washington's unpleasant experience may have encouraged him to invite his old and trusted companion Dr. James Craik to enter the service. His letter, dated April 26 (Fitzpatrick, 7: 479–80) indicated a guarded regret that he could no longer offer Craik a choice of the top positions, since these were no longer available.

98. Smith (1: 192, 324).

Congress, with its usual procrastination, referred the Shippen-Cochran plan to the Medical Committee, which reported back to the House on February 27, but no action was then taken. In the meantime, a plan submitted by Benjamin Rush on the same date was turned down, and the Shippen-Cochran plan was enacted into law on April 7, 1777, with a few minor modifications suggested by John Adams, Elbridge Gerry, and Thomas Burke.[99]

After three long months, during which the Medical Department had remained without an official head, Shippen was finally appointed "Director General of all the Military Hospitals for the Army" on April 11. An unfavorable vote was barely averted by some clever maneuvering on the part of his supporters in Congress, who were able to force reconsideration of an earlier motion which would have named to the Director General's post Philip Turner of Connecticut, a veteran of the French and Indian War and a surgeon of great skill and experience.[100] On the same date John Cochran was appointed to be "Physician and Surgeon General of the Army in the Middle Department" and, Jonathan Potts "Physician and Surgeon General in the Northern Department." Cochran received an additional designation as "Director and Surgeon General of the Flying Hospital." [101]

A day later Washington, not having received notice of Cochran's appointment, departed from his well-known principle of not exerting his own prestige in such matters and wrote the following exceptional recommendation to Congress:

> If the appointments in the Hospital are not filled up, before the receipt of this, I would take the liberty of mentioning a Gentleman, who I think highly deserving of Notice, not only on Account of his Abilities, but for the very great Assistance, which he has afforded in the course of this

99. Duncan (*Medical Men*, pp. 193–94) discusses the delays in Congress, as does Burnett (2: 320–21). The entire plan, as printed in Ford, *Journals*, 8 (1888), pp. 224–25, is available in Duncan, *Medical Men*, pp. 194–98.

100. Thacher, *Medical Biography*, 2: 153; Pilcher, p. 12. Although Turner is known to have been present at the capture of Ticonderoga, Cochran does not seem to have met him at that time (Warren, p. 189).

101. Owen, p. 72. Cochran's commission (the signature of John Hancock is an authentic replacement) is presently in the possession of James L. Mitchell of Atlanta, Ga. For his refusal of the assignment of Deputy Director of the Northern Department, see JC to PS, February 29, 1777 (Ely Autograph Collection, NJHS), *infra* p. 216. Cochran's duties as Director and Surgeon of the Flying Hospital are outlined in Duncan, *Medical Men*, pp. 207–8.

winter, merely in the nature of a Volunteer. The Gentleman is Doctor John Cochran, well known to all the Faculty and particularly to Doctor Shippen, who I suppose had mentioned him among the Candidates. The place for which the Doctor is well fitted, and which would be most agreeable to him, is Surgeon General of the Middle Department. In this line he served all the last War in the British Service, and has distinguished himself this Winter particularly in his attention to the Small pox patients, and the wounded, which but for him and Doctor Bond, must have Suffered much, if not been totally neglected, as there were no other Medical Gentlemen to be found.

If the appointment of Surgeon General is filled up, that of Deputy Director of the Middle Department would be acceptable. I have been thus full in my recommendation, because Doctor Cochran, in a manner had my promise of one of the Capital appointments in the Hospital, upon a presumption, that I should have had some hand in the nomination, by the Resolution of Congress impowering me to fill all Commissions under the Rank of Brigadiers's General.[102]

A week later Cochran exercised his newly acquired right of appointment by naming Jonathan Horton to serve as surgeon at Mendham, near Morristown. Unfortunately the young man soon died, having developed "contagious putrid fever while attending in an uncommonly assiduous manner." [103]

Obviously the new arrangements could not please everyone. John Warren, for example, complained bitterly to Jonathan Potts that "Gentlemen, some of whom had never before been engaged in the Service, are put into places of profit and honor, whilst those who have surmounted ten thousand difficulties and exposed themselves to innumerable dangers in establishing Hospitals from a state of Chaos to regularity are overlooked." [104]

Warren's letter points up one of the problems which had helped to

102. GW to President of Congress, April 12, 1777 (Fitzpatrick, 7: 398–99).

103. Horton was appointed on April 18, 1777 (Stryker Collection, 10411, New Jersey State Library, Trenton) and died on May 24, 1777 (Morris County Court Record Book, MG 529, NJHS). Cochran had better luck with two other Jersey mates, Robert R. Henry (Wickes, p. 284) and Charles McKnight (Thacher, *Medical Biography*, 1: 383).

104. Neill, "Potts," p. 30, quoting Warren on May 16, 1777. Warren, efficient and warmly recommended by General Greene on December 16, 1776 (Force, series 5, vol. 3, col. 1246), had nevertheless managed in some way to make himself persona non grata to Shippen (see warning of Cornelius Baldwin, in Warren, p. 134). Despite his relationship with the hero Joseph Warren, he was not selected as a "sub-director" by Shippen (Batchelder, p. 507). Deeply offended and "unwilling to sacrifice his honor," he

destroy Morgan and was to continue to plague Shippen and Cochran—namely, the unhappy relationship between the regimental surgeons and the general hospital medical officers. The former have been described as ignorant, factious and turbulent, dishonest as to furloughs and discharges, and a disgrace to the profession.[105]

Fully aware of the necessity of improving the quality of the regimental surgeons and mates, Shippen and Cochran now joined in an appeal to medical students, apprentices, and young practitioners, urging them to join the service:

> The liberal provisions made by Congress in the new medical arrangement, Joined with a humane desire to prevent the repetition of the distresses which afflicted the brave American soldiers the last campaign, have drawn men of the first abilities into the field, to watch over the health and preserve the lives of the soldiers—many of them from very extensive and profitable practice, and every species of domestic happiness. Dr. William Brown of Virginia, Dr. James Craik of Maryland, and Dr. Thomas Bond, jun. of Philadelphia, are appointed Assistant Director Generals. Dr. Walter Jones of Virginia and Dr. Benjamin Rush of Philadelphia, Physician and Surgeon Generals of the Hospitals of the middle department. Under these none but gentlemen of best education, and well qualified, are employed as senior Physicians Surgeons,&c. The Eastern and Northern departments are filled with gentlemen of the first characters in those countries; and the public may depend on it, that the greatest exertions of skill and industry shall be constantly made, and no cost spared to make the sick and wounded soldiery comfortable and happy. As a consequence of the above liberal arrangements of the Honorable Congress, we do, with great pleasure, and equal truth, assure the public (notwithstanding the many false and wicked reports propagated by the

---

requested and obtained the assignment as senior physician and surgeon of the Boston military hospital (Warren, p. 149). With a brood increasing annually, he managed to hold on to this sinecure for six long years, resisting all attempts to dislodge him. Like Shippen, he gave anatomical lectures for pay throughout the war (Guerra, p. 515). See also *infra* n. 194.

105. For the difficulties of attracting competent regimental surgeons, see GW to Shippen, March 1, 1777 (Fitzpatrick, 7: 220), and GW to John Hancock, March 14, 1777 (*ibid.*, pp. 287–88). For a perhaps too dismal portrait of the typical regimental surgeon, see Batchelder, pp. 512–13. At one point Washington was convinced "that the regimental surgeons are aiming to break up the general hospital," but General Greene seems to have realized the fundamental importance of the regimental hospital (Gibson, pp. 120–22). John Warren (Warren, pp. 96–97) also felt that the regimental surgeons worked for the annihilation of the general hospital. For Washington's efforts to "cultivate harmony" between the regimental and general hospital medical personnel, see Kinnan, pp. 34–36 (July 28, 1776), pp. 50–51, 98 (August 7, 1776).

enemies of American liberty, and only calculated to retard the recruiting service) that all the military hospitals of the United States are in excellent order, and that the army enjoy a degree of health seldom to be seen or read of.

W. SHIPPEN, Jun. Director General of the American Hospitals.

JOHN COCHRAN, Physician and Surgeon General of the Army in the Middle Department

Head Quarters, Middle Brook, June 4, 1777.

. . . It is requested that the above may be published in all the newspapers on the continent.[106]

Apparently the new regulations of Congress were subject to various interpretations and succeeded only in accentuating the persistent disagreement between hospital and regimental surgeons. The latter, formerly accountable only to their line officers, bitterly resented the scrutiny of their activities now being granted to Dr. Cochran as Physician and Surgeon General of the Hospitals. One resolve of Congress was aimed expressly at line officers who took the liberty of ordering patients back to their regiments without going through the formality of obtaining a discharge from the hospital director, and against those officers who preferred to seek private medical care at government expense when the services of a general hospital were readily available.[107]

Such intrusion on the traditional prerogatives of line officers was bound to lead to difficulties. Late in May 1777 the controversial Major General John Sullivan wrote to Shippen ordering that a hospital be set up at Princeton under the command of Frederick Ridgely, one of his regimental surgeons. Shippen firmly refused to do so, citing a congressional edict to the effect "that every sick soldier shall be sent to a continental Hospital, as soon as any other diet or lodging becomes necessary for him, than what is allowed to all Soldiers." [108]

106. *The Pennsylvania Evening Post*, June 5, 1777.

107. The resolve of April 22, 1777 (Owen, pp. 74–75) includes the first proposal for a Corps of Invalids; this concept was given substance in the resolves of June 20 and July 16 (Owen, pp. 77, 79–81). Enlisted men and officers admitted to the Corps of Invalids were no longer subject to the command of their regular superiors.

108. Shippen to Sullivan, May 29, 1777 (Papers of the American Revolution, LC). Shippen was relying on a strict interpretation of a resolve of Congress, one which he may have influenced, since it was passed at the same session on October 9, 1776, at which he obtained virtual equality with Morgan. The order that "no regimental hospitals be for the future allowed in the neighborhood of the general hospital" was resented

Sullivan soon seized on an opportunity to discredit the features of the new plan which both his line and medical officers considered objectionable and impractical. At the end of June he wrote to Washington, complaining that some of the sick from his division had been deliberately refused admission to the general hospital. Washington referred the matter to Shippen, but it was Cochran who wrote Sullivan a blistering letter of denial and even insisted on an apology.[109]

Sullivan, of course, could not take such a deliberate affront to a general officer lying down. His somewhat inchoate and blustering reply is full of veiled threats and attempts at self-justification, but adds nothing substantial to the facts under dispute. Sullivan again wrote Washington, enclosing a copy of Cochran's letter and appealing for some redress. But Washington tactfully refused to become involved, and suggested instead a court of inquiry, a procedure which the impatient general had already ordered. Apparently Cochran and his men were not represented at this packed hearing, and the testimony supplied by the notoriously antagonistic regimental surgeons and their orderlies was obviously biased.[110] The only apparent result of this disagreeable controversy was an even stricter interpretation of the rules for admission to the general hospital. Cochran seems to have come through entirely unscathed, with an enhanced reputation as an advocate of equal rights for medical officers.[111]

During his first year of active duty Cochran's circuit in New Jersey

---

by the regimental surgeons and led to the abuses which cost so many unnecessary lives. Shippen and Rush (Lee, *Memoir*, 2: 169) both insisted "that no regimental hospital will [now] be necessary"—all this despite the early warning of General Greene who had observed Morgan's difficulties in New York (Greene, *Nathanael Greene*, 1: 227–29).

109. Sullivan, once described by Thomas Burke of the Medical Committee as the "marplot of our army" (Burnett, 2: 496), had already had similar confrontations with the first Director General, Benjamin Church, at Cambridge (Gibson, pp. 116–17), and with Morgan (Burnett, 2: 150). Cochran's letter of July 3 is reproduced in "Additional Letters," *infra* p. 218. The other pertinent papers are Sullivan to JC (Sullivan, 3: 635–37); Sullivan to GW, July 5 (George Washington Papers, LC); GW to Sullivan, July 7 (Fitzpatrick, 8: 364–65); and Sullivan to GW, July 10 (Sullivan, 1: 413–14).

110. For the report of the Court of Inquiry, dated July 6, 1777 (George Washington Papers, LC), see Saffron, "Confrontation."

111. For Washington's unqualified support of Cochran's position, see The Orderly Book of Colonel Walter Stewart, July 4–October 21, 1777 (Item 1082, Library of the National Society of the Daughters of the American Revolution, Washington D.C.) for July 17, 1777: "Doctor Cochran is to inspect into the state of the sick and issue such orders respecting them as will appear proper; that no sick be sent from camp to the general hospital without his certificate."

had taken him from Morristown to Middlebrook and Pompton. By mid-July he was at "the Clove" headquarters. Later in 1777, when Washington moved his troops into Pennsylvania, Cochran found himself on very familiar territory, not far from his boyhood home in Chester County.[112] At the battle of Brandywine (September 11, 1777) Cochran had an unusual opportunity to show his surgical skill and bravery under fire when the intrepid Lafayette, having dismounted briefly to rally the wavering troops, received a bullet through the calf of his left leg. With blood running out of the top of his boot he was forced to the rear, where Cochran hastily slapped on a bandage just in time to avoid being captured along with Lafayette by the advancing British. They then joined the retreat to Chester Creek, where Lafayette was carried into a house and set on a table so that Cochran could complete attending to the wound, and he may have accompanied the young Frenchman to the general hospital at Bethlehem. This incident, of course, served to cement their already friendly relationship.[113]

After Brandywine many wounded were sent to Princeton, Trenton, and other Jersey points. Cochran is known to have opened a surgical hospital at Hope Lodge, Whitemarsh, which was maintained during the months of October and November. His own work there, however, was interrupted by a distressing incident.[114] Earlier in the year the surrender of Ticonderoga to the British and the advance of Burgoyne on Albany had made the situation of Cochran's little family at Livingston Manor one of potential danger. Apparently the demands of duty with the flying camp had prevented him from visiting Gertrude as frequently as the Livingstons would have liked. Walter writes with some concern:

> As you are but two days ride from here George Washington cannot be so unreasonable as to deny you the liberty of coming up to consult and de-

112. The temporary hospitals later established at Coatesville, Downingtown, and Lionville were within easy riding distance of his birthplace, which he must have revisited on many occasions.

113. The best account of this celebrated incident is in Gottschalk, *Lafayette*, ch. 4; Barclay (*Personal Recollections*, p. 237) has Washington ordering the surgeon to attend the boy "as if he had been my son." Lafayette was still limping more than a month after the injury. For the presence of Cochran at Bethlehem, see Tilton MS, 3: 248 (Delaware Hall of Records[Dover]).

114. Wallace, p. 136.

> termine how and where you are to place your family in Safety during the Campaign. This is absolutely necessary [as] I am entirely at a loss. I think you ought to ask the General's advice in this matter—he certainly can give you the best.[115]

The removal of Schuyler from command on August 4, 1777, and his replacement by General Gates naturally caused considerable resentment among his Cochran-Livingston relatives, and may have produced among the women a desire to see the whole mess resolved quickly. Gertrude and her three boys started out for Bethlehem, but the unsettled conditions in that area made her decide to return to Tinicum,[116] where early in November Cochran's oldest son John

> met his melancholy death occasioned by the fall from a Horse. Tho the best assistance arrived in time to give him relief, tho he was trepanned with the utmost care and Judgement yet the fracture proved his death in four days . . . the poor mother is in the most distressed condition imaginable. Cochran was obligated to return to his Duty and she has not a Relative near to give her the least Consolation.[117]

There can be no greater evidence of Cochran's deep attachment to the cause of independence and his devotion to duty than the fact that he is to be found back at Whitemarsh headquarters no later than one week after his son's burial. He then made brief visits to Valley Forge to inspect the proposed site of winter quarters and make an important appointment.[118] On December 12 he was at Buckingham Hospital, supervising the admission of the sick then pouring in from Princeton, Bordentown, and Trenton.[119] A week later this indefatigable worker

115. WL to JC, July 14, 1777 (Livingston Papers, NYHS).

116. See WL to JC, August 10, September 10, 1777 (Livingston Papers, NYHS) for Gertrude's journey and arrival at Tinicum. Schuyler was later acquitted with the highest honors by Congress (December 3, 1778).

117. WL to PS, December 3, 1777 (Schuyler Papers, NYPL). The letter places Cochran back in camp as early as November 19. See also Orderly Book of General Heath, Book 16, p. 125 (NA).

118. Weedon (*Orderly Book*, pp. 135, 141) places Cochran at the Valley Forge area on November 19 and 25. On the latter date he was to confirm or replace Samuel Tenney of New Hampshire as "surgeon general to this army." Benjamin Rush offered to assist the overworked Cochran at this distressing period (Butterfield, 1: 169–70).

119. The hospitals, reopened after Brandywine and Germantown, had rapidly become "cesspools of infection." There is an implied criticism of Shippen in a letter from Washington to Governor William Livingston (Fitzpatrick, 10: 223–40), and the hospitals were ordered closed despite Shippen's objections (Shippen to GW, December 12, 1777 [George Washington Papers, LC]; Fitzpatrick, 10: 150).

finally arrived at Bound Brook, New Jersey, to consult with General Greene on the medical services under the latter's command.[120] But by New Year's eve he is once more at Valley Forge. There he found health conditions becoming progressively worse as the shocking lack of drugs, clothing, footgear, blankets, and housing began to take their inevitable toll.[121] As men huddled together to protect themselves from the fierce cold, scabies soon became rampant. This skin disease required isolation in separate barracks where those about to receive an application of sulfur in "hog's lard" could be "subjected to medical treatment away from the others." [122] The rising threat of smallpox led to a general inoculation under Cochran's direct supervision and the opening of an additional isolation hospital at Yellow Springs.[123] Impossible living conditions brought on wholesale resignations of line officers, and these in turn led inevitably to a lowering of morale among their regimental surgeons, many of whom disappeared without official leave from camp during the holidays. This unhappy state of affairs is indicated in Cochran's revealing, conciliatory letter of December 31 to Albigence Waldo, a young surgeon, deferring the grant of a furlough.[124] It is interesting to note that Waldo finally did receive an honorable furlough on January 8, when inoculation had been completed. He speaks with righteous contempt of the absentees, "one of whom is to be broke for lying and deceiving in order to get a furlow, and I wish his cursed tongue was pull'd out for giving an example of Scandal to the New England Surgeons, tho' the Connect' Ones are well enough respected at present." [125] On January 10, Cochran or-

120. General Orders, December 20, 1778 (Fitzpatrick, 13: 442). While en route with Gertrude, Cochran showed his usual spirit when he came to the defense of his old friend, James Parker, imprisoned for refusing to sign the oath of allegiance. "Mrs. Cochran and the Doctor much piqued . . . fought it out with the Governor [Livingston] who said Mr. Parker was as well as he, the Dr. said he knew better that he had attended him for ten years and that if he remained in confinement his disorder would terminate in a Dropsy." Under the additional threat that Mrs. Parker's "death would be laid to his door, . . . another order was made out, he is entirely obliged to the Dr. for his liberty" (Mrs. Walter Rutherfurd to her husband, Dec. 16, 1777, in *Family Records and Events*, ed. Langston Rutherford [New York: De Vinne Press], 1894).

121. The lowered morale of the unruly patients was shown by rioting and desertion (GW to Officers, January 30, 1778, in Fitzpatrick, 10: 405).

122. For scabies at Valley Forge, see Martin, pp. 110–11; Kapp, pp. 139–40; Hand, pp. 200, 212; and Washington, *Orderly Book*, p. 11.

123. For this important installation and Washington Hall, see Gibson, pp. 152–53.

124. Waldo, p. 316; see also "Additional Letters," *infra* p. 220.

125. Waldo, pp. 321–22; see also the comments of Thoms, pp. 490–91.

dered inserted in a Philadelphia paper a stern warning demanding the immediate return of all regimental surgeons then on unauthorized leave. Congress had already given the Director General authority to deal with refractory mates or those who were inattentive or absent without leave. There is at least one record of a medical malefactor who was to be reprimanded before the entire regiment. In order to avoid similar incidents it was ordered that "passes signed by Dr. Cochran be deemed valid in his Department." [126]

Adding to the lowered morale and discontent among the medical officers was the celebrated *Symetry* affair. On the night of December 30, 1777, a British brig, the *Symetry*, foundered on the coast near Wilmington, Delaware. It was taken as a prize by General William Smallwood, whose duty it was to guard the mouth of the river and harass enemy shipping. The cargo proved to be a veritable bonanza, consisting of staples, rum, drugs, and arms. Perhaps of even greater importance were the large quantities of cloth for uniforms, hats, and footwear, sufficient to provide for four British regiments. When this valuable material was brought at Washington's request to Valley Forge, the line officers decided to distribute the cargo among themselves at a moderate price, excluding the medical men and other potential purchasers. The reaction among the Maryland surgeons to this indignity was swift and violent as their memorial indicates:

> We the Subscribers, highly sensible of the unjust arbitrary & unprecedented Determinations of a Committee of Field Officers conven'd for the purpose of settling the mode and distributing the Articles on board the prize Brig; thereby excluding us the Privileges of Purchasing—Actuated by Principles of just Resentment—Do hereby from this date resign every Charge entrusted to us as Surgeons and Surgeon's Mates to this Division—We shall take the earliest opportunity of making our Resignation to *Doctor Cochran*, the proper Person to receive them—Signed—
>
> Jn H. Briscoe—Surgeon to 2nd Maryland Regt.
> Jn Hindman——D—to 5th M.R.
> Jn Nelson——D—to 6th M.R.

126. "Additional Letters," *infra* p. 220. For the reprimand of a Dr. James Sacket, approved by Washington, see Fitzpatrick, 11 (April 14, 1778): 269n. Sacket resigned on April 24, 1778. For an even more glaring example of dereliction of duty, see the complaint of Colonel Lachlin McIntosh to Governor Richard Caswell of North Carolina concerning a Dr. Samuel Conley, who was charged on March 20 with "Inhumanity in leaving many of his brave countrymen to Perish without his assistance" (Reed, vol. 2). For passes authorized by Cochran, see Weedon, *Orderly Book*, p. 294.

Ricd Pendel—D—to 4th M.R.
Reuben Gilder—D-to Delaware Regt.
Ricd Sappington—Surgeon Asst. to 3rd M.R.
Walter Warfield—D—to 1st M.R.

With his power of persuasion Cochran was able to convince young Sappington to remain in service. The others seem to have carried out their threat to resign.[127]

Cochran sent the letter on to Washington, who seems to have agreed that an injustice "to the Gentlemen of the medical line" was involved: "This morning was laid before me a letter from the Regimental Surgeons written to Dr. Cochran. These gentlemen feel themselves so much hurt by the discrimination made by the Regulations between them and the officers of the Division that they have sent in their resignations." Washington later ordered that no further distribution be made, but insisted that the medical books belonging to Robert Boyes, the British surgeon of the *Symetry*, be returned to him "since we do not war against science." However, the scarcity of medical texts was so great at this period that as late as September Washington had to sternly admonish surgeon Nicholas Way for having retained them.[128]

Cochran now made a determined effort to obtain closer cooperation from the regimental surgeons. Becoming increasingly concerned with the overcrowded conditions at the general hospitals, he ordered the construction of two huts for the sick of each brigade; these were to be 15′x25′x9′, have two windows and one chimney, and be located not nearer than thirty or more than one hundred yards from the brigade. After the construction of these huts was completed Cochran was able to have the following order issued on January 21 with greater equanimity:

> It being impossible for the Surgeon General of the Flying Corp. to make provisions for the sick, unless they are sent to places properly furnished for the purpose, all officers and regimental surgeons are therefore to apply to the Chief Surgeon (Assistant Director) present in camp and take

127. For contemporary accounts of the *Symetry* affair, see Waldo, p. 322; *The Pennsylvania Evening Post*, January 15, 1778; and Tilghman to Clement Biddle, January 2, 1778, in Reed, 2:104. For the mass resignations of the Maryland and Delaware surgeons tendered to Cochran on January 9, see the memorial in the Revolutionary War Records (NA). Sappington did not resign; Warfield later rejoined the service.

128. GW to General Smallwood, January 13, 1778 (Fitzpatrick, 10: 309). For the letter to Nicholas Way, September 6, 1778, see *ibid.*, 12: 407. Much later Cochran ob-

> his directions where to send the sick. A contrary practice has been attended with great inconvenience to the sick and probably has occasioned the death of several men. Many have been sent to hospitals already crowded with patients or to places where no provisions had been made.

On the same day it was ordered that "Patients are not to be sent to the general hospital without express permission of the Surgeon of the Flying Hospital. He is to supply Regimental Surgeons with medicine chests as soon as possible." [129]

While Cochran was struggling under these adverse conditions to maintain the health of the troops within his medical purview, the Rush-Shippen feud was gathering momentum in the halls of Congress. Shippen had not long enjoyed the prestige of office before finding himself a target for the same criticism which had been leveled against Morgan. Cochran made every effort to avoid becoming involved in the controversy. Nonetheless, the contentious Rush and young Tilton were both outspoken in condemning the notoriously evil conditions existing in the general hospitals. The first blast came from Rush, now Shippen's implacable foe, who wrote letters to Duer and Washington in December 1777 denouncing Shippen as neglectful of the plight of the sick, and characterizing him as utterly incompetent. Regardless of who was responsible it was true that conditions could not have been much worse. While serving at the Princeton hospital the conscientious Tilton fell victim to the dreaded "putrid fever" and came close to losing his life.[130] Fortunately, as we have seen, Wash-

---

tained special permission from Governor William Livingston of New Jersey to import medical goods from New York (William Livingston to JC, May 8, 1780 [Livingston Papers, Rutgers University Library—Special Collections]).

129. Valley Forge Orderly Book, January 13, 1778 (NA); see also the orders of Washington (Fitzpatrick, 10: 333; 11: 260), and Hand, pp. 223, 271–72. The building of these huts and the order to furnish the regimental surgeons with chests would seem to demolish Tilton's contention that camp hospitals were being entirely neglected before his experience at Basking Ridge in 1780. The more-practical Cochran seems to have disagreed with Shippen on this crucial matter, doing all in his power to conciliate the overly sensitive regimental surgeons. In this matter of regimental hospitals Cochran had the active support of Baron Steuben, the newly appointed Inspector General, who also had strong opinions on sanitary measures concerning bedding and clothing (Duncan, *Medical Men*, pp. 243–44).

130. For a little-known vignette of Tilton as a "well-meaning and learned gentleman," written before he became ill, see Buettner, pp. 53–57. Tilton describes vividly his 1777 illness, narrow escape, and subsequent visits to other, even more deeply infected hospitals in *Economical Observations*, pp. 59–60. See also Duncan, *Medical Men*, pp. 222–23.

ington now brushed aside Shippen's objections and ordered the closing of the two major New Jersey hospitals, and this act undoubtedly saved many lives. From this point the feud between Rush and Shippen grew in intensity, resulting in ever-increasing partisanship within the department. With the continued support of his relatives Shippen won this preliminary battle in Congress; but Rush resigned his appointment as Surgeon General, refusing to serve further under a man he considered both incapable and indifferent.[131] He then returned to his seat in Congress and membership on the Medical Committee, more than ever determined to make his position understood.

With inoculation completed, the brigade and flying hospital huts in use, and a large new building at Yellow Springs under construction, Cochran was at last in a position to pay a long delayed visit to the Manor to console his grieving wife. During these few weeks of leisure he exchanged thoughts on several occasions with William Smith, the New York Loyalist attorney who was living unmolested at Livingston Manor. According to Smith's diaries, Cochran was somewhat despondent at this point and uncertain of the final success of the movement for independence, having admitted to his wife that soldiers might be traced by their blood in the snow for want of shoes. He was seen as being both chagrined and "disaffected" by the disgraceful treatment meted out to his brother-in-law at the hands of the Adams faction in Congress, and disturbed by the growing opposition to Washington by Gates and his followers. Cochran had a healthy dislike of the New

131. For the Rush-Shippen feud, see Rush to Shippen, December 2, 1777 (Butterfield, 1: 169–70), requesting a "military Inspector" to check on the quality of medical care as well as "sheets with which [Foster] abounds." Rush to William Duer, December 8, 18, 1777 (*ibid.*, pp. 171–72, 175–76), recommends Dr. John Jones as Inspector General, calls "a battle [with Shippen] inevitable" and threatens resignation. Rush to GW, December 26, 1777 (*ibid.*, pp. 180–82) condemns overcrowding at Princeton. The Duer letters were read in Congress. On January 27, 1778, Tilton and Moses Bloomfield, Cochran's old friend, appeared before a committee examining Rush and Shippen (see Burnett, 3: 59, and Hand, pp. 271–72). Rush and Shippen also testified, and the former finally resigned rather than continue serving under Shippen. See Witherspoon to Rush, February 2, 1778 (Burnett, 3: 66–67) and Rush to Morgan (Burnett, 3: 67n.), giving Rush's reasons for resigning. On February 6 the "Purchasing power was taken from the hands of the Director General and given to the Deputy Director General"—that is, to Jonathan Potts (Owen, pp. 95–96). Since the latter was a devoted supporter of Shippen, there was little or no change in the matter of procurement. In fact, unnecessary competition between the Medical Department and the Commissary resulted in an escalation in the cost of provisions (Ephraim Blaine to Potts, May 2, 1778 [Potts Papers, HSP]).

Englanders, accusing them of having stolen all the arms captured during the Burgoyne campaign, and of having doomed to failure the projected invasion of Canada by Lafayette and Conway by their refusal to march north of Albany. Although he was fond of the Frenchman, he felt that the Canadian venture was too "vast [a] project to be entrusted to a Youth of but 22 years who had never seen any service but in this country." He admitted that "Quarrels between Washington and Gates had run very high" and that there had been threats of mass resignations if the "much-despised" heads of the cabal succeeded in their plan to replace the commander in chief. Cochran also commented on the spiraling inflation; saddles were at such a premium that he had been offered one hundred pounds for his own, and a similar sum for a brace of brass pistols.[132]

From another long and impassioned letter written by Philip Schuyler on February 18, 1778, it appears that Cochran must have been echoing the political sentiments of his brother-in-law, who was still rankling at his replacement by Gates at Saratoga. Schuyler again defended his medical comrade Samuel Stringer as a patriotic physician who had been much abused by Congress, going so far as to urge his reinstatement. Schuyler also blamed the failure of the Canada expedition on Gates, and resented the fact that for seven long months his enemies in Congress had been able to hold up action of the committee appointed to enquire into the causes of the loss of Ticonderoga.[133]

After the collapse of the ill-fated Canadian expedition, first proposed by Gates and the Board of War in order to undermine the authority of the commander in chief, an unhappy Lafayette returned to the dismal atmosphere of Valley Forge. It was during this harsh and

132. Alarmed at the prospect of a smallpox epidemic in camp, Cochran had recommended the construction of a new hospital at Yellow Springs spa (now Chester Springs), some ten miles from Valley Forge (see *supra* n. 123). While the work was in progress, a local surgeon, Dr. Samuel Kennedy, kept the patients isolated in three barns. This conscientious patriot fell victim to an infectious disorder just as the troops were about to move from camp in June (Gibson, pp. 152, 329). According to Smith (1: 291–92), Cochran left Valley Forge on January 12, 1778. Smith considered him sincere and highly motivated, but at the same time naive and politically unsophisticated.

133. PS to Gouverneur Morris, February 18, 1778 (Gouverneur Morris Papers, CUL, *infra* pp. 271–72). On March 5, 1778, we find William Duer recommending his friend Stringer to the attention of Robert Morris (Sparks, *Correspondence*, 3: 109).

discouraging period that Cochran's cheerful disposition and buoyant good nature made a lasting impression on the young Frenchman. Apparently Cochran was endowed with an unusually good voice, and his rollicking songs, including a famous one with the singular refrain "Bones, Bones, Bones," afforded a never-failing source of amusement to Washington, Lafayette, and "the family" at headquarters.[134] Of more practical importance was the significant improvement in the supply of hospital drugs and other essentials brought about by the transfer of the capable Jonathan Potts from the Northern Department to assume the newly created position of Deputy General of the Medical Department in charge of supplies. As early as February 6, the date of his formal appointment, he had sent an impressive quantity of drugs from Albany to Valley Forge. By mid-April the Apothecary John B. Cutting could report to Potts that "we have begun to supply the Regiments in Camp . . . Dr. Cochran has given orders to the Division on the left to bring their Chests first, and we propose going through the whole Army in the order in which they now lay." [135]

When Benedict Arnold reported to Valley Forge late in May he was still suffering severely as a result of the fractured right thigh bone incurred at Bemis Heights, and was unable to engage in field service. He had brought with him his aide-de-camp, Matthew Clarkson, another casualty of the northern campaign. Cochran took care of both these men personally, covering the distance between his quarters at Moore Hall to camp every day in order the change their dressings. Yet Arnold's wound continued to plague him long after he took command of Philadelphia on June 19, 1778.[136]

134. Cochran was familiarly known as "the good Doctor Bones." For his unusual prowess as singer and dancer, see the letter of Lafayette to GW, January 5, 1779 (Gottschalk, *Letters*, p. 72) and the letter of Lafayette to JC in "Appendix A," *infra* pp. 263–64.

135. Cochran acknowledged receipt of the drugs on March 22 (Potts Papers, HSP). Distribution of the newer, lighter chests to the regimental surgeons began before April 16, following Cochran's excellent suggestion for "calling in of the larger chests which are too compleat and capacious for field service . . . the standing chests [at Yellow Springs] acquire a great variety of useful articles which are not essential in camp." For the contents of the chests, see Grieffenhagen, p. 127. Concerning supplies of wine, molasses, and oil, seek Craik to Potts, April 7, 26, May 2, 1778 (Potts Papers, HSP). On May 30 Washington ordered the enlistment of women nurses, "for he can no longer bear having an army on paper and not have them in the field" (General Orders, Fitzpatrick, 11: 407).

136. Pinkowski, p. 234.

In the halls of Congress the Medical Committee continued to study the accusations against Shippen, advising Rush: "We wish to proceed in the business so as to obtain the most perfect information of the malpractices, if there are any of the Director-General." As a direct result of the charged atmosphere, Shippen's request for a million dollars was cut in half; for it was "alleged that great quantities of delicacies and wines destined for the sick were being consumed by the well," that is, by the line officers and their surgeons. Even the highly esteemed Henry Laurens, a good friend of the Lee family, joined those who were insisting on "an enquiry into the conduct of the Director-General and all the rest." Richard Henry Lee, who now saw trouble ahead for his brother-in-law, ended one paragraph with the warning "*Cave quod agis.*" [137]

As Shippen's influence continued to decline, Congress showed its propensity for playing politics and began to interfere more directly in the internal affairs of the poorly managed department. As usual the more shrewd Yankees managed to find plush assignments for their partisans. Isaac Foster, one of these, considered himself exempt from the routine orders of Shippen. Even Washington's old friend and personal physician, James Craik, found himself virtually superseded by this favorite of the New England bloc, as this excerpt from a letter to Potts shows:

White Plains, 29 July 1778

> Since I came over to the North River, I have been a Gentleman at large. Foster has taken the supreme command and has managed his card so well at Congress, that he is continued Deputy-Director, and is Purveyor. He tells me he has plenty of stores, and shall want nothing from us, that he can purchase what he wants, and has plenty of medicine.
>
> Cochran and his people continue to act as before by the General's desire, tho' Burnet is the person appointed by Congress. There is certainly a great necessity of a new organization, and that as soon as possible [138]

137. Ballagh, 2: 45–46. Concerned about the possible effect of "new arrangements" on his own career, Cochran sought the support of Henry Laurens. On June 1, 1778, John Laurens writes his father, recalling the endorsement of Cochran by Washington, and adding: "He joined the army when our affairs were a very unfavorable aspect—he is remarkably tender of his patients—if I have any doubts of him it is that like all the rest of his department he may lose time by a convivial disposition" (*S.C. Hist. Gen. Mag.* 6 (1905): 107).

138. A Bunker Hill man and a favorite of the New England bloc, Foster amassed a

As preparations began for the impending attack on Philadelphia, Washington was anxious to know the full strength of his command. He had found the hospital reports, which were supplied somewhat irregularly by the Medical Director, to be overly optimistic. Although hitherto a firm Shippen supporter, he suspected that there was a serious oversight somewhere and called on the Adjutant General to report on the obvious discrepancy between the number of sick absentees reported by the regimental officers and the official hospital returns. Two line officers were ordered to inspect and discharge the remaining sick—mostly men recuperating from the effects of inoculation—who could not immediately continue with the troops.[139] Shippen admitted that his returns had been delayed by the removal of the sick to new hospitals, but insisted that the Army was "in fine order, plentifully supplied with everything but Cloaths." [140] Now more anxious than ever to demonstrate his interest and efficiency, Shippen wrote to the head of the Medical Committee, Gouverneur Morris, urging the completion of a new, unified arrangement of the Medical Department and quoting Cochran in support:

> Much good will arise to and expence be saved for the public by making only one System, & that much in the manner you have before you, a great many useless and ignorant officers will be discharged, men of science will be enlisted & no more employed than are necessary—many offer now for places, I put them all off till the examination which should be held immediately.[141]

---

large quantity of "private stores" while still on duty, in preparation for his retirement (Burnett, 4: 249n). For the Danbury hospital, see Graves, pp. 11–12, and Batchelder, p. 509.

139. Although on May 15, 1778, Washington had found the Yellow Spring Hospital, under the general supervision of Cochran, to be "in fine order" (Craik to Potts [Potts Papers, HSP]), on May 27 there were still 3,000 men under inoculation and therefore considered unable to march. See Washington to R. H. Lee (Fitzpatrick, 11: 451, 488), ordering regimental surgeons to report exact sick returns to Cochran. For the use of nonmedical officers to check returns, see Washington, *Orderly Book*, pp. 13, 23–24, 26, and Saffell, p. 363.

140. Shippen's sycophantic letters, replete with good tidings about the number of sick, were at variance with the facts as reported by others. On April 13, 1778, he thinks that a favorable report "should reduce the Tongue of Malice itself"; on October 5 he is optimistic that the hospitals will soon be emptied of all but those who "are proper subjects of a Chelsea"—that is, the London home for disabled war veterans (George Washington Papers, LC).

141. Shippen to Gouverneur Morris, June 17, 1778 (Gouverneur Morris Papers, CUL—Special Collections), included in "Appendix B," *infra* p. 273.

Congress now insisted that all officers, including surgeons, take an oath of allegiance to the United States of America. Cochran took his before Lord Stirling on May 20, 1778, but had difficulty in getting co-operation from some distant medical officers. In fact a few of them had not complied with this order as late as 1781.[142]

On June 18, 1778, it was learned that the British were preparing to abandon Philadelphia. Washington ordered General Charles Lee to intercept them in New Jersey and hurried to his support. Cochran was the senior medical officer at the bloody but inconclusive battle of Monmouth, being ordered on June 29 "to direct what is to be done with the wounded and sick. He [was] to apply to the Quarter Master and Adjutant General for assistance." [143]

In the fall of 1778, Lafayette obtained permission from Congress to return to France. Having been entertained at every stop on his journey north from Philadelphia, the exhausted youth fell severely ill with lobar pneumonia when he arrived at the Brinckerhoff Mansion, Fishkill, on the first of November. Washington, greatly concerned, ordered Cochran to give up all other duties in order to devote his time exclusively to the care of the young Frenchman. Lafayette ran a very high fever for more than a week, and at times his chances for survival appeared dim. But by November 12, following a severe nasal hemorrhage, he was out of danger, and on December 2 he had recovered sufficiently to resume his journey, still under the care of John Cochran. By this time Lafayette had become genuinely attached to his physician, and when the two men arrived in Boston on December 7, they were entertained lavishly by John Carter and his wife, Philip Schuyler's daughter.[144] After more than a month of merrymaking,

142. Book 165, p. 31 (NA); JC to Townsend, September 1, 1781 (*infra* pp. 143–44).

143. Stryker, *Monmouth*, p. 234. On July 28, 1778 (Craik to Potts [Potts Papers, HSP]), Jabez Campfield and George Draper, two of Cochran's associates, were at Morristown, presumably still caring for the Monmouth casualties. Cochran urges Craigie to refill the depleted regimental chests. On August 8, 1778, as the bulk of the army moved into New York state, Cochran was ordered to share responsibility for the flying hospital with his New Jersey colleague, William Burnet (Fitzpatrick, 12: 289). Burnet was then serving as Physician and Surgeon General in the Eastern Department; on October 20, 1778, during the former's absence, Cochran was ordered to assume his duties (Fitzpatrick, 13: 118).

144. For the episode of the illness, see Thacher, *Military Journal*, p. 185; Gottschalk, *Lafayette Joins the American Army*, pp. 303, 305. John Carter was the alias of John Barker Church, an Englishman who had eloped with Schuyler's daughter, Angelica. A specu-

Cochran saw his charge safely on board the *Alliance*, receiving from the grateful Lafayette his own brace of pistols as a gift.[145] John, who seems to have loved nothing more than a good time away from home, had already announced that he would not be back at the Manor in time for the Christmas holidays as originally planned.[146] This seeming indifference precipitated a severe bout of illness on the part of the still despondent Gertrude, and led Walter Livingston to write reprovingly:

> You have very near broke the heart of [your] tender and affectionate wife, her almost inconceivable distress of mind and violent Rheumatick pains has emaciated her to such a degree that all who see her think her life is in danger. . . . your Commission is of very little Consequence when compared with her life. You must either never part with her or resign.[147]

The mildly repentant wanderer, having lingered in Boston until January 11, 1779, did not return to the marital bed before January 19—an absence from home of almost six weeks. Apparently Gertrude's attack of rheumatism was aggravated by "melancholy over the loss of [our] poor little boy Jack," and it was therefore quite impossible for Cochran to proceed directly to headquarters, as he would have wished.[148] Instead, he wrote to Washington's secretary, James

---

lator who made a fortune selling rum and other commodities to the military, he later returned to England where he was laughingly referred to as the "French Commissary." See Mills, pp. 214–16.

145. Lafayette to GW, January 5, 1779 (Gottschalk, *Letters*, p. 72). He speaks of his "good doctor who has attended me with his usual care and tenderness." For the gift of the pistols see Wilson, *Memorial History*, 3: 95–96. Lafayette's letter to Cochran ("Appendix A," *infra* pp. 263–64) is dated June 10, 1779; its arrival is mentioned in JC to PS, September 12, 1779 (Schuyler Papers, NYPL). There can be no question of the sincerity of Lafayette's affection for Cochran. For example, see the postwar references in the *Hamilton Papers*, 3: 604; 4: 144, 283, 653. Writing to Washington as late as January 22, 1792, Lafayette adds "best compliments to Hamilton, Knox, Jefferson, Jay, Major Washington, Cochran, and all other friends" (Gottschalk, *Letters*, p. 360).

146. Cochran originally intended to move his family to the Bound Brook, N.J., headquarters immediately after the Christmas holidays (JC to James Parker, December 1, 1778 [NJHS]; see also WL to Robert Livingston, December 18, 1778 [Livingston Papers, NYHS]).

147. WL to JC, January 7, 1779 (Livingston Papers, NYHS). Cochran's convivial propensities may have led to an escapade in which he lost his gold watch. His friend Antony Wayne ordered Major John Stewart to sign a receipt for the watch which was advertised to be auctioned off in order "to save the Doctor blushes from the recollection of [the] circumstances" (Wayne Papers, vol. 8, September 28, 1779 [HSP]).

148. JC to PS, January 19, 1779 (Schuyler Papers, NYPL), speaks also of Lee's malice towards Washington. Gertrude's health remained precarious for some time (JC to PS, February 11, 28, 1779 [Schuyler Papers, NYPL]).

McHenry, himself a physician and an admirer of Cochran, explaining his predicament. Cochran suggested that his principal assistant, Dr. George Draper, be authorized to direct the hospital during his absence. He later wrote to Washington in the same vein. Schuyler also intervened on behalf of his brother-in-law, with the result that the sympathetic commander gave "Dr. Cochran . . . permission to return to the manor of Livingston whenever he pleases." [149] Fortunately, weather and health problems at the Middlebrook winter and spring encampment never approached in severity those of Valley Forge. Indeed, things were so quiet that Dr. William Brown, Physician General, was encouraged to arrange a course of lectures on the "practice of physic," anatomy, and surgery to benefit the medical staff.[150] Cochran was able to spend a good deal of time at the Manor, reporting to the Jersey headquarters at infrequent intervals until early in June, when the successful moves against Stony Point and Verplanck's Point by the British put the entire mid-Hudson region in jeopardy. Washington moved to the latter area, where Cochran rejoined him, writing to Schuyler: "Gitty greatly improved; she must have exercise and since she cannot get it without me I will keep her within a few miles of the Army." [151]

The anticipated attack on Fort Clinton (now West Point) failed to materialize. Instead, Wayne turned the tide by his recapture of Stony Point.[152] It was in late summer, during the relative lull in war activities, that Washington wrote Cochran a familiar letter displaying that sense of humor which was seldom permitted to surface in his writ-

149. JC to James McHenry, January 24, 1779 (Henry E. Huntington Library). Cochran did visit Middlebrook on April 26, 1779, carrying a letter from Schuyler (GW to PS, April 27, 1779, in Fitzpatrick, 14: 446–48). Permission was readily granted (Fitzpatrick, 14: 448). It was on January 8, 1779, while Cochran was absent from headquarters, that Washington wrote to the Committee on Conference a critique of the Medical Department. He urged one director, authorized to move medical officers freely from one district to another; "more latitude to the regimental surgeons"; and the use of regimental hospitals under the supervision of the "Surgeon General of the flying hospital"—that is Cochran, rather than the Director General (Fitzpatrick, 13: 489–90).

150. The lectures were announced on February 11, 1779 (Fitzpatrick, 14: 100–101).

151. Cochran and his wife stayed at Smith's Place, near camp.

152. In preparation for the attack, Wayne wrote to Cochran on July 2 (Wayne Papers, HSP) requesting "two good and Careful surgeons, As the Health and Lives of the men may much depend upon the skill and attention Desire you to appoint gentlemen of ability furnished with every necessary in their way." For a humorous account of how Wayne inspired the men to storm Stony Point, see the Cochrane MS (Yale University Library).

ings. It demonstrates rather convincingly the cordial relationship existing between the two families.[153]

Meanwhile, the committee appointed to consider the circumstances surrounding John Morgan's dismissal had brought in a report on March 13, 1779, which commended the former Director General. The memorial which Morgan then submitted to Congress was so full of invective that it was amended without legal permission by the committee chairman, William Henry Drayton, and by Morgan himself, thus affording Laurens, as always friendly to the Lee faction, an opportunity to soften the blow to Shippen by means of delaying tactics. Nevertheless on June 12 Congress voted decisively for Morgan's complete vindication, and three days later the exultant Morgan submitted to Congress a letter charging Shippen "with malpractice and misconduct in office." [154]

Shippen, now becoming increasingly aware of the difficulty of his position, had already taken steps to avoid the disclosures sure to arise from a full-fledged congressional investigation of his administration. A month earlier he had written to Gouverneur Morris, reversing an earlier stand on the need for another reorganization of the department. The rather rude reply is indicative of the increasingly antagonistic mood of Congress towards Shippen.[155]

In the summer of 1779, long before the fall of Charleston and the capture of the Medical Department of the South, the need for additional personnel in that region was becoming apparent. Acting under direct orders from Washington, Cochran sent Mace Clements and Miles King from his own command in the Middle Department to the South, and was preparing to "send one or two more." Yet, months would pass before the restrictions on moving surgeons freely from one department to another would be completely abolished. The shortage

153. Fitzpatrick, 16: 116–17. According to Lossing (*Pictorial Field-Book*, 2: 201n), this letter was presented to the New-York Historical Society by son James. See facsimile reproduction, *New-York Historical Society Quarterly Bulletin* 1, no. 1, (1917): 6–7, and "Appendix A," *infra* pp. 264–65.

154. For the official references to the Morgan reinstatement proceedings, see Burnett, 5: 130n, and Gibson, pp. 240–42. On June 24, Washington told Morgan he did not know when the Shippen trial would begin, being too occupied with the Arnold court-martial (Fitzpatrick, 15: 309–10).

155. Gouverneur Morris to Shippen (Gouverneur Morris Papers, CUL—Special Collections). See letter of June 17, 1778 ("Appendix B," *infra* p. 274)," referred to in n. 141, *supra* p. 52. Gouverneur Morris had been a member of the Medical Committee since April 18, 1778 (Owen, p. 100).

of capable surgeons did not prevent Cochran from attempting to maintain good standards. On August 11, Washington wrote to a line officer who had complained of the inefficiency of a regularly appointed regimental surgeon: "But as you represent him to be unqualified for his office I shall direct Dr. Cochran to have him examined and retained or dismissed as his qualifications may justify." It is interesting to note that the man resigned two weeks later.[156]

As the year 1779 came to a close and the impending trial of the Director General was the talk of the department, the morale of many medical officers plummeted to a new low. The New Englanders seem to have taken particular offense at their shabby treatment by Congress. As that body dawdled on the matter of half-pay, bounty lands, and other benefits already granted to the line officers, there was a halfhearted move towards a mass resignation to take place on January 1, 1780. This threat, however, had little effect on a stubborn Congress, then thoroughly disenchanted with the titular head of the department.[157]

When the army returned to winter quarters at Morristown in the fall of 1779, Cochran rented for his family the house of another army surgeon, Jabez Campfield, who had just returned from serving with General John Sullivan's expedition against the Indians.[158] From the original site of the two-story gambrel roof structure on King's Highway, Cochran could look across the village green to the Ford mansion, where Washington had set up headquarters.[159] The winter proved to be one of unparalleled severity, the hardships of the soldiers surpassing even those of Valley Forge. With drifts four to six feet high, many of the regiments were forced to remain in tents until February.[160]

156. Clements and King were sent to join General Charles Scott in the South (GW to Scott, July 27, 1779 [Fitzpatrick, 15: 492]), and GW to Colonel Michael Jackson, August 11, 1779 (*ibid.*, 16: 81–82). The surgeon, Calvin Scott, resigned on August 28.

157. Nathaniel Scudder to Nathaniel Peabody, December 6, 1779 (Burnett, 4: 532–33). See also Packard, 1: 608, and Warren, pp. 198–99.

158. Campfield returned from Sullivan's expedition on October 2, 1779. His diary of the expedition is preserved in the New Jersey Historical Society (Wickes, pp. 194–95).

159. Mills (pp. 209–19) devotes an entire chapter to the Campfield house, occupied by the Cochrans on December 17. Better known as the Hamilton-Schuyler house, the structure which now stands at 5 Olyphant Drive, near Morris Avenue, is administered by the local chapter of the Daughters of the American Revolution. For some years the Letter-Book was on display there. Cochran stored medical supplies there (Fitzpatrick, 17: 282) and may have used herbs grown in the garden (Ives, p. 12).

160. Torres-Reyes (p. 5) speaks of the "six long winter months of unparalleled and continuous severity."

The thickness of the ice made it possible to drive teams of horses from the Jersey shore to Staten Island, and this unusual phenomenon was put to military use in mid-January 1780, when Cochran accompanied Lord Stirling, several thousand men, and 300 sleds over the frozen Amboy Bay in an unsuccessful attempt to capture a British fort on Staten Island. The rigors of this disappointing episode, the scarcity of alcoholic beverages, then considered so essential in freezing weather, and the utter lack of basic medical equipment are well described in Cochran's humor-tinged letter to Andrew Craigie, the Apothecary General.[161]

Dr. James Tilton, then in charge of the general hospital at Basking Ridge, seven miles south of Morristown, was permitted by Cochran to erect the well-ventilated, experimental "hutts" of his own design. These contributed to a drastic reduction in the mortality which might well have been anticipated during that cruel winter. Tilton's undoubted success made him even more conceited and quite contemptuous of authority. His later insistence that as many sick as possible be kept in the smaller camp hospitals, as well as his demand that the regimental surgeons be treated as equals of the general hospital personnel, undoubtedly stemmed from this favorable Morristown experience.[162]

Early in 1780, Gertrude's niece, Elizabeth Schuyler, finally persuaded her father that she be permitted to visit Morristown in order to help her uncle care for the sick soldiers, a task that she and her aunt performed faithfully every day. The Cochrans were among those who had subscribed four hundred Continental dollars for an "assembly" in camp; at one of the dances the dark-eyed, soft-spoken girl succeeded in attracting the attention of the sophisticated beau, Alexander Hamilton. He haunted the Cochran home night after night, and tradition has it that the tired surgeon returning chilled after a demanding day in the field was unable to stretch out on his favorite sofa, firmly occupied

161. The Craigie letter of January 18, 1780, is included in "Additional Letters," *infra* p. 226; see also Thacher, *Military Journal*, p. 225.

162. Dr. John Jones, the famous surgeon whom Tilton admired, had early inveighed against overcrowding in general hospitals. For the most recent study of the location and construction of Tilton's huts, see Torres-Reyes, pp. 83–84. By February 15 the hospital was in full use, and Tilton requisitioned enough wood to serve for a month or two (Weedon, *Orderly Book*, p. 149). As a former regimental surgeon Tilton was unusually sympathetic to this group. For an insight into his self-conceit, see Tilton to Nicholas van Dyke, Aug. 6, 1779 (HSP).

by the young lovers.[163] Gertrude, the prudent aunt, became somewhat concerned at this tempestuous wooing, and may well have hastened the arrival of her brother Philip. The latter came at Washington's invitation at the end of April with two other delegates, ostensibly to act as a liaison between Congress and the Army.[164] After a brief stay with the Cochrans, Betsey Schuyler's parents rented a house of their own, which soon became another center of gaiety. The young couple announced their engagement in May, shortly before the Schuylers left for Albany. When Baron Steuben, under whose gallant protection Philip had placed his enamored daughter, reviewed the troops at Bound Brook in honor of the Chevalier de la Luzerne, the newly arrived French minister, Gertrude Cochran, her niece, and other Schuyler and Livingston relatives were prominent among the ladies present to grace the occasion.[165]

From mid-March Morristown was in a flurry as the long delayed court-martial of William Shippen, which Washington, bowing to the demand of Congress, had ordered at the end of the previous year, finally began its deliberation. The trial brought a host of witnesses to the small community, many of them physicians, but Cochran seems to have done his best to avoid showing partiality in the controversy.[166] It is not without significance, however, that when Benjamin Rush came to testify against Shippen he was entertained at dinner on March 20, 1780, by his old Trenton comrade-at-arms.[167]

163. Mills (pp. 209–13) has a good account of the romance. See also Lamb, 2: 234–35; Wilson, *Memorial History*, 3: 95–96; and Desmond, pp. 89–91.

164. Schuyler, John Mathews, and Nathaniel Peabody arrived on April 28, 1780 (Burnett, 5: 132–34). On May 10, Schuyler wrote to Congress: "We have omitted observing that the Medical Department are destitute of those necessaries which are indispensable to the sick."

165. The Chevalier de la Luzerne, second French minister, presented his credentials to Congress on November 4, 1779. For the parade, see Humphreys, *David Humphreys*, 1: 158.

166. Shippen may have had a last opportunity to eliminate Morgan as a prosecutor. There is an unusual letter from General Daniel Brodhead dated November 23, 1779, indicating Morgan's desire to return to active duty (Pennsylvania Archives, series 1, vol. 12, p. 191).

167. The arrest was postponed for six months despite Morgan's persistence. Finally on December 17, 1779, Washington wrote to Morgan: "It is my intention to arrest the Dr. as soon as it can be done" (Fitzpatrick, 17: 282). For the court-martial itself, see Bell, "Court-Martial," pp. 220–39, and Gibson, pp. 242–50. There are also unpublished letters of Shippen, Rush, and Potts among the papers of John Laurance, the trial judge (NYPL). Potts seeks to defend Shippen. Marshall describes how Shippen nullified Morgan's attempts to obtain testimony (Duane, pp. 234, 249).

The Shippen indictment had two important results: one was an immediate tightening of the congressional funding for medical services, and this penury was to plague Cochran until the end of the war.[168] The other was that, with Shippen under technical arrest, many of his administrative duties were automatically shifted to Cochran's shoulders.[169] The Director's efficiency, questionable in the best of circumstances, undoubtedly deteriorated even further under the pressure of preparing his defense. Washington increasingly sought the counsel of Cochran, who was authorized to communicate with the Medical Committee and other key figures as the de facto head of the department. Shippen, now anxious to disclaim any involvement in the Morgan dismissal, sought and obtained an open letter from Richard Henry Lee in which he piously denied that Shippen had made any effort to discredit Morgan with Congress. Instead he placed the entire onus for Morgan's cavalier treatment on an obvious scapegoat, Samuel Chase of Maryland, then about to undergo scrutiny by Congress as a speculator in needed stores. Chase was characterized by Lee as the man who had almost single-handedly led the drive in Congress against Morgan.[170]

Cochran's first move as the acting head of the medical corps was to approach the congressional committee in Morristown with the request that the surgeons serving until the close of the war receive the same retirement pay allowances which Congress had recently granted to line officers. He then must have suggested to Philip Schuyler that he

168. Gibson, pp. 231. Robert Morris boasted about his curtailment of Medical Department expenditures during and after the period of the Shippen trial. The close ties between Shippen and Potts, the Purveyor-General, made the latter suspect in some quarters. His name was later linked with that of Foster in an order to turn over all stores bought for public use. Craik warns Potts in a friendly letter, urging him to "keep Dr. Cochran and the Army well supplied; their wants are much noted"; and Potts wrote to Congress in his own defense upon his retirement in October 1780 (Gibson, pp. 257–59).

169. Before and during Shippen's period of technical arrest (January 3 to August 18, 1780), Cochran was called upon to make important decisions. From February 1780 on he was authorized to sign the monthly returns on the general hospitals (NA, 3911, 8901, and 8905); on April 8, 1780, he was consulted by the physicians of Connecticut as the source of authentic information relating to the medical establishment of the Army (Connecticut State Library); and on April 11 he wrote a highly critical letter to the Medical Committee ("Additional Letters," *infra* pp. 227–28).

170. Shippen to Lee, April 10, 1780, in *Southern Literary Messenger* (May 1860), pp. 344–55. Lee to Shippen, May 7, 1780 (Ballagh, 2: 178–80).

inform the Medical Committee in Philadelphia about the distressing state of the hospital affairs. William Houston made the following informative reply to Schuyler:

> It is painful for me to say, I cannot be surprised at it. The prodigeous number of idle officers in that Department is a publick scandal. There is, I am told, no Hospital here [Philadelphia] nor within twenty miles of the town, and yet, I suppose, there are not less than a score of hospital officials who are doubtless entitled to whatever they wish to draw from the Purveyour's store as well as ordinary rations. You must remember the Return made here last winter before the hospital was moved, when there were 50 hospital officers and 133 patients. It is not a Trife will supply the officers here, as many of them are high in office, though I cannot hear of anything they do and it is to be supposed the same circumstances exist in other places.

Houston insists that the Medical Committee has the power to correct the situation: "Difficulties will arise but a little Resolution and Perseverance will reconcile them." [171] Such complaints about Shippen's Philadelphia friends must have been widespread, and he now tried to fill the Philadelphia hospital in order to justify their presence in the city.[172] Although Shippen's long, drawn-out trial, with its unseemly denunciations and incriminations, had finally come to a close by the end of June, the Director was unable to resume his duties until the records of the trial were approved by Congress.[173] British successes in the South during the spring of 1780, and the capture of many medical officers at the fall of Charleston on May 12, resulted in a serious disruption of services in that area, and this situation demanded immediate attention.

171. William Houston to PS, May 13, 1780 (Burnett, 5: 139). Malachi Treat also had some suggestions for Schuyler. On April 26, 1780, he wrote that he was not disappointed about the half-pay and bounty lands since "each Department has more persons employed than are necessary for the public good, and as our System among the others in unwieldy and Burthensome it is necessary that Congress should reduce the Numbers, before it can with Propriety grant us what our Services and Merit may deserve" (Schuyler Papers, NYPL). This opinion of a prominent hospital surgeon may well have influenced Congress in its radical elimination of many supernumerary medical officers.

172. In the *Pennsylvania Evening Post* (April 26, 1780) a notice signed by Thomas Bond, Jr., requested the commanding officers of Continental battalions in New Jersey, Pennsylvania, Delaware, and Maryland to send "such sick as are in a situation to be removed to the general hospital in Philadelphia."

173. Fitzpatrick, 19: 181–82; Tilton MS, vol. 4: 353 (Deleware Hall of Records, Dover).

On July 15, 1780, Washington sent Cochran to Philadelphia with the findings of the Shippen court-martial. Cochran was also instructed to discuss with Congress the mounting problems of the department, "in much disorder already," to urge some positive action which might prevent further deterioration and thus avoid "the same calamities which prevailed in 1776."

Cochran did stay on in Philadelphia for more than one week, pleading with the Medical Committee for much-needed supplies, for some back pay for his officers, many of whom had been made literally destitute by inflation, and for retirement privileges similar to those already granted to line officers. He also asked for authority to transfer medical officers to new posts or to field service as duty might require.[174] Shippen seems also to have been in Philadelphia that week; a cryptic note from James Lovell, the Massachusetts delegate, to Nathaniel Peabody, dated July 22, 1780, seems to indicate that the conscientious Cochran did indeed take a dim view of Shippen and his coterie, still enjoying a leisurely existence on inactive status in Philadelphia: "A thought struck me from seeing [Cochran's] behavior to the *Family of Bethlehem* particularly to the *Virgin* that he is quite capable of giving anecdotes that may be depended on." [175]

Apparently, John Mathews of the Congressional Committee, having spent some time in Morristown, had a better understanding of the disturbed state in which the department found itself, and agreed with Cochran in the matter of reassigning men from one department to another as required by necessity. Like Houston, Mathews took a dim view of the number of medical officers in Philadelphia "with no visible employment," and his important letter carries an implied criticism of the Director General.[176]

174. For the report of the Medical Committee on the meeting with Cochran, see Owen, p. 135 (July 21, 1780). Cochran was reasonably successful in this, his first confrontation with Congress. Potts, as Purveyor-General, was given $200,000 "for the use of the general hospitals in the middle district" (*Journals of the Continental Congress* 17 [1780]: 648).

175. Lovell to Peabody (NA, MS file, no. 3619). Apparently Shippen was alluded to as "the virgin of Bethlehem." In WL to JC, August 23, 1780 (Livingston Papers, NYHS) he speaks of the possibility that Cochran "go to the South this Winter." If such a trip was ever made, there is no evidence to substantiate it.

176. Mathews to Medical Committee, August 10, 1780 (Burnett, 5: 320–21). This letter indicates how actively Congress was debating the new restrictions on the size of

Congress received the court-martial proceedings on July 18, 1780, and debated the issue until August 16 before exonerating Shippen of all charges except that of speculating in hospital stores. The delegates then proceeded to consider the Medical Department's "new arrangement," which contemplated a drastic reduction in the number of senior medical officers on active duty. On September 9, Washington, fearful of political skullduggery in regard to his favorites, again took the unusual step of writing to three members of Congress, declaring that "Dr. Cochran and Dr. Craik, for their services, abilities, experience and close attention, have the greatest claim to their country's notice." [177] There is no mention of Shippen in this letter, and Washington must have known or surmised that the Director was about to retire.

John Mathews replied to Washington's letter on September 15, 1780. He admitted that there was "a new arrangement for the Medical Department now before Congress, and nearly completed, by which there will be a great reduction of officers," but cautioned that Congress "will not be too much influenced by the spirit which has given a well-grounded alarm to the gentlemen concerned." [178] On September 30 the "new arrangement" became law and on October 6 and 7 the congressional ax fell with a vengeance, sweeping away many Shippen satellites, including the efficient Jonathan Potts. [179] He was replaced as Purveyor General by Thomas Bond, Jr., another member of the Philadelphia circle. Bond's own term, however, proved to be a

---

the Medical Department at the very time that Cochran was complaining about a shortage of good young surgeons. See also Binney's caustic comments (Gibson, p. 260).

177. The letters went on September 9, 1780, to Joseph Jones, John Mathews, and James Duane (Fitzpatrick, 20: 18–19). Acting on Cochran's advice (JC to Duane, September 9, 1780, "Additional Letters," *infra* pp. 229–30), Washington also commended Drs. Latimer, Hagan, Tilton, Townsend, and the apothecary, Craigie.

178. Mathews to GW, September 15, 1780 (Burnett, 5: 372–73) concerns the impending new arrangement of the Medical Department and the reduction of officers. Jones wrote to James Madison on October 2 (*ibid.*, pp. 398–99) suggesting that Cochran and Craik deserve the attention of Congress for long and faithful services. Madison replied on October 10 (*ibid.*, pp. 417–18) indicating that the two senior surgeons had not been forgotten.

179. Although Duncan (*Medical Men*, p. 329) considers the reorganization plan of September 30 "presumably the work of John Cochran," there is no evidence to support this view. Indeed, JC to Duane, September 9, 1780 (NYHS), attributes the new plan, as being as close to the British system as circumstances will permit, to Shippen. But Shippen disavows the plan as "mean, vulgar and contemptible" (Shippen to Lee, Octo-

difficult one as he met with one rebuff after another from the tightfisted Robert Morris.[180]

Many veteran medical officers previously prominent in the Revolutionary service decided to retire at this point, being unwilling to be "deranged" to the newly created, egalitarian rank of "Hospital Physician and Surgeon." These resignations left the Middle Department without many competent surgeons, much to the distress of Cochran, who on October 6, 1780, had been commissioned "Chief Physician and Surgeon of the Army attached to the General Staff." On the same day Shippen was reappointed to his former post, but "with difficulty," and though this action was tantamount to an official vindication, he knew that his position was basically untenable. He seems now to have accused Cochran most unjustly of wanting to supplant him.[181] Fortunately, Shippen received at this time, either by chance or design, what amounted to a virtual ultimatum from President Joseph Reed of the Philadelphia College to return to his professorship in anatomy or be replaced.[182] In fact, he had continued to retain his academic standing for a full four years after entering the Army, spending much of his time giving courses in anatomy for pay while serving as Director General. His letter of resignation to Congress, dated January 3, 1781, and the letter to Washington the following day, both gave a desire to resume teaching as the reason for his retirement. Shippen's resignation surprised no one, and his departure was mourned by none but his Philadelphia cronies.[183]

Cochran, undaunted by the radical changes recently ordered by

---

ber 27, 1780, Lee, *Memoir*, 2: 172). The substance of the reorganization plan probably originated with the Medical Committee of Abraham Clark, Ezekiel Cornell, and Theodoric Bland, assisted by other members of Congress and possibly by John Jones. Potts fell victim to his unswerving loyalty to Shippen.

180. The papers of Robert Morris show a lack of communication between Bond and the budget-minded financier, and this situation led to serious consequences for the Medical Department.

181. *Journals of the Continental Congress* 18 (1780): 908; JC to Duane, October 20, 1780 "Additional Letters," *infra* p. 232). For Shippen's indecision, see his letter to Lee (Lee, *Memoir*, 2: 172).

182. Joseph Reed to Shippen, December 8, 1780 (Pennsylvania Archives, series 1, vol. 8, p. 643). Reed was later accused of having offered Shippen an easy way out of his embarrassment (Brunhouse, p. 104).

183. James Duane's motion of November 24, 1780, that Shippen "repair to headquarters," may have brought about the final decision to resign on January 3, 1781. Congress accepted immediately (Owen, p. 160). In his letter of the following day to

Congress, persisted in efforts to secure equal benefits for his medical officers. Finally, on November 6, 1780, he obtained the crucial support of Washington in the matter of retirement pay.[184] Cochran soon left on a preliminary inspection tour of the medical facilities along the Hudson, where Washington proposed to spend the winter. Later in the month Chastellux, the famous French traveler, visited the Fishkill hospital. Although he does not mention Cochran by name, he may well have been the "Doctor" of the hospital, "who had seen me pass by and recognized me as a French general officer [and] with great politeness came to inquire if I wanted anything and to offer me every service." Chastellux had high praise for the "zeal, perseverance and attention" of the Medical Department, and was impressed by the high regard in which medical men were held by the public and military alike.[185]

As 1780 drew to a close Cochran stayed briefly with his family at the John Ellison house in New Windsor. He later thanked Timothy Pickering, the recently appointed Quartermaster General, for building "a small place for our servants and kitchen." [186] From then until the end of the war the Army wintered in the vicinity of Newburgh, and Cochran spent much of his time at Fishkill and other medical installations in the area. It was while on a visit to the Manor on December 10, 1780, that the ever-hopeful William Smith, still elated by the recent defection of Benedict Arnold, audaciously suggested that Cochran approach Washington to effect a reunion with Britain.[187] The Cochrans may have stopped at the Manor on their way to Albany for the Schuyler-Hamilton wedding, which took place on December

---

Washington, Shippen explains that Congress considered his duties as Director General "incompatible with those of Professor of Anatomy" (George Washington Papers, LC).

184. The memorial to Congress, dated November 4, is co-signed by Cochran, Craik, Latimer, and Hagan (Tilton MS, vol. 4: 359 [Delaware Hall of Records, Dover]). GW to Congress, November 5, 1780 (Fitzpatrick, 20: 293–94); GW to JC, November 6, 1781 (Fitzpatrick, 20: 307).

185. Chastellux, 1: 87, 265–66. The two men may have met again at the Preakness camp (Baker, pp. 197–99) or at John Ellison's in New Windsor, where both men can be placed in December. After the war Chastellux wrote to Cochran asking him to sponsor Jean-François Coste, the chief medical officer of the French Expeditionary Forces, for the Order of the Cincinnati (Benjamin Franklin Papers, vol. 23, p. 127 [American Philosophical Society]).

186. JC to Pickering, December 16, 1780 (NA, 2238).

187. Van Doren, p. 395; see also Smith, 2: 358.

14. On his return Cochran dined with Washington (December 26) and three days later left for Philadelphia, apparently having been advised to anticipate developments in the matter of Shippen's impending retirement.[188]

Congress proceeded with unusual alacrity to the discussion of a successor. On January 9, 1781, the names of John Cochran, James Craik, and William Brown were brought up for discussion. The lifelong friendship of Washington and Craik has led some writers to believe that the former might have favored Craik's appointment to the directorship. There is no evidence, however, that Washington took any active part in persuading Congress, which on January 17 proceeded to appoint John Cochran Director General of the Hospital of the United States.[189] Possibly suspecting Washington's preference in the matter, Cochran may well have been telling the truth when he later wrote to Craik that he would have preferred to remain in his old position with fewer responsibilities.[190]

The year 1781 proved to be the most significant and challenging in John Cochran's long military career. Fortunately, we can refer to the extensive correspondence in his letter copy book for this period, which illuminates the old and new problems he encountered with this office. For almost an entire year the department had been functioning without an authoritative head, and the entire corps was dispirited and fragmented. Adding to the general discontent was the stark fact that many medical officers, unpaid for two years, were unable to supply the needs of their impoverished families. Of the fifteen veteran officers reappointed on October 7, 1780, only eight remained on active duty. A penurious Congress, now completely dominated by the economy-minded Robert Morris, was reluctant to approve the replacements now strongly recommended by Cochran.[191]

188. Dr. Samuel Adams mentions the dinner (Hunter, p. 638). Cochran also brought with him a letter from Hamilton to Washington, dated December 19 (GW to Hamilton, December 27, 1780 [*Hamilton Papers*, 2: 526]).

189. Cochran was nominated by James Mitchell Varnum and elected on January 17 (Owen, p. 161). His letter of acceptance addressed to Samuel Huntington on February 3 ("Letter-Book," *infra* p. 93) was read in Congress on February 19 (Owen, p. 166). For Washington's alleged preference, see Phalen (p. 19), who gives no evidence.

190. JC to Craik, March 26, 1781, "Letter-Book," *infra* p. 106.

191. On May 24, 1781, Cochran pointed out to Congress that there were many vacancies caused by resignations, and urged replacements ("Letter-Book," *infra* p. 118).

Others who had found themselves threatened by the "New Arrangement" were three New Englanders—Isaac Foster, Philip Turner, and John Warren—all of whom had been holding on to relative sinecures in their peaceful section of the country. The Foster case proves clearly that speculation in hospital necessities by officers of the corps was not confined to Shippen, and must have been more widespread than is generally realized. As early as 1778, Foster had begun to build up his own stores. His attempt to remove these from Danbury as private property when he resigned, followed by Washington's stern threat to retain them by force if necessary, form an unpleasant episode in the medical history of the Revolution.[192] Turner now applied political pressure in an unsuccessful attempt to have a hospital established at New London, a move which Cochran opposed as entirely unnecessary. Turner did not leave the service until June 13, alleging that only a deep sense of loyalty had overcome his original impulse to spurn the degrading new rank and retire at once.[193]

But it was the notoriously difficult John Warren who gave Cochran the greatest aggravation by defying repeated orders of Congress and the commander in chief to close the Boston hospital and report to headquarters for reassignment. Warren's resort to political chicanery in an attempt to maintain his desirable position was in marked contrast to the conscientious efforts of Cochran to heal wounds and satisfy the legitimate wants of the men under his command.[194]

Only Thomas Bond, Jr., the Shippen admirer who had been passed over completely in the consideration of a new Director, seems to have

192. GW to JC, February 12, 1781 (Fitzpatrick, 21: 217). As early as October 19, 1780, Potts and Foster had been cautioned about stores (Owen, p. 154).

193. Cochran denied the need for this hospital, which had been established under political pressure by Jonathan Trumbull on May 10, 1780 ("Letter-Book," *infra* p. 110; Owen, pp. 132–33). Frustrated in his attempt to obtain this sinecure, Turner resigned, declaring that his demotion "under the late election of officers was a designed affront too notorious for me to Honour" (NA, 93, 3787, June 11, 1781). He later claimed that Cochran had misunderstood him and that he had not resigned, but as late as 1788 his claim had not been settled (NA, Miscellaneous Record Books, vol. 138, pp. 101–3). Not until April 22, 1808, did Congress decide in his favor (Graves, p. 19).

194. Prodded by Robert Morris, Congress on October 10, 1781, ordered the closing of three hospitals, including the one at Boston (Peters to JC, "Appendix A," *infra* pp. 265). Cochran conveyed this information to Warren on October 20, ("Letter-Book," *infra* p. 155–56), but on October 22 suggested that he "stand fast." Eight months later Warren was still in possession, at which time (June 18, 1782) Washington ordered Cochran to close the hospital immediately (Fitzpatrick, 24: 357).

been disgruntled at Cochran's appointment, declaring that neither Cochran nor Craik was qualified to head the department.[195]

On a more pleasant side the new Director was gratified to learn on January 19, 1781, the very day of his confirmation, that his persistent efforts had been successful in one direction; henceforth, medical officers who served until the end of the war, or who were honorably discharged, would receive equal treatment with line officers in respect to half-pay for life.[196] In one of his first official acts Cochran ordered Malachi Treat to evacuate partially the hospital which then occupied the much deteriorated "Pennsylvania Hutts" at Jockey Hollow, and transfer the sick to Trenton. This decision was made just as the Pennsylvania line was reacting to congressional parsimony by breaking into mutiny.[197]

In February the inevitable smallpox made its appearance at New Windsor, necessitating a general inoculation of soldiers, wives, children, and camp followers.[198] With this work completed Cochran was in a position to accompany Martha Washington on a pleasant three-week jaunt up the Hudson, during which they stopped at Livingston Manor, among other places, before reaching the Schuyler mansion in Albany.[199]

Upon returning to camp on April 5, 1781, Cochran came down with an attack of pleurisy which kept him confined for the rest of the month.[200] During this period Washington wrote to Cochran again

195. JC to Craik, March 26, 1781, "Letter-Book," *infra* p. 106.

196. Owen (p. 162) reports the action of Congress on January 17, 1781, in response to the memorial and the Washington letter (see n. 184, *supra* p. 65). On March 22 this was amended to give medical officers the option of accepting the equivalent of five years pay at one time (Gibson, p. 305).

197. Treat to GW, January 27, 1781 (George Washington Papers, LC). Despite the unsatisfactory conditions the hospital was only gradually disbanded. Monthly sick reports continued until June (see "Letter-Book," *infra* p. 183).

198. GW to Heath, February 2, 11, 1781 (Fitzpatrick, 21: 170–71). Baxter (p. 453) credits Cochran with unusual kindness to the children and wives of the enlisted men. In spite of several so-called general inoculations, smallpox remained a menace to the troops throughout the war.

199. On March 3, 1781, Cochran arranged for a barge to pick up Martha Washington at Fishkill Landing (Sparks, *Washington*, 2: 302, NYHS). The trip of eighteen days must have covered March 6–24. See JC to Craik, March 26 ("Letter-Book," *infra* p. 106).

200. GW to Heath, April 12, 1781 (Fitzpatrick, 21: 450). See also JC to his officers, May 1, 1781, "Letter-Book," *infra* p. 113. By April 30, Cochran had recovered sufficiently so that he could invite several young medical officers for dinner (Thacher, *Journal*, pp. 310–11).

expressing his concern about soldiers incorrectly reported "Sick absent in the service of the Hospital . . . [being] apprehensive that many of the men are not in being, or cannot be accounted for." He urged the new Director to provide more accurate returns of all hospitals, a task which Cochran conscientiously attempted to fulfill in spite of poor coperation from John Warren and others.[201] In addition to his administrative duties, Cochran was often called upon to treat the families of officers on Washington's staff, and Martha herself seems to have had great confidence in his abilities. Through a series of letters we can trace the gradual decline of Mrs. Eliza Webb, a youthful victim of tuberculosis, who succumbed despite the best efforts of Cochran and Craik, who often collaborated on the most friendly basis.

Late in May, Cochran left an ailing Martha Washington under the care of Craik and traveled to Philadelphia. There he confronted an intransigent, politically motivated Board of War, which on May 28, 1781, had assumed supervision of all matters relating to the Hospital from the more sympathetic Medical Committee.[202] Through correspondence and personal appearances he again made clear his views on such matters as promotions, back pay, depreciation of currency, and free postage. Cochran as always acted in the best interest of the men under his command.[203] It was while advancing his thoughts about a general reorganization of the department that he sensed, possibly for the first time, the resistance inspired by James Tilton's *Oeconomical Observations.* This controversial paper, which bears the date January 1,

201. On April 30, 1781, Washington requested "returns from all the Hospitals under your Direction this side Susquehanna River" (NA, Orderly Book, no. 162, p. 15). A return of Cochran to Robert Morris is dated July 23, 1781 (Papers of the Continental Congress, vol. 22, pp. 61–62). By this time Morris was already at the height of his power and a veritable financial dictator.

202. See the request of Charles Stewart for "restoratives" for Martha (May 21, 1781, Henry Clinton Papers [William L. Clements Library, University of Michigan]). Craik later brought Martha to Philadelphia, where Cochran must have consulted with him. During the Newburgh period, when Martha's illness delayed the commander's final departure to Virginia, Cochran remained in constant attendance (Cochrane MS, Yale University Library). See also Cochran to Webb, March 4, 1781 ("Additional Letters," *infra* p. 235); Ford, *Correspondence,* 2: 344, 361, 367.

203. JC to Samuel Huntington, May 24, 1781 ("Letter-Book," *infra* pp. 116–18). This outspoken letter was referred to the Board of War. For the action of Congress, see Owen p. 175. While still in Philadelphia, Cochran wrote to the New Jersey Assembly, requesting the depreciation in pay recommended by Congress (June 22, 1781, Stryker Collection). The order to pay is dated June 10, 1782 (Auditor's Acct. Bk. A, p. 331 [New Jersey State Library]).

1781, had undoubtedly been circulating for months behind closed doors.[204] Indeed, on June 17 the Board of War had already placed itself firmly on record as being in favor of promotion by seniority or length of service. This was a radical concept which Cochran, with his dim view of regimental mates as some "kind of cattle the politicians would call in," was bound to view with dismay.[205]

Cochran remained in Philadelphia for a month, attempting to make his views clear. But on July 14, 1781, in spite of Cochran's demurrer, the Board of War recommended to Congress that in future no distinction be made between hospital and regimental surgeons in the matter of promotion, and that a line officer preside over all medical examining boards. Congress, hesitant to approve so radical a departure, ordered the Board of War to submit all relevant correspondence to Washington, who in turn transmitted the papers to a special board of officers then convened at Dobbs Ferry, requesting their advice on the controversial issue. Cochran met with this board in person to plead for caution, but the concept of promotion by seniority naturally appealed to the general officers present and they voted in favor of it. They seem, however, to have reversed themselves immediately by conceding to the Director the right to examine, certify, or reject all candidates for appointment or promotion. It was these recommendations, which in effect represented an incomplete victory for the leveling forces headed by Tilton, Jones, and Morris, that Congress voted into law on September 25.[206] Four days later Cochran was grat-

204. As recently as 1971, Torres-Reyes (p. 84) considered the original of this salient document to have been lost. A year earlier, however, it had been discovered in the library of the New-York Historical Society and has since appeared in print (*Robert Morris Papers*, 1: 323–34). For the early circulation of the paper among members of Congress, see Tilton to Rodney, March 11, 1781 (Tilton MS, vol. 4: 380 [Delaware Hall of Records, Dover]).

205. For the opposition of Cochran to "regular succession of Promotion of Physicians and Surgeons," see JC to Tilton, June 3, 1781 ("Letter-Book," *infra* pp. 118–19). For the opposing view of the Tilton-Morris-Jones group and Cochran, see the excellent résumé in the *Robert Morris Papers*, 1: 334–37, as well as Saffron, "The Tilton Affair."

206. See the most trenchant statement of Cochran to Robert Morris on this matter ("Letter-Book," July 26, 1781, *infra* pp. 129–31). Washington transmitted this letter with other pertinent papers to the Board of Generals on August 1, received their decision the following day (Papers of the Continental Congress, no. 148, vol. 2, pp. 269–70), and forwarded this to the Board of War on August 5 (Fitzpatrick, 22: 463; see also notes in *Robert Morris Papers*, 1: 389–91). On June 4, 1781 ("Additional Letters,"

ified to learn that the five surgeons he had recommended for promotion as early as June 4 had finally been approved, though with some reluctance since Congress felt that "the department [was] E already furnished with a sufficient number of officers of different ranks." [207]

It is of some interest to note that of the three guiding principles elaborated in Tilton's *Oeconomical Observations*, two were not at all original and were indeed perfectly acceptable to Cochran. He had no objection to the separation of the office of Purveyor General from the command of the Director General, such a separation having actually been in effect, on paper at least, since February 1778. Nor did Cochran dispute the importance of keeping the sick in small units at the regimental or brigade level when their maintenance in huts or even tents proved feasible.[208] It was only in his insistence on maintaining high standards of professional ability, and in his refusal to bow meekly to political pressure, that Cochran found himself in opposition. Nor did he hesitate to inveigh against the "Philadelphia Triumvirate," which he thought had wrongly influenced Morris and Congress in this controversy on promotion.

Bond fared no better than others with the tough Robert Morris. On July 2, 1781, the latter refused to authorize a new hospital in Philadelphia, suggesting with justification that it "would be much cheaper and better . . . to agree with the Pennsylvania Hospital to receive the Continental Patients at hard dollars." The hospital authorities did agree to receive all but the "putrid cases" which were to be sent to the "bettering house." [209]

---

infra p. 236), Cochran asks for the promotion of five mates, noting resignations; one month later seven of the fifteen authorized surgeons had resigned (JC to Board of War, June 30, 1781 ["Letter-Book," *infra* pp. 123–24]).

207. Congress accepted the final recommendations of the Board of War on the matter of seniority on September 30, 1781 (Owen, p. 180). It also agreed, albeit reluctantly, to the promotion of the five men recommended by Cochran (September 25 [Burnett, 6: 225]). For the adverse reaction of Cochran to the closing of the hospitals, see the correspondence with Warren, Bodo Otto, and Peters ("Letter-Book," October 20, 1781 *infra* pp. 155–60) and with Joseph Young (October 22, *infra* p. 163).

208. As early as December 31, 1777, Cochran had written to Waldo: "We shall soon have regimental Hospitals erected, and general ones to receive the Superabundant. . . ." ("Additional Letters," *infra* p. 220).

209. *Robert Morris Papers*, 1: 208, 236. On July 30 he found the "distress of the Hospital real" and advanced the sum of 2,000 hard dollars (*ibid.*, p. 413).

Cochran, having been apprised of Washington's designs on New York City, realized the need for a large medical installation in the Newburgh area. His request for a four-hundred-bed hospital was frowned upon as being too grandiose by Colonel Thomas Pickering, who decided that Cochran would have to do with "so much as will answer his instant wants." [210] After Yorktown the hospital was completed according to original plans, and eventually remained as the only medical installation in the Hudson valley.

With the southern campaign entering a peak of activity the Board of War requested belatedly in mid-September that plans be submitted for providing the medical officers now urgently needed by the troops under Generals Greene and Lafayette. Cochran, who from September 30, 1781, had been granted complete authority over medical affairs to the Carolinas, had already struggled with this problem, having sent several younger men to the South, and he would shortly transfer some of his best officers to Virginia.[211] Nevertheless, he hesitated to deplete the already meager northern staff any further. Congress now showed the high favor in which Cochran's views were held by ordering on September 20 that "the appointments be made in accordance with Dr. Cochran's wishes," even though an alternate plan prepared by James Craik carried Washington's blessing. As a result the men already appointed by Deputy Surgeon General David Oliphant of the southern command were confirmed, and Oliphant was authorized to make additional appointments on the spot as he thought

210. "Dr. Cochran has called for 400 Bunks, Straw etc. Is it not very curious that not one Gentleman of the Faculty should think of, or care for the situation of their Dept. till the campaign opens" (Colonel Hugh Hughes to Pickering, July 7, 1781 [NA, 26291]). "Dr. Cochran cannot for some time to come want all the bunks he demands, and the making of them, excepting so much as will answer his instant wants must not interrupt the capital works you have in hand" (Pickering to Hughes, July 9, 1781 [NA, Book 82, p. 10]). Cochran, nevertheless, persisted in his efforts to have a permanent installation erected in the area between the Clove and New Windsor (Tilton MS, vol. 3: 309 [Delaware Hall of Records, Dover]) and eventually succeeded (GW to Knox, November 8, 11, 1782 [Fitzpatrick, 25: 324, 329–30]). Blanchard (Balch, p. 131) describes a hospital near West Point as having unrepaired barns, with sick lying in single beds on straw, but with coverlets, and with bread and meat prepared by convalescents.

211. As early as January 23, 1779, Congress had reacted positively to the Cochran-inspired letter of Washington (see n. 149, *supra* p. 55, relating to the movement of medical officers; and Owen, pp. 110–11). The reorganization of September had extended the control of the Director General to the Carolinas, but not until March 22, 1781, did Cochran become the first Surgeon General to control all the medical officers of the United States Army (Owen, pp. 171–72).

necessary.[212] Although Cochran had earlier indicated that Washington wanted him "to continue in the Field this Campaign," he did not move to Virginia with Washington's staff, apparently conceding that honor to Craik, a Virginian by adoption. Instead, he seems to have spent much time in Philadelphia, where he could keep himself informed through channels of developments in the medical situation, prepared to supply further reinforcements if needed.[213]

In November, while Robert Morris was continuing his audit of Shippen's accounts, the Board of War produced still another, even more elaborate and radical "Ordinance for constituting and rearranging the Hospital Department." Clearly inspired by Tilton, this scheme would have gone even further in eliminating senior officers from positions of authority and in removing distinctions between hospital and regimental personnel, thus melding the entire Medical Department into one uniform corps.[214] Meanwhile, Cochran's letter to his old friend, Thomas McKean, President of Congress, denouncing many of the radical proposals then in the air, seems to have had the desired effect.[215] By the end of the year the tide of reform had ebbed, and a new committee rejected the "Ordinance" as completely useless, later making some insignificant revisions in the 1780 plan.[216] Tilton now came in for his share of criticism in the alleged mismanagement of the hospital in Williamsburg, Virginia, which he commanded. In coming to Tilton's defense Cochran took the opportunity, tongue in cheek, to chide the would-be reformer about "a vast variety of whim-

212. The various plans for supplying officers for the southern army were considered on September 17, and the Board of War voted to recommend the plan of Cochran (Owen, pp. 180–81). These plans are in the Papers of the Continental Congress, no. 148, vol. 2, ff. 259–75, with that of Cochran , dated June 4, on f. 273. See *Journals of the Continental Congress* 21 (1781): 981n.

213. In Philadelphia on Sept. 17, 1781, Cochran became a member of the Friendly Sons of St. Patrick and assisted at the gala on Jan. 1, 1782, when Washington was "adopted" by the order (Campbell, p. 45).

214. For the Shippen audit, see the Robert Morris Papers, Diary L, p. 59 (LC). For the elaborate proposed ordinance, see Owen, pp. 184–92. See also the note in Burnett, 6: 147, which reviews the erratic steps taken by Congress relating to the Medical Department from July 17 to the end of the year.

215. JC to McKean, October 9, 1781 ("Letter-Book," *infra* pp. 150–53).

216. On January 3, 1782, Congress passed a greatly modified version of the radical reorganization plan of November 3, 1781. The only important change involved the elimination of the titles of Chief Physician and Surgeon of the Army and Chief Hospital Physician in favor of the simple title Physician (Owen, p. 194).

sical systems which have been offered to Congress." He added as a final thrust: "I do not apprehend any essential alteration will be made." [217]

As the year 1781 drew to an end Morris continued to deny financial support to the distressed Medical Department, persisting in his efforts to close the hospitals at Yellow Springs, Albany, and Boston. In two highly critical letters he refused to "advance one shilling" to Bond and Oliphant for supplies, claiming that his consultant, the eminent Dr. John Jones, considered the estimate exorbitant and the medicines useless.[218] Morris even had the audacity to question the necessity of establishing a temporary hospital in Wilmington for the southern casualties, even though the move had been approved by Cochran with Washington's sanction.[219] Cochran must have returned periodically to Philadelphia at least until May, since the last entry from that city in his letter copybook is dated May 4, 1782.

It was at this rather late date that the Tilton-inspired thesis about the usefulness of regimental hospitals received official recognition in Congress. On May 12, 1782, Washington, replying to a suggestion from the Secretary of War, wrote: "Under proper Regulations and Restrictions, I am persuaded that the Measure of Regimental Tents will be very useful. I have desired Doctors Cochran and Craik to give us their Sentiments." A May 12 letter signed by Cochran, Craik, and Latimer, on which Washington based his opinion, gives convincing proof "that the mode recommended has been practiced in our army these several years when Circumstances would permit." [220]

217. See JC to Tilton, January 1, 1782 ("Letter-Book," *infra* p. 167). Acting on the advice of Cochran, Washington notifies Colonel Francis Mentges: "You cannot have any immediate control over the Physicians and Surgeons" (Fitzpatrick, 23: 423–24 [January 2, 1782]).

218. *Robert Morris Papers,* 2: 269. In all fairness it should be noted that by October 1 even Bond admitted to Cochran that the southern hospital was "pretty well supplied" ("Letter-Book," *infra* p. 148). Morris and the Medical Department continued to spar until the end of the war. On January 4, 1782, Morris told Cochran that he could not give priority to the Medical Department in the matter of pay. On February 19, 1782, he accused Bond of applying monies already received "to different purposes than those which were intended" (Official Letter-Book, Robert Morris Papers, LC).

219. GW to John Dickinson, December 3, 1781 (Fitzpatrick, 23: 368–69), and December 15, 1782 (*ibid.*, p. 392).

220. Replying to a letter from the Secretary of War, Washington on May 18, 1782 (Fitzpatrick, 24: 263) encloses the cosigned letter of Cochran, Craik, and Latimer

In June 1782, when the active phase of the war was almost at an end, Cochran was ordered to prepare a standard set of procedures relative to the examination and admission of candidates for the Corps of Invalids. This group had originally been established in 1777 and supervised by Colonel Lewis Nicola, but had hitherto remained rather loosely organized. With the end of hostilities in sight many of those permanently disabled were anxious to return to their families, and on December 9, 1782, Cochran helped to establish a Retirement Board for those who wished to be pensioned rather than remain in the Corps of Invalids.[221] Although Congress now reasserted the seniority principle of promotion for the medical corps, Washington later expressed certain misgivings that it might be "unproductive of general good".[222]

In the fall of 1782 there developed another of those unpleasant situations involving rank and precedence which frequently plagued the Continental Army. In 1780 and 1781 Cochran and his family had occupied quarters at John Nicoll's house in New Windsor, although the most desirable place in the Newburgh area for officers was John Ellison's house overlooking the Hudson. This had been occupied successively by Washington and Knox. When Knox, however, moved to the command of West Point, Cochran immediately rented part of the house for his family without first consulting the efficient but humorless Thomas Pickering. All would have gone well were it not for the unexpected reappearance in camp on October 5 of General Gates after two years of relative obscurity. Pickering, who had already angered Cochran by refusing to build him a bedstead similar to the one he had made for Gates, was now caught between two fires. He demanded that Cochran give up his quarters, since the general would accept no other and Washington was anxious to mollify the overly

("Additional Letters," *infra* p. 238). Although the three men agreed on the virtues of the regimental hospitals, Cochran remained unclear as to who was to pay for the regimental supplies (JC to GW, August 6, 1782 ["Additional Letters," *infra* pp. 240–41]).

221. For the classification of the members of the Corps of Invalids, see General Orders, August 3, 1782 (Fitzpatrick, 24: 460–61). See also *ibid.*, 25: 411; 26: 297; 27: 38. Henceforth the problems of veterans and compensation would involve Cochran and his colleague General Henry Knox for many years, with their collaboration continuing for a full decade after the war had ended (Feinstone Papers, August 13, 1792 [American Philosophical Society]; *Hamilton Papers*, 16: 587 [July 10, 1794]).

222. Fitzpatrick, 24: 356 (July 26, 1782).

sensitive Gates by keeping him close to headquarters. Cochran firmly refused to give up his place to Gates or anyone else unless equally suitable quarters were provided. With his occasionally excoriating tongue he accused Pickering of "Ignorance of [his] Profession of showing Partiality in Favor of those under [his] own inspection," of forcing Cochran to sleep "on three small [stools] and in consequence of catching a cold have gotten a return of fever," and of cooping up Cochran's "second in command in a small house" with no adequate supply of fuel. Cochran ended with the same threat he had made to Sullivan five years earlier: "Should you conceive your Feelings injured by the reply to your Scurrility, I am ready to give you any satisfaction, where Pen and Ink are not concerned." Fortunately, Cochran himself found the solution to this disagreeable situation. He expressed a willingness to take up quarters with the De Puyster family across the river, and Washington, happy to find any way out of the dilemma, readily granted permission.[223] Gates was pleased and Cochran's honor sustained; indeed, the two men are known to have dined amicably together a few weeks later.[224] Cochran and Pickering also soon patched up their differences.[225] This episode reveals Cochran as a gentleman, fully aware of the privileges due "an officer of my relative rank in the Army," and determined to command respect for the medical officer commensurate with his status. As in the Sullivan and *Symetry* affairs, his conduct seems to have received at least the tacit approval of the commander in chief, and undoubtedly helped bring about the long-deferred recognition of equality between line and medical officers.

Cochran's last year of military service was relatively quiet, but

223. For the correspondence relating to this tempest in a teapot, see JC to Pickering, October 15, 23, November 2, 4, 1782 ("Additional Letters," *infra* pp. 241–44); Pickering to JC, October 15, 1782 (NA, Box 84, p. 198), November 3, 1782 (NA, Box 85, pp. 233–34). See also Pickering to Gates, November 7, 1782 (NA, Box 84, pp. 226–27); Gates to GW, November 7, 1782 (George Washington Papers, LC); JC to Gates, November 8, 1782 ("Additional Letters," *infra* p. 245).

224. On December 15, Cochran dined with General Gates, General Howe, and several medical officers (Thacher, *Journal*, p. 388).

225. By November 11, Pickering had agreed to build a kitchen and "double hutts" for Cochran near his new quarters, but requested that the kitchen not be more elaborate than "temporary use requires," and hoped that for the huts Cochran would supply wood from dismantled hospital quarters. For this correspondence, see NA, Box 81, p. 268; Box 87, p. 261; and NA, 93, 24351, item 10. For a later exchange about firewood, see NA 93, 24259, and NA, Box 86, p. 171, both dated May 2, 1783.

not totally devoid of interest for students of his career. In February 1783 he called attention to the plight of invalid officers residing at home for whom no adequate provisions had been made by Congress.[226] He is known to have been at Albany from mid-February to early March, besieging the legislature with his old claim of 2,000 acres on the Mohawk River. He describes with glee how he won the battle "which exceeded the attack at Trenton; for to pay the King's debt was a bitter pill, but so it was that I crammed it down." [227] Back in camp by March 10, 1783, he may have heard the two inflammatory "Newburgh Addresses," and was almost certainly present when his hero, Washington, made the memorable speech at "The Temple" on March 15, which stilled forever the threat of a confrontation between the Army and Congress. Although the health of the troops was generally excellent at this time, one minor problem, the "itch," persisted, demanding a continual supply of brimstone.[228] At the end of April Cochran wrote Washington that some medical officers, in desperate need of money, would accept the five years of full pay offered by Congress in lieu of half-pay for life.[229] The staff itself had by now been reduced radically by resignations or retirements, but the loyal Cochran stayed on, undoubtedly at the urging of Washington. Shortly after the celebration of the peace treaty he became one of the original members of Baron Steuben's Society of the Cincinnati,[230] and

226. See JC to Pickering, February 2, 1783 ("Additional Letters," *infra* p. 246), and Pickering to Nicholas Quackenbush, February 3, 1783 (NA, 93, M.R.B. 86, p. 37). Congress reacted quickly and favorably to Cochran's plea for sick officers' allowances (Owen, pp. 213, 216).

227. JC to PS, March 9, 1783 (Schuyler Papers, NYPL). Years later (February 1, 1790) Cochran petitioned New York state for an additional 850 acres of bounty land (Assembly Papers, vol. 15, p. 222 [New York State Library, Albany]). No evidence of success in this matter can be found.

228. JC to Captain Lillie, March 25, 1783, refers to the sulfur supply ("Additional Letters," *infra* p. 250). Throughout the war this one drug was in constant demand.

229. The overly officious Morris boasted to Rush that he had reduced medical expenditures in one year from $5 million to $1 million dollars. Even allowing for exaggeration and a devalued currency, it was this neglect which caused Cochran to appeal directly to Washington for support (Gibson, p. 231; "Additional Letters," August 6, 1782, *infra* p. 240). Morris, who had sold Potts twelve cases of surgical instruments before entering on his official duties (Owen, p. 118), could not find enough money on August 5, 1781, for a Morristown cutler to complete an order (Joseph Morgan to [JC?] NA, 93, 29276).

230. The organization meeting on May 13, 1783, took place at Baron Steuben's quarters, Verplanck House, Fishkill. On February 2, 1784, at a meeting in New York City, Cochran was appointed to a committee charged with the preparation of bylaws (Schuyler, *Institutions*, p. 23).

in June he requested from Washington, already preparing to leave Newburgh, a formal certificate of service. It was received along with a brief but sincere personal letter, both of which follow:

TO DOCTOR JOHN COCHRAN

Head Quarters, August 10, 1783.

Dear Sir: It was not 'till Yesterday that I received your favor of the 25th of June. I now acknowledge the receipt of it, and thank you very sincerely for the kind Expressions of Benevolence and regard which you are pleased to extend to me; And to assure you, that I shall retain a cheerfull remembrance of past Services, and wish you every felicity in your future Life.

I take pleasure in sending you the Certificate requested. And am with much Regard etc.

CERTIFICATE TO DOCTOR JOHN COCHRAN

Head Quarters, Newburgh,
August 11, 1783

This certifies that Doctor John Cochran, during the present War, has been in the Service of the United States, acting in different medical Capacities, until the 17th of January 1781, when he was appointed Director of the Military Hospitals. That during the most of the Time, he has been under my immediate Inspection and Command; and in the various Stations in which he has acted, has discharged their several duties, with that Attention, Skill and Fidelity, as have gained my approbation.[231]

Almost the last formal order issued by Washington to his faithful surgeon was one of great significance for the future of our country. Relating to medical supplies for the forts of the interior, the General's letter urged Cochran to use his customary good judgment in providing for the welfare of the thinly dispersed troops: "As the preservation of the health of the Troops and perhaps the very existence of the Posts, which may be established on the Western Waters, will depend very much on this arrangement, I shall rely on your Activity and precision in having the business executed in the most effectual and satisfactory manner." [232]

Washington was forced to remain at Newburgh until August 18,

231. JC to GW, June 25, 1783 ("Additional Letters," *infra* p. 251); GW to JC, August 10, 11, 1783 (Fitzpatrick, 27: 95–96).

232. GW to JC, August 10, 1783 (Fitzpatrick, 27: 95).

1783, detained by the stubborn illness of Martha, who remained under Cochran's constant supervision during this period. This close relationship between the two families gives validity to the tradition, which has never been challenged, that Washington turned over the furniture of the Newburgh headquarters to the Cochrans on his departure.[233] Cochran, Pickering, Knox, and other officers are known to have remained at camp for several months, winding up affairs. It was here that Washington's Rocky Hill, N.J., address was read to the troops on November 3. On the same day John Cochran and his old friend from New Jersey, William Burnet, were among the many officers who were formally separated from the Army. On November 4, General Knox invited Cochran to come to West Point to help compose "a proper answer to the general's farewell orders." [234] On the same day Washington ordered Cochran to reduce even further the number of medical officers. Cochran's last return is dated November 11, 1783.[235] Of the entire medical staff only William Eustis and Samuel Adams with two mates continued to man the new building erected under Cochran's supervision at New Windsor, which would now remain as the only permanent medical installation in the north. Just how faithfully Cochran carried out his very last duties appears in this brief note from Robert Morris:

> Office of Finance 20 Decem. 1783
>
> Sir,
>
> I have received your favor the fifteenth Instant and entirely approve the Arrangements mentioned in it. Accept my Thanks for this Instance of Attention to the Public Interest, and believe me, With Esteem and Respect your most obedient and humble Servant.[236]

233. Baxter, p. 478.

234. According to Phalen (p. 16), Cochran was formally separated from the service on November 3 (Knox to Pickering, November 4, 1783 [NA, 3, 26550]; GW to JC November 4, 1783 [Fitzpatrick, 27: 230–31.

235. On November 4, 1783, Washington requested Cochran to "transmit me as soon as possible a List of such officers of your Department as it will be absolutely necessary to retain" (Fitzpatrick, 27: 230–31). On November 11, 1783, Cochran signed his final official Army returns (NA, 39121–D06).

236. Robert Morris Papers, LC. The Cochran letter has not been located.

New York City

During the relatively restful period before the ratification of the Articles of Peace, while matters of administration continued to occupy his attention, Cochran must often have given serious thought to his postwar plans. He had developed a close association with the great personalities of the new nation during his absence of seven years from New Brunswick, and the thought of returning to the arduous practice of a country physician had little allure for the fifty-two-year-old soldier, who had spent much of his mature life in the saddle away from home and family. It seems significant that as early as September 1781 he signed himself "John Cochran of the City of New York, physician" in witnessing the will of John Nicoll of New Windsor, and early in 1783 he is known to have had a New York address to which medicines could be shipped. When the Cochrans finally left the Newburgh area for New York late in the year they first occupied a house in Duke Street, but this proved to be either too small or inconveniently located. By the following May John Cochran and Walter Livingston had acquired jointly the twin houses of Richard Harrison at 95–96 Broadway, opposite the Lutheran church. For the better part of a decade the Cochran home was to remain a center of hospitality, where Schuyler and Livingston relatives mingled with prominent generals and political figures who "were entertained in a most princely manner." [237]

During the immediate postbellum period Cochran was frequently

237. *Abstracts of Wills*, 12: 243. See also Pickering to Knox (NA, Book 87, p. 229). The move to Broadway is noted in the *New York Packet* of May 3, 1784. The letter of Cochran and Walter Livingston to Richard Harrison, April 17, 1784, is in the Livingston Family Papers (NYHS). At this period Walter Livingston was serving as Commissioner of the United States Treasury. A year later Cochran was concerned about a payment on the house, having been unable to sell the house in New Brunswick (JC to PS, February 24, 1785 [Schuyler Papers, NYPL]). For the social life of the Cochrans, see Lamb, 2: 215. It should be remembered that James Duane, mayor of the city from 1784 to 1788, was married to Maria, a sister of Walter Livingston. Among the Cochran house guests were Anthony Wayne and John Paul Jones (Cochrane MS, Yale Univer-

called upon by John Pierce, the Paymaster General, to assist him in cases of retired medical officers applying for commutation.[238] A distinguished war reputation soon brought Cochran a wide patronage among the citizens of the city, and he was undoubtedly called into consultation by such old military companions as Malachi Treat and Charles McKnight. Along with these two men and Doctors Thomas Jones and Nicholas Romayne, Cochran formed part of the Columbia (formerly King's College) clique, headed by Alexander Hamilton and John Jay, which dominated the Board of Regents of the recently established University of the State of New York. Cochran resigned from the board in 1787, when Columbia was exempted from the provisions of the law of 1784 and permitted to function independently, but remained a trustee of Columbia College until he left New York City.[239]

Cochran soon found himself accepted by the most eminent physicians of the city and was on friendly terms with the celebrated Drs. Samuel Bard and John Jones. In 1787, when the medical faculty of Columbia was being reconstituted by Bard, Cochran, a man who held no medical degree, received the signal honor of being invited to join this distinguished group. He modestly declined the offer of a professorship, pleading the press of other duties and advancing years. Yet his younger colleague, Charles McKnight, did accept a lectureship in anatomy.[240]

It seems obvious that Cochran's continuing contact with his former

---

sity Library). Lamb (2: 221) tells that Wayne presented Cochran with a magnificent silver-hilted cutting sword; later the silver was melted down to make six goblets. Cochran is known to have been active in the Society of the Cincinnati and St. Andrews Society (Franks, *Directory* [1786], pp. 72, 73, 76).

238. In Pierce to Andrew Dunscombe, September 29, 1784 (NA, 28972), the former acknowledges the assistance received from Cochran. He even supplied a certificate of service for Thomas Tillotson, who had testified so viciously in the Sullivan affair (NA, Miscellaneous File 4598).

239. Sherwood, p. 551. Cochran remained a trustee of Columbia College until May 5, 1794, when he resigned "unable to attend from disposition" (Columbia College Minute Book, May 5 [Columbiana, Columbia University]). Son James, while a state senator in 1815, helped defeat a bill proposing incorporation of the Medical Institution of the State of New York, a rival school opposed by James's friend David Hosack, and by Samuel Mitchill and William MacNeven (Stookey, p. 158).

240. JC to PS, January 28, 1785 (Schuyler Papers, NYPL). Wilson (*Memorial History* 3: 18) has Cochran active in the affairs of the New York Medical Society. Franks *Directory* for year 1786 lists twenty-five physicians in a population of 23,614.

war companions, who kept pouring into the exciting capital of the new nation, and his many social activities, diminished his interest in the practice of medicine.[241] Like many another military man, he eventually decided to apply for one of the major political appointments then becoming available. Cochran must have derived some added pleasure in being selected over Thomas Pickering on May 8, 1786, for the position of "Receiver of Continental Taxes for the State of New York." [242] At this time he probably limited his medical work to an occasional consultation, turning over to Charles McKnight the bulk of his practice.[243] The new post did not provide the lucrative sinecure Cochran had anticipated, since Congress soon reduced the original allowance for office maintenance. Indeed, the many problems and responsibilities he now was forced to handle may well have aggravated a gradual tendency to hypertension. The land-poor Cochran was certainly no great businessman, as his later correspondence with Schuyler clearly shows, and he often experienced temporary financial difficulties.[244]

In April 1788, Cochran found himself a central figure in the disturbing incident known as the "Doctors' Mob." Accounts of the episode vary, but it appears that a certain Dr. John Hicks instigated the three-day reign of terror by waving at a boy a partially dissected arm supposedly belonging to the child's recently buried mother. Hicks then fled from Dr. Richard Bayley's anatomical room at the New York Hospital, hiding behind the chimney of Dr. Cochran's house in hopes

241. When a set of hounds arrived in New York from Lafayette, destined for Mount Vernon, Washington was grateful to Cochran for caring for them, "since war is declared against the canine species in New York." Washington refused to write a letter of recommendation for Cochran for an appointment, unwilling "to hazard the mortification of a refusal," but speaks warmly of "his friendship and inclination to promote your interests" (Fitzpatrick, 28: 233n., 240–41).

242. Rufus King to Pickering, June 17, 1786 (Burnett, 8: 146). King noted that Cochran had applied for the position but denied knowing his sponsor. Cochran was nominated by Judge John Laurance on May 3 and elected on May 8 (*Journals of the Continental Congress* 30 (1786): 228, 239). His acceptance is dated May 11 (Papers of the Continental Congress, no. 78, vol. 6, f. 315; Burnett 8: 351n.).

243. For Charles McKnight, see Duncan, *Medical Men*, pp. 346–47. At his untimely death in 1791 he was considered to be without peer as a surgeon. The loss of this disciple and dear friend must have been a severe blow for the ailing and harassed Cochran.

244. The memorial of Cochran (dated July 18) for additional funds was read on July 31, 1787, and denied on October 2 (*Journals of the Continental Congress* 33 (1787): 443–44, 589). For Cochran as a victim of the Susquehanna land fever, see JC to PS, April 4, 1783 (Schuyler Papers, NYPL).

that "because he had relenquished practice his home would not be searched." The mob, in violent pursuit, seems to have suspected that Hicks would seek the protection of so highly respected a physician, and the pursuers ransacked the house from cellar to garret, infuriated at not discovering their quarry, whom they would undoubtedly have torn limb from limb. Cochran and McKnight were among the four physicians who sought safety in the town jail. They were released in a day or two, but only after the wounded Baron Steuben had persuaded Mayor Duane to order the militia to fire into the still-threatening mob, killing several men.[245]

Shortly after this unpleasant experience, Cochran seems to have had the first of a series of mild strokes which precluded any possibility of a return to the practice of medicine. He realized correctly that his New York state position would terminate upon ratification of the Federal Constitution, and again became concerned about his future status. The day after Washington's inauguration, which he undoubtedly attended, Cochran wrote him a personal letter, outlining his situation and soliciting continuation in an office similar to the one he then held.[246] On August 1, 1790, the new President, recalling the assurance made eight years earlier to "retain a cheerfull remembrance of past services," appointed his old comrade-at-arms Commissioner of Loans of the United States for the State of New York.[247] This post proved to be even less of a sinecure than the previous one, since all his activities were now under the scrutiny of Alexander Hamilton, the Secretary of the Treasury, who refused to permit family connections to interfere with a demand for efficiency in office.[248] There is good reason

245. For somewhat varying accounts of the incident, see Duer, p. 21: Walker, p. 142; and Lamb 2: 306–7. See also Ladenhaim.

246. May 1, 1789 ("Additional Letters," *infra* pp. 256–57).

247. GW to Hamilton, September 25, 1789, mentions Cochran as one of "a great variety of characters who have made a tender of their services" (Fitzpatrick, 30: 413). The federal appointment is dated August 7, 1790, and the annual salary was $1,500.00 (*Hamilton Papers*, 6: 537 [August 6, 1790]). Cochran's commission, signed by Washington, is now in the possession of James L. Mitchell of Atlanta, Ga.

248. Hamilton agreed that the work in the New York office was more taxing than in other states, but refused to show partiality by raising Cochran's salary (*Hamilton Papers*, 6: 302–4 [March 16, 1790]). See the jocular note of Cochran on this subject, February 2, 1791 (JC to Joseph Hardy, in William Duer Papers 3: 13 [NYHS]). See also the note of JC to PS where the former offers the use of his home to Hamilton and his family, who are coming to New York from Philadelphia (July 12, 1791).

to believe that Hamilton had no elevated opinion of Cochran's ability as a man of finance, but by virtue of the latter's position, Hamilton was forced to consult with him on such important issues as the establishment of the Bank of New York, and on Hamilton's pet project, "The Society for the Establishment of Useful Manufactures."

All might have gone well had it not been for the bankruptcy of William Duer in April 1791, which led to a national scandal and brought Cochran much personal grief as well as official pressure.[249] At one point his offices were invaded by irate creditors who threatened to use force if necessary to inspect the record of Duer's most recent stock transfers prior to the crash. To bring matters even closer to home it was Walter Livingston, Duer's intimate associate in Army contracts and land speculation, who suddenly found himself on the verge of financial ruin. Walter managed to survive only through the generous assistance of Philip Schuyler, who could not resist the pleading of his sister Gertrude.[250] The panic of 1792, attributed to the Duer debacle, further tested Cochran's endurance. He now found himself in another awkward position on account of the unintentional error of a clerk, one of sixteen hemmed into an office "in a small and inconvenient house." William Seton, a New York businessman who was asked by Hamilton to look into the matter, concluded that Cochran was "certainly a worthy honest Man, but for conducting such an intricate and extensive system . . . it requires more ability and actual knowledge . . . than he is equal to." [251] Perhaps as a result of this affair the government found more adequate office space for Cochran in Federal Hall shortly before his retirement.[252]

In July 1792, Cochran sent his son Walter to study law in Albany with his elder brother James; for New York City "is a bad place for a

249. For the Duer bankruptcy, see *Hamilton Papers*, 11: 189 (March 25, 1792). For the distress of Walter Livingston, see JC to PS, July 3, 1792 (Emmet Collection, NYPL, *infra* p. 258), and JC to James Parker, July 19, 1792 (Parker Papers, NJHS). The sale of some Mohawk Valley land by Cochran to John J. Morgan of New York City on May 10, 1792, may also be related to money problems brought on by the panic (indenture in possession of Mrs. Franklin B. Manierre, Cazenovia, N.Y.).

250. See PS to Hamilton (*Hamilton Papers*, 11: 186–90 [March 25, 1792]), which illuminates the Livingston-Duer affair, and puts Livingston in an unattractive if not criminal light.

251. William Seton to Hamilton (*Hamilton Papers*, 11: 345–46 [April 29, 1792]).

252. [New York City] *Minutes of the Common Council* (1793), 2: 10–11, 13.

boy to acquire knowledge in his profession . . . where study and application are necessary." [253] James was then occupied in completing construction of a family mansion on the Mohawk River property, and thoughts of retirement must have increasingly entered Cochran's mind. An incident which occurred just before the house was completed might have proved serious, and indicates a lamentable lack of judgment on the part of James. Convinced that the atrocities attributed to Joseph Brant, Mohawk leader of raids into Cherry Valley during the Revolution, had been exaggerated, James invited Brant, then on his way from Canada to negotiate a treaty with Congress, to spend the night as his guest at an inn near Palatine. Brant's presence aroused the ire of local inhabitants, who were bent on revenge, and the Indian had to be spirited away to a place of safety to prevent an ugly episode.[254]

Despite his illness and preoccupation with business matters Cochran found time to write Schuyler recommending "a Nesbit, a mechanical genius, [who] excells in constructing Locks for inland Navigation." It is of some interest to note that Schuyler, who had years earlier acted on Cochran's suggestion about a flax mill, now proceeded to become one of the pioneer canal builders in the United States. Family tradition has it that it was by means of a self-made, crude model of the proposed locks that Schuyler was able to persuade the doubting German settlers on the Mohawk of the practicality of this pet project, an early link in the waterway which eventually became the Erie Canal.[255]

Cochran's few remaining years of active life were plagued by personal financial problems as well as by the realization that his days of usefulness were ended.[256] By mid-summer of 1793 his condition had

253. JC to PS, July 17, 1792 ("Additional Letters," *infra* pp. 259–60).

254. Stone, 2: 337, 492. Apparently in early June 1792 the house had not yet been completed and occupied.

255. JC to PS July 17, 1792 ("Additional Letters," *infra* p. 259, and Cochrane MS, Yale University Library). Schuyler later became the leading promoter of the Inland and Lock Navigation Company which began the improvement of the Mohawk River in 1792 and eventually formed part of the Erie or State Barge Canal. During this work Schuyler must often have visited the Cochran home at Palatine.

256. In the accusations against Hamilton by Archibald Mercer, Cochran and Walter Livingston were involved as bondsmen for Theodosius Fowler, who failed in his contract to supply the western army (*Hamilton Papers*, 13: 220–22).

deteriorated to such a point that he sent Washington a pathetic letter, offering to resign in favor of his son James.[257] Apparently this request did not meet with a favorable response, and Cochran held on to his position until late in 1794, when another stroke interfered so seriously with his ability to function that James believed the end was near. Cochran managed to survive, but Hamilton was forced to recommend his replacement. On February 3, 1795, General Matthew Clarkson, whom Cochran had treated many years before at Valley Forge, was named as his successor.[258] The Cochran family must have moved to the Palatine estate in the summer of 1795, for Duncan's New York City directory for that year no longer lists Cochran's name.

The finely built, commodious, square house situated on a slight elevation, with a commanding view over the flat land skirting the Mohawk River Valley, must have supplied a comfortable place of retirement for the old veteran. Under the loving care of Gertrude, surrounded by his two sons, and stimulated by the visits of numerous travelers, he lived on for another thirteen years in peace and contentment. Family tradition expands on the hospitality which made the Cochran house famous for miles around.[259]

257. JC to GW, August 1, 1793 ("Additional Letters," *infra* p. 260). James wrote that his return to Albany "depends a good deal upon my father who is mending very fast. He does the business of his offices, tho he cannot as yet go down to his office" (James Cochran to Down Fonda, August 7, 1793 [Gratz Collection, HSP]).

258. James Cochran to Rufus King, January 2, 1795 (Rufus King Papers, NYHS). Both John Jay and Schuyler had already appealed to Washington on his behalf. According to James, "My father is confined to his room and will in all probability not live long, as he is liable to frequent attacks of his old complaint; he is now however tolerably well." On January 12, Hamilton described to Washington Cochran's deteriorating condition and "with extreme regret and reluctance" urged that he be replaced "with all convenient dispatch" (*Hamilton Papers*, 18: 33). John's name appears for the last time in Duncan's *Directory* for 1794 (p. 37).

259. Cochran must have seen and admired the site in the Mohawk Valley during the French and Indian War. Although the tract of 2,000 acres had been granted to him by the Crown on October 7, 1763, there were interminable delays caused by the need for surveys and legal action against intruders. After the Revolution the New York state legislature reluctantly recognized the claim (Assembly Papers, vol. 14, p. 415). See also JC to PS, March 9, 1783 ("Additional Letters," *infra* p. 248), and JC to PS October 10, 1783 and January 28, 1785 (Schuyler Papers, NYPL). The house with "four, great corner chimneys" is well-described in Greene, *Mohawk Turnpike*, pp. 175–76. Within sight of the famous old stone Palatine church, the house, rebuilt according to original plans after a 19th-century fire, is still standing, surrounded by 500 acres of Cochran's bounty lands. The recently widowed Gertrude was drawn by the Baroness de Neuville, who with her husband visited the Cochran home around 1808.

John breathed his last on April 7, 1807, and Gertrude survived him by exactly six years. In 1817 the two brothers abandoned the Palatine home for new quarters in the rapidly growing town of Utica. Unwilling to leave the parental remains behind, they transferred these to a cemetery in Utica. As the town grew they were again transferred to the Forest Hill Cemetery, where, under a simple slab on a small mound of earth now lie the remains of the fourth and undoubtedly the most efficient Director General of the Medical Department of the Continental Army.[260]

Biographers are generally noted for unusual sympathy with their subjects, and this writer is no exception. Aside from an inordinate sense of loyalty to his friends, which occasionally brought him grief, I can find no real flaw in Cochran's character. He reveals himself in his correspondence as a man of goodwill, integrity, and dedication. People of all ages, including younger men such as James McHenry, were attracted to him by some undeniable charm, and felt that they could pour into his sympathetic ear their most intimate problems. His constant good humor kept associates cheerful under adversity, and letters to subordinates show how earnestly he sought to improve the morale of his officers as well as the quality of medical care. He shunned controversy, but could rise to heights of indignation when he considered himself unjustly treated. Cochran was a truly modest man, one who felt subordinate to a great cause. As a result his own administration

260. The obituary notice in the *Albany Gazette* of April 9, 1807, reads incorrectly: "Died at his residence in Palatine on the 6th inst. in the 79th year of his age." I have been unable to locate a will of John or Gertrude. The earliest biographical sketch appeared four years later (*American Medical and Philosophical Register* 1 [1811]: 465–68). Probably based on material supplied by a son, it was copied, often word for word, by all subsequent writers. The remains of John and Gertrude, first interred in the Water Street Cemetery, Utica, were transferred in 1875, on the centennial celebration of the battle of Bunker Hill, to Forest Hill Cemetery (Erastus Clark MS, The Oneida Historical Society, Utica, N.Y.) The sons of Cochran were men about town in Federal New York (Dunlap, 2: 418). For their subsequent careers, see Bagg, pp. 439, 443, and Lossing, *Hours*, pp. 207–8. Son James and grandson John Cochrane both served in Congress (*Biographical Dictionary of the American Congress* [1961 ed.] pp. 713–14). For John Cochrane, see *Dictionary of American Biography*, s.v. "Cochrane, John."

was singularly free from the rancor and divisiveness which had plagued the Medical Department throughout most of its existence. It is to such relatively little known medical men as John Cochran, James Craik, William Burnet, and their colleagues—men who gave the efforts of their best years under the most trying of circumstances—that Americans owe a long-belated recognition of gratitude.

THE LETTER-BOOK OF SURGEON GENERAL JOHN COCHRAN

1781–1782

Note on Editorial Procedure

The letters in the Letter-Book are published as written, but abbreviations have often been spelled out, and certain misspellings, archaisms, as well as obvious slips of the pen have been corrected without comment. Capitalization has usually been kept as written, but commas have been occasionally eliminated or inserted to insure readability. The erratic chronological order in the Letter-Book as bound has been corrected. Letters from secondary sources where the originals were not available have been reproduced as found.

Note on the Manuscript of the Letter-Book

The Letter-Book had its origin on February 3, 1781, two weeks after Cochran received formal notification of his election as Director General of the Medical Department. It ends abruptly, and for no obvious reason, some fifteen months later, the last entry, from Philadelphia, being dated May 4, 1782. Apparently it was mislaid at this time, much to Cochran's consternation (see JC to Craigie, June 19, 1782, "Additional Letters," *infra* p. 239), and the date of recovery is not known. It is doubtful whether a continuation ever existed.

Once recovered, the manuscript remained in the possession of descendants, being studied and excerpted by various members of the family (Biddle, 1879; Cochrane, 1884; Baxter, 1897; Chard, 1944, 1946). Stephen Wickes, the medical historian of New Jersey (1879), acknowledges a personal relationship with the then owner, Brigadier General John Cochrane, but does not seem to have had access to the manuscript. The Letter-Book first appeared on public view about 1923 when the so-called Schuyler-Hamilton (Campfield) house became the official headquarters of the Morristown chapter of the Daughters of the American Revolution. Loaned by several descendants of John Cochran, it remained there until 1939, when it was removed by Mrs. Thornton Chard of Cazenovia and New York. Now in the possession of her daughter, Mrs. Franklin B. Manierre, the manuscript has been for the last thirty years on loan to the New York Academy of Medicine.

While in Morristown a typescript of the manuscript was prepared by Mabel Day Parker (1933), and at the Academy another typescript was made by Gertrude Annan. Both of these were of considerable help in preparing the present version. The manuscript consists of ninety-one leaves, 12¾" x 7¾", bound in marbleized boards with a leather spine. The general condition is good. The four sheets preceding the first letter contain three repetitious and incomplete sketches of Cochran's military career; the form of an appointment for surgeons wishing to enter the service; and a signed receipt from Sam C. Wells for forty dollars paid to him by Cochran.

The existence of the manuscript is noted in the *Proceedings of the New Jersey Historical Society*, 10 (1925): 217; 14 (1929): 25; 15 (1930): 152; 50 (1932): 87–88. It is also recorded in the *Guide to the Depositories of MSS Collections in the United States New Jersey* (preliminary volume), Newark: The Historical Records Survey, 1941.

New Windsor February 3rd 1781

Sir

I received your Excellency's Favor of the 18th of January, Yesterday, inclosing an Act of Congress appointing me Director of the Military Hospitals

I thank Congress for this additional Mark of Honor conferred on me, & you Sir, for the polite & obliging manner, in which you were pleased to communicate the same.

If my past conduct, in the Station of Physician & Surgeon General to the Army, which I have filled for near four Years, has been acceptable to that honorable Body, I hope my future Endeavours to perform the Duties of my new Office, will not be less so.

As far as my Abilities will enable me to execute the Trust reposed in me, they shall be most faithfully Exercised, & whatever Errors may fall to my Lot, they will proceed from a Want of Judgement & not from Intention

I was also favored at the same time with an Act of Congress containing the Alterations made in the Plan for conducting the Hospital Department of the 30th of Septemr and the permanent Emolument allowed to the principal Officers of the Department, which I doubt not will be satisfactory

I have the Honor to be with the utmost respect & Esteem

Your Excellency's

most obedt. and

very humble servant

John Cochran DMH

His Excellency Saml. Huntington Esqr.
President of Congress

The earliest dated letter in Cochran's Letter-Book, addressed to Samuel Huntington, President of Congress

In the possession of Mrs. Franklin B. Manierre, on deposit at the New York Academy of Medicine

To Samuel Huntington

New Windsor, Feb. 3d 1781

Sir—

I received your Excellency's favor of the 18th of January, yesterday, inclosing an Act of Congress, appointing me Director of the Military Hospitals.

I thank Congress for this additional Mark of Honor, conferred on me, and you, Sir, for the polite and obliging manner in which you were pleased to communicate the same.

If my past Conduct, in the station of Physician and Surgeon General to the Army, which I have filled for near four years, has been acceptable to that honorable Body. I hope my future Endeavours to perform the Duties of my new Office, will not be less so.

As far as my Abilities will enable me to execute the Trust reposed in me, they shall be most faithfully Exercised, and whatever Errors may fall to my Lot, they will proceed from a want of Judgement and not from Intention.

I was also favored at the same time with an Act of Congress containing the Alterations made in the Plan for conducting the Hospital Department, of the 30th of September and the permanent Emolument allowed to the principal Officers of the Department, which I doubt not will be satisfactory.

I have the Honor to be with the utmost Respect and Esteem
your Excellency's
most obedient and
very humble servant
John Cochran D. M. H.

To Isaac Ledyard

New Windsor, Feb. 26th 1781

Dear Sir—

Inclosed you have General Washington's orders to Capt. Berrien for the delivery of all Hospital Stores in his possession to the Bearer, who will be the officer of Colonel Hazen's Regiment sent with a party, to take them by Force in case of a Refusal. You will therefore send a careful Person with him to take a list of such articles as may be received, and take Charge of them. I suppose the officer will receipt for them. You have his instructions sent to you open, accompanied with a Line to Col. Hazen to furnish the party for the Danbury Service. It was thought most prudent not to send a party the Distance of Windsor, lest some trouble might be the consequence. You have his Excellency's Letter to Messrs Hooker at Windsor for the Delivery of the stores in their Hands, which I hope will be sufficient. I have indorsed it to your Order, and wish how soon the matter may be accomplished. I suppose you will direct the Person who goes to Danbury, after he has got possession of the stores, to proceed to Windsor.

I hope he is a man of prudence and will conduct himself with discretion.

I am Dear Sir

Your most obedient and very humble servant

John Cochran, D. M. Hospls.

P. S. It will be well to wait on Col. Hazen to know when the Party sets out, that your man may keep pace with him.

To Messrs. Hooker

New Windsor, February 26th 1781

Sir—

Agreeable to the within requisition of the Commander in Chief you are to Deliver the Hospital Stores above alluded to in your possession, to the order of Doctor Ledyard, Asst. Purveyor to the Hospitals of the United States.

I am Gentlemen

Your most obedient and very humble servant

John Cochran, D. M. H.

Copy of General Washington's Letter to Messrs Hooker at Windsor, Connecticut, relative to Hospital Stores.

New Windsor, February 25th 1781

Sir—

I am informed that Doctor Foster late Purveyor to the Hospitals in the Eastern District, has deposited in your hands sundry articles procured by him for Hospital use and, with Directions not to deliver them to the public officer on the Plea of their having been procured on private credit. All Purchases made by public officers for the public use, are necessarily presumed to be on public credit, and a detention of them on the plea, I have mentioned cannot be justifiable. If admitted it would sanction the worst abuses.—The service too, would be particularly injured by a Compliance with Dr. Foster's directions to you, as the Hospitals are in great distress for want of stores, and I must therefore request and require you will immediately deliver them to the order of the Director General, for which this will be your justification.

I am Gentlemen

Your most obedient and humble servant

George Washington

To Samuel Huntington

New Windsor, February 27th 1781

Sir—

I was honored with your Excellency's Favor of the 18th of January, inclosing a Resolve of Congress, for establishing an Hospital at or near New London, for the purposes therein mentioned. This letter came to my hands only last Night, which will take off any Charge of Negligence, in not Attending to the Contents, at an earlier Period.

As I have no returns of an Hospital at New London, I am uncertain whether there is one open at that place, and however necessary it might have been to establish it at the time the resolve passed, yet, as I am informed, it rarely happens, at this time that any Continental Prisoners of ours are carried in or exchanged at that place, there can be no use in continuing it.

It was the Commander in Chief's orders to my Predecessor in Office and repeated to me, to have the Hospitals as much concentrated as possible. Many Evils have attended their being scattered over the Country. They were the Receptacles of idle Persons, who could not be prevailed on to join their Corps [and] being at a Distance, were seldom inspected and tended to a vast consumption of Hospital Stores, to the great Prejudice of the Service. I shall make further Enquiry into this matter and if necessary to keep the Hospital up at the Above Place, I could wish Doctor Turner to take charge of it, in preference to any other Person, as well on account of paying Attention to your Excellency's recommendation, as to his own Conveniency and the public good.

I have but a very slight acquaintance with Doctor Turner's Medical Abilities, but from the Character given of him, it would be a pity to lose so good and so old an officer, and I would do anything in my Power consistent with my Duty, to retain him in office.

I am with highest respect and Esteem
Your Excellency's
most obedient and
very humble servant
John Cochran D.M.H.

To Thomas Waring, Morris[town]

New Windsor, February 28th 1781

Dear Sir—

I received your Favor from Morristown, inclosing a return of the sick, which I am happy to find are few in Number, and the Cases not bad. It is probable you will have some little addition to the Number on hand, from the Detachment of the Marquis de La Fayette, I hope they will be taken as good care of, as the Nature of the Circumstances we are in will admit. The Want of Necessary Stores for our Hospitals, afford a gloomy prospect.

I do not know that there is any probability of your being sent to the Southward, nor would I wish to order an officer of the Department on a Tour of Duty, by which his Health or private Interest should be injured, especially when others might be found, to whom that Duty would be perfectly agreeable, but the Nature of Military Service is such that it is always expected every Officer will obey orders, otherwise the worst of Evils might be the Consequence, and the Department brought into disrepute.

The Gentlemen of the Corps which I have the Honor to superintend, may be assured that every Endeavor of mine shall be exerted to render them as happy as possible.

I am Dear Sir

Your most obedient and very humble servant

John Cochran D. M. H.

To Dr. George Stevenson, Morristown

New Windsor February 28th 1781

Dear Sir—

I was favored with yours of the 19th Instant, yesterday and thank you for your Congratulations on my Appointment to the Directorship of the Hospitals. Whether I shall answer the Expectations of the

Public in General, or of my friends in particular will greatly depend on the Gentlemen of the Department, by a faithful Discharge of their Duty and a strict adherence to the Rules laid down by Congress in the Plan for conducting the Hospital Department.

I believe you are persuaded that you have my Patronage and every good intention to your Welfare, therefore should be very sorry that your situation should ever be such as to put it out of your Power to comply with any Orders you may receive from your superiors. It is very evident that you cannot live on the Air and unless Money is furnished you cannot proceed to Virginia, where I do not believe you will be ordered, but should you be so unfortunate, as it so badly accords with your Circumstances, on Application of Dr. Treat, I am persuaded he will order another in your Place, you first making known to him your particular situation.

I am

Dear Sir

Your most obedient and very humble servant

John Cochran D. M. H.

To Abraham Clark

New Windsor, Feb. 28th 1781

Sir—

Inclosed are the returns of the sick and wounded in the Hospitals (except that [at] Yellow Springs) for the Month of January, together with the Regimental and Flying Hospital return for the month of February, which show the healthy state of our Troops and in our present circumstances of Want, is very favorable. Tho' we have few Deaths, yet the poor fellows suffer for want of necessary supplies, which I hope will soon be afforded them, otherwise there will be little occasion for Physicians and Surgeons. I hope some pay is ordered to be advanced to the Officers of the Department without which it cannot much longer exist. Many of us have not received a shilling in near two years nor can we procure public clothing.

I have a letter from Dr. Craigie our Chief Apothecary now at Boston, informing that Doctor Foster the former Deputy Director to the Eastward had absolutely refused giving up the Medicines, Instruments, &c purchsed by him for public use, which deranges us much. There is a Quantity of Hospital Stores at Windsor and Danbury in Connecticut under the same Circumstancesn which he has refused also. I have taken a short cut, and by stealing a march on him, may probably obtain part if not the Whole.

It appears very extraordinary that a public officer purchasing stores &c. on public credit shall, when out of office, retain large quantities of those Articles in his hands on Pretence That his Accounts are not settled, when perhaps the public owe him nothing and the sick are perishing for want of these very stores. As soon as I can obtain a perfect return of the officers, &c. in the Hospital Department, I will transmit it to the Medical Committees previous to which I beg to have a return of those who have resigned since the new arrangement took Place.

Since setting down to write I received a letter from Doctor Ledyard our assistant Purveyor at Fish Kill, telling me that he could not possibly proceed to Windsor in Connecticut in Quest of the stores already mentioned, for want of money, not being able to raise as much as "would put a Hoop on a Cask or a Board on a Box" if the sum [were] waiting.

I have the honor to be with respect and Esteem Sir
Your most obedient and very humble servant
John Cochran D. M. H.

To Isaac Ledyard

New Windsor, March 4th 1781

Dear Sir:

When I received your Favor of the first instant, which was this Day, I was writing to the Medical Committee, inclosing Hospital Returns and pressing the Necessity of the Department being furnished with money, and gave them an extract from your Letter of the deplorable State and Consequences of being without cash to carry any Plan into Execution. I know not what to advise you. I hope you have sent some one with the officer to Danbury to take charge of the stores. Those at Windsor must take their Chance until come Method can be fallen on to raise the wind to carry our scheme into Execution. If in the mean time, either from public or private Credit you can proceed to the Business, I will be answerable for the expense attending the procuring the stores. I shall set out for Albany tomorrow and propose returning in three weeks.

I am yours &c.

J. Cochran D. M. H.

To Thomas Bond, Jr.

New Windsor March 25th 1781

Dear Sir

I was favored with yours of the 20th Ult. about 15 days ago on my way to Albany which accounts for my not anwering you until now—as I only returned last night.

I am sorry to inform you that I found that Hospital entirely destitute of all kinds of stores, except a little vinegar which was good for nothing—and frequently without Bread or Beef for many days, so that the Doctor under those circumstances was obliged to permit such of the patients as could walk into town, to beg provisions among the inhabitants.

The stores from Danbury are arrived at Fishkill, I am informed, so that I propose a small supply to be sent there from that Quarter-provided those you mention to be on the way, arrive in time for the people who are to be inoculated.

On my return I found a letter from Mr. John De La Mater informing me that he had an offer from you of continuing in service, as your Clerk and pay master to the Hospital Department, the latter of which he conceives will give him full employ; you are the best judge of this matter, therefore will act accordingly—He wishes to have his pay fixed, and to have his appointment, and that his chief place of residence should be at Danbury, the propriety of the latter I am at a loss about. From long acquaintance with him, I believe him to be a very honest man, and very capable of business. I shall write and inform him that the matter rests with you, and that I have wrote you on the subject—I much approve of Dr. Wilson's going to Virginia and if Jenifer accompanies him, he will have an excellent assistant, and if joined by the two mates Dr. Treat informs me he has ordered there—I hope they will be sufficent for that service.

I have already mentioned the gentlemen you recommended to the medical committee, to fill the vacancies of Hospital Physicians and Surgeons, and in the strongest terms, except Dr. Cowell, with whom I am Little acquainted, either as to his medical abilities or his industry—These being ascertained, he claims his promotion of course—from long service, and I shall recommend him with pleasure; but I think it is probable Congress will introduce some of the deranged Seniors; this however proper, will discourage the Mates, who are a very useful part of the Department, and on whom much dependence must be placed.

As it will be improper for me to leave Head Quarters until Latimer comes up, whom I expect shortly, or Craik arrives, you cannot expect me in Philadelphia. I think you had better make out an estimate for the ensuing campaign, with the assistance of Dr. Treat and present it to the Medical Committee, you and he are better judges of the requisites for the hospitals, that I can be, from the nature of the different services we have been employed in for some years.

I pity our distressed condition on the score of money, and unless a sufficiency can be procured at the opening of the campaign, we are undone. Foster being dead, it is probable I shall be able to procure the stores at Windsor, Connecticut, as soon as money can be furnished to the Assistant Purveyor to attend to that Duty.

I am Dear Sir

Your most obedient and humble servant

John Cochran D. M. H.

To Malachi Treat

New Windsor March 25th 1781

Dear Sir

I arriv'd last night from Albany, when I received both your favours of the 2d and 17th Instant, and thank you for your attention to the several matters recommended to your care, I am happy that the Malignant Fever which appear'd in Philadelphia has abated, and I hope every thing has been done to give general satisfaction, and the poor unhappy sufferers comfort.

I wish to see Doctor Latimer here as soon as possible, for until he or Doctor Craik arrive, I do not think myself justifiable in leaving Head Quarters—I am sorry my friend Latimer is so much out of humor. I do not mean to say he has no reason for chagrin, but let him bear his share with christian patience and live by faith as you do. If I am only wanted in Philadelphia to solicit cash and give in [an] estimate, I believe I may as well be any where else, we can have no more of the Fox than the skin, as the old saying is, and if he has not been sufficiently skinned I wonder at it—for I do not believe there is a single shilling in the Treasury.

I shall write Doctor Bond on the subject of the estimate, Tho Congress say that it shall be made by the Director. Yet why cannot you and Doctor Bond make out an estimate and deliver it in, for if I was to make a Thousand, the Medical Committee will be the judges at last, and give no more than what they please, which was the case with the last, nor do I find they have furnished [us] with cash to purchase to the amount—tho it has been dock'd and approved of, some three or four Months ago. The state of our Finances are such that it will be impossible to lay in a magazine for the campaign therefore we must in a great measure depend on purchasing as we go. Were I on the spot with you I must depend on yours and the Purveyor's assistance in enabling me to make out an estimate, as being better acquainted with the Hospital consumption of stores &c. than I can be, from the nature of the different services in which we have been employed for some years past.

As soon as the stores arrive, which you suppose to be on the way, we shall begin inoculation which I wish might be postponed altogether, for it will consume a great Quantity of stores, which are much wanted in the hospitals, and fear will not be replaced.

Doctor Young showed me your letter enclosing a resolve of Congress respecting the depreciation &c. which made him happy, and poor fellow he wanted comfort as much as any man I ever saw; His situation is truly pitiable, and hope something will turn up which will give him relief.

It gives me pain that Doctor Hagan has so much of the volunteer about him; as an hospital officer, he must conform to the orders of his superiors or there is an end to all discipline and neither you nor I can be answerable to the other Gentlemen of the Department for suffering such a step.

The obstinancy of Tilton has nothing in it surprising, considering the man, I had rather see him *pancreviated* than the Physicians *nobsquibled*.

I am Dear Sir with esteem
Your most obedient humble servant
John Cochran D. M. H.

To Barnabas Binney

New Windsor, March 25th 1781

Dear Sir—

I received your favor of the 27th Ultimo about 18 days ago, on my way to Albany, and as I did not return before last night, that will account for my not attending to you sooner. I thank you for your very polite congratulations on my appointment and the favorable sentiments you are pleased to entertain of my disposition, and the willingness you express of serving under my superintendance. In return I only wish to act such a part as will entitle me to a continuation of your future approbation, and that of every gentleman in the Department.

I hope your resignation has not been accepted by Congress, and that you still continue one of our body, for it gives me the highest pleasure and satisfaction to see retained in the service such Characters, as have abilities and discharge their duty, with faithfulness; this I think without flattery, I can say of you, having been an Eye witness to your assiduity.

If your resignation has not been accepted, and you are willing to continue in the department, I wish to know where it would be most convenient for yourself to be employ'd. The circumstances of your family might require a choice. I believe there will be no necessity of a Physicians going to Virginia. I hope those already sent, will be sufficient for that service.

I am Dear Sir

Your most obedient Humble servant

John Cochran D.M. H.

To Philip Turner

New Windsor, March 25th 1781

Dear Sir

I was favoured with yours of the 27th ultimo, when on my way to Albany, from whence I did not return till last night which accounts for my not paying an earlier attention to the contents.

Give me leave to render you my thanks for your kind congratulations on my appointment, and the obliging manner in which you express your readiness to serve under my superintendance.

I should be happy in accomodating matters to your wish, but I fear it is out of my power. It is not with me to give any other Rank to an officer of the Hospital Department, than what is fixed by Congress, and there does not appear to be a necessity of continuing an Hospital at, or near New London, for the purpose set forth in the resolve of Congress, however necessary it might have been at the time the resolved passed, as it is not probably any prisoners may arrive there in future to be exchanged more than at any other seaport, or at least not in such numbers, as to justify the keeping an Hospital open for their accomodation.

It was his Excellency's orders to my predecessor, and repeated to me, to have the Hospitals as much contracted s possible, and it becomes more necessary at this time, than heretofore considering the diminution of the numbers of the hospital staff, and the vast scarcity of stores, for want of which the sick are suffering in every Quarter.

I had a letter from the President of Congress, recommending you in the genteelest terms, to the charge of the Hospital. I gave him my reasons, which I hope were satisfactory. It gives me pain to think that an old and faithful officer, in the service of the public, should be supplanted by any set of designing men, but if you can reconcile it to yourself to serve in the station Congress have allotted you, you may command every indulgence in my power, consistent with my duty and the public good.

I shall be happy to be made acquainted with your determination on this head as soon as may be, that I may arrange matters accordingly before the campaign opens.

Several of the Hospital Physicians and Surgeons have resigned since the new arrangement took place, owing I believe, principally to their not being able to subsist themselves, in the service, for it is upwards of two years, since many of us have received a shilling from the Continent, and there is as little prospect now of pay as there was two years ago.

Doctor Craik succeeds me as Physician &c to the Army, and Doctor Burnet, who was deranged, succeeds him as chief hospital Physician.

I always entertained the highest sense of your disposition toward myself and thank you for your attention to my character with the member of Congress. My appointment was unsolicited, and a rank to which I never aspired, being perfectly happy where I was.

I am with esteem and regard

Dear Sir

Your most obedient and

Very humble servant

John Cochran D.M. Hosp'ls.

To James Craik

New Windsor March 26th 1781

Dear Craik

The enclosed act of Congress appointing you chief Physician and Surgeon to the Army in my room, came to hand a few days since, under cover from the Department of Congress.

Give me leave to offer you my congratulations on this appointment, as I know it is more agreeable to yourself than your former station, and more acceptable to the commander in chief, and the whole Army. You will not think me guilty of adulation, when I assure you that I would rather have complimented you on the accasion of you being appointed Director than where you are, for many reasons, and I believe every member of Congress will do me the justice to acknowledge that I gave you the preference upon every interview I had with them when conversing on the subject. I know of none who are dissatisfied with my appointment unless it be my old friend Tom[m]y [Bond] for what reasons I am at a loss to conjecture. He has been heard to say that neither you or I were qualified for the station of Director, and that neither of us would get it. I have not yet found out, by what means he became acquainted with our abilities, or who made him a judge of what Qualifications were necessary to constitute a person fit for the Directorship. I think he will be prone to find fault with me, from some little specimens he has afforded already. I hope to act such a part as to be out of the power of friend or foe.

I shall be happy to see you once more with us, I purpose to be the greatest part of my time in the field, perhaps you will say no thanks to you for that a resolve passed a few days after you left Philadelphia, ordering the Director to repair to Head Quarters and to make that the chief place of his residence.

I am just returned from an 18 days tour up the North River as far as Albany to attend Mrs. Washington, we had an agreeable jaunt, excepting the badness of the roads, but we met with so much hospitality, wherever we went that compensation was made for the difficulty in traveling.

We are so squeezed for paper that I can only afford you a half sheet for cover and all.

I hope Mrs. Craik and family are all well, my poor little boy lays ill of a fever. Mrs. Cochran's compliments. I have many excuses to make for my silence through the winter, but must leave them until I have the pleasure of offering them *propria persona* or *viva voce* if that words better please.

I am Dear Sir

Your sincere friend and very humble Servant

John Cochran D. M. H.

To William Burnet

New Windsor March 26th 1781

Dear Sir

The enclosed act of Congress appointing you chief Physician and Surgeon to the hospitals, in the room of Doctor Craik removed to the Army, came enclosed from the president to my hands yesterday.

You will give me leave to congratualte you on your appointment, and hope from your acquaintance with the Hospital duties to receive no small addition to the Department. There is little to be done at present, therefore no great call for your attention immediately, but you will be so obliging as to inform me where you would choose to act at the opening of the campaign that I may arrange matters accordingly; as it is my wish to make everything as agreeable to the Department as possible. It is my desire particularly to accommodate my old friend and neighbour in a manner most agreeable to his wish.

I am with sincere regard and esteem

Dear Sir

Your most obedient and very humble servant

John Cochran Director Mily. Hosp'ls.

To George Campbell

New Windsor March 26th 1781

Dear Sir

On my arrival from Albany a few days ago, I was favored with yours of the 8th of March, and am sorry for your Distresses and wish it was in my Power to alleviate them. Were I to inform you my own situation with a wife & Family, and not a Friend to give me assistance, as not having it in their power, perhaps you would be brought to think that you are not altogether the only sufferer. If Congress is not in a Capacity to do something for us by the opening of the Campaign, we are all undone; however I hope for better Times, and no doubt the Period is not at a great distance, when we shall have a proper supply. Congress have passed some late resolves respecting our depreciation & Pay, which puts us on the same footing with every officer in the Army, and the Nominal sum of the Whole shall be equal to specie.

I would be far from advising you to your Hurt, but would wish you not to quit the Dep't if you can possibly continue in service. There are several Vacancies of Hospital Physicians & Surgeons, which will probably be filled up shortly. I have recommended you among the four oldest mates for these Vacancies, which would be a very pretty Emolument for Life. You may be assured of Experiencing every Indulgence in my power consistent with my Duty and the public Good. I thank you for your Congratulations on my appointment. Whether my present station will contribute to my future Happiness, time only must discover, but if I have no better Success than my Predecessors, my Lot must be unfortunate indeed. A determined Resolution to conform to the Rules of Right, and that support which I have some reason to expect from every Gentleman of the Department will, I hope, protect me against the Malevolence of my Enemies (if I have any) I say, if I have any, for sure I am that I never put a Thorn in any honest Man's Breast.

Pray let me hear what resolutions you are come to, that I may arrange my matters accordingly. If any one should be continued after the War, & even should you continue a Mate, you might expect to be retained in preference to many others; which would be equal to 720 Dollars per *Annum,* a very pretty salary.

Dear Sir,

Your most obedient and very humble servant

John Cochran D.M.H.

To Thomas Bond, Jr.

New Windsor March 26th 1781

Dear Sir

Since writing the enclosed I am informed from Doctor Campbell that in a conversation with you in Philadelphia you mentioned my acting with [in]consistency, in seizing the stores purchased by Doctor Foster, for publick use, while I advised Mr. Voorhees to retain in his hands, those he had, until his accounts were settled. I believe my letter to you on the subject does not convey either advice or even an approbation of his conduct. I think I infom'd you that he did not chuse to comply with the requisition of Dr. Wilson in behalf of Doctor Potts, late Purveyor, until his accounts were settled, and had assurances to receiving his own pay, and money to discharge the debts he had contracted on accompt of the public. The stores were always in my power, and I could take them when I saw fit, and what I did respecting the stores of Doctor Foster, was by the express command of his excellency the commander in chief, and whatever may be your opinion of the consistency or inconsistency of my conduct, I hope to act such a part as will enable me to stand some scrutiny. I mean to do what is right, and if any errors fall to my lot, they will be those of judgement and not intention, and could wish to conduct myself in such a manner as to entitle me to the approbation of every Gentleman in the Department.

I am Dear Sir

Your most obedient and very humble servant

John Cochran

To Abraham Clark

New Windsor April 2d 1781

Dear Sir—

I was favored with yours of the 20th ultimo, and hope you will soon be able to procure a supply of money for our Department, the want of which, is attended with many Disadvantages, as well to the officers of the Hospital as to the sick.

I had a letter a few Days since from Dr. Treat informing me that 3 months pay would be furnished to the officers of the Hospitals as soon as a return could be obtained, which I here inclose tho' not altogether as accurate as I could wish. I have not heard from Dr. Tilton since I came into office, nor do I know where to direct to him or I should have called on him before this time. It is probable I may hear of him when I do go Philadelphia which will be as soon as some Person arrives on whom I can depend to relieve me. Doctor Turner is willing to serve, provided, I will give him his Rank and the Charge of an Hospital at or near New London. I have wrote him that I can give him no other Rank than what is conferred by Congress, and there does not appear to be any occasion for an Hospital at or near New London. I have requested him to give me his sentiments on the subject of serving that I may make my arrangements accordingly.

I am Sir with esteem and respect

Your most obedient and very humble Servant

John Cochran D.M.H.

To Malachi Treat

New Windsor April 2d, 1781

Dear Sir

I was favored with yours of the 24th ulto. and have, agreeable to your request, furnished Mr. Clark with a return of the officers belonging to our Department, tho not as accurate as I could wish. I have several Lists of Mates, no two of which agree, I have therefore been obliged to make it out as well as I could. I wrote Dr. Bond some time ago, to be so obliging as to call on Doctor Shippen for a return of the mates. He sent me a return, some of Whom are in Carolina and were never appointed, others have resigned and their places filled up, which has embarrassed me much. I will take it as a favor, if you will call on Dr. Shippen and procure me an exact List of the Mates appointments.

I cannot go to Philadelphia before Craik or Latimer arrive here, or some other Person to relieve me. I hope it will be in my Power to set out about the 20th instant. I am happy to find that you have in some measure put a stop to that infernal Fever and that your Hospitals are in as good a way as Finances &c will admit of. Where is our Friend Tilton? I can hear nothing of him or from him. Does he still insist on the Demolition of all Chiefs and will not serve. If he does, I shall be sorry for it, for with all his positiveness he is a most excellent officer, and deserves much of his Country for his assiduity.

I am Dear Sir

&c John Cochran D.M.H.

To an Unidentified Surgeon

New Windsor April 2d, 1781

Sir

I was favoured with yours of the fourteenth Ultimo, which I should have answered by the return of the post, but it did not come to hand in time for that purpose. I am sorry your case respecting your Finances are so similar to every Gentleman of our Department. Neither myself nor any of the Gentlemen who have served with me, have received a shilling from the Public in twenty three months, which has, as you may reasonably suppose, reduced us to some difficulties. There is no money belonging to the Department, otherwise would answer your Demands, therefore can only recommend it to you, to have recourse to your Friends for that assistance you mention as the only resource. I hope for better times. I am informed that three months pay is ordered for the Staff, which no doubt will be paid immediately. A return of the Hospital Department was only wanting for that purpose, which I have sent to Congress this Day. As the Department is much reduced in Numbers, I am obliged to call on all those who are not immediately employed, to the vicinity of Head Quarters, to be in readiness to attend to whatever duty the service may require.

I am, Sir,

Your very hble serv't.

John Cochran D.M.H.

Paper is so scarce that I am obliged to take a Leaf out of an Orderly Book.

To Abraham Clark

April 30th, 1781 New Windsor

Sir—

I herewith send you the Hospital returns of sick and Lame &c, also those of the Army and Flying Hospital since the first of February. They are not as compleat as could be wished for, owing probably to miscarriages. I have sent the Originals, not having paper enough to transcribe them into Form. Several of the Hospital Physicians & Surgeons complain that they have not paper sufficient to make out the necessary Hospital Return, therefore are obliged to omit them on that account.

I have from all Quarters the most melancholy Complaints of the sufferings of the sick in the Hospitals, for want of stores and necessaries that you can conceive, and unless some speedy remedy is applied, the consequences must be very fatal. Doctor Warren who has charge of the Boston Hospital represents his situation in a very distressed condition, and prays most earnestly for relief.

As soon as my strength will enable me, I propose setting out for Philadelphia. On the 5th instant, I was taken with a Pleurisy which has confined me till yesterday and has left me very weak. I have desired Dr. Treat, with the Purveyor, to give in an Estimate of stores &c for Hospital use for the ensuing Campaign, which I hope has been done.

I am Sir,

Your most obedient and very humble servant

John Cochran D. M. H.

To David Townsend, Charles McKnight, William Eustis, John Warren, Thomas Waring, James Mann, Malachi Treat, and Bodo Otto

New Windsor May 1st 1781

Dear Sir

His Excellency the Commander in Chief, apprehensive that many of the men returned sick, absent and in the service of the Hospitals are not now in being, or cannot be particularly accounted for, has requested me to furnish him with a particular and accurate Return from all the Hospitals under my Inspection, of every man in said Hospitals, specifying their names, the Corps they belong to, and the time of their admission. He also wishes these returns may comprehend the Continental soldiers, who wait on the Medical Gentlemen or are otherwise employed in the Department, and that the particular service they are in, their Names, the Corps they belong to and the time they have served in that capacity, be specified. It is expected the utmost punctuality will be observed in making this return.

You will also furnish me with a return of the Hospital Mates doing Duty with you, with their names, and Dates of appointments and by whom appointed, as I have not been able to obtain a List of them from any Quarter, and without an accurate return of them to the Medical Committee they cannot receive their Pay.

Your very humble servant

John Cochran D.M.H.

To Philip Turner

New Windsor May 8th 1781

Dear Sir

I received your favor of the 17th ultimo and am exceeding sorry that it is not consistent with your feelings and that it would affect your Delicacy to attend the Hospitals in general, in the Character of Hospital Physician and Surgeon. I wish I could reconcile it to the Principles of Duty and the good of the Service, to indulge you with the Charge of an Hospital at New London, agreeable to your Desire, but on consulting the Commissary General of Prisoners, and others well acquainted with the Circumstances of this affair, I am informed that it rarely happens that any Continental Prisoners are sent to New London for Exchange, either seamen or soldiers, for whose use alone an Hospital could with propriety be established. I will allow there may be many sailors and others belonging to private ships &c. sent there for exchange, but it surely cannot be expected that a General Hospital should be opened for the purpose of attending those people, more than in every Parish in the State, to accomodate the sick of every private family—therefore as you could not with propriety attend the private sick at public Expence and having few or no Continentals to take up your attention, should I not (by coming into the measure you propose) be charged with conferring on you, a sinecure, for which I should be blamed by every gentleman of the Department, who might think himself injured by not being indulged in like manner. I am convinced that it is a consequence which would naturally follow and I am led to believe that you have too great a regard for my reputation to see it wounded on any account.

The resignations in the Hospitals since the new arrangement have been very frequent and I do not know whether Congress will be induced to fill the vacancies, therefore the Nature of the service will require every officer to be ready to attend where his services may be most wanted. As it is uncertain what may turn up in the course of a few Weeks and what medical assistance may be wanted, I am ordered by the Commander in Chief to call upon every medical Gentleman not immediately attached to some particular Duty, to repair to the vicinity of Head Quarters to be in readiness to perform any duty that may be assigned them. I therefore would be happy to see you at Fishkill, where, if you arrive before I return from Philadelphia, which will be about the 10th of June, you will wait my return and be assured nothing in my Power shall be wanting to render you every service consistent with the public good and my Duty.

I am Dear Sir

Your most obedient and very humble servant

John Cochran, D. M. H.

To Abraham Clark

New Windsor May 8th 1781

Sir

By last post, I received a letter from Doctor Hagan inclosing his appointment from Congress, as Hospital Physician and Surgeon, together with his resignation, intimating that he considered himself no longer an officer of the Hospital. As this is the first instance of an Hospital Physn &c. offering his resignation to me since I have been in office, I have acquainted him that I have referred his case to the Medical Committee, not being fully satisfied that it lay with me to grant his request.

I have also the resignation of Doctor Josiah Bartlett, Mate to the Hospital, on Duty in Boston, which I have taken the Liberty to acquiesce in, from the Principle of the Mates being appointed by the Director and one of the chief Hospital Physicians & Surgeons, which gives by implication a right to Discharge.

I hope to see you in a few days and am with respect and esteem

Sir

Your humble servant

John Cochran D. M. H.

To Francis Hagan

New Windsor May 8th 1781

Dear Sir—

I received your favor dated at Annapolis, some time ago, which I have not answered, because in the fluctuating state of your manoeuvers, it was impossible for me to know where to direct to you.

I also was favored with yours of the first Instant enclosing your Appointment of Hospital Physician and Surgeon by Congress, on the new Arrangements together with your Resignation, considering yourself no longer an officer of the Public. As yours was the first instance of an Officer of your Rank offering me their resignation, I was at a Loss to determine as to the propriety of accepting of it. I consulted the Commander in Chief on the Subject. He informed me that as he had never been consulted on the appointment of these Gentlemen, he could give me no information about the Matter. In Consequence of which I have transmitted the Whole to the Medical Committee for their Consideration informing them that you no longer considered yourself an Officer of the Hospitals.

It affords me but a melancholy Prospect when Gentlemen who are capable and willing to do their Duty, take their Departure from us, when God knows, with what kind of Cattle their Places will be supplied.

I wish you success and am,

Dear Sir,

Your most obedient and very humble Servant

John Cochran

To Samuel Huntington

Philadelphia May 24th 1781

Sir:

The melancholy situation of the Medical Department has induced me to lay the Distresses of the sick and the necessity of the surgeons before you with a request that your Excellency would be pleased to lay them before Congress.

The Hospitals are in the utmost distress for Want of Necessaries for the sick, in some of them we have not stores, and in others the supplies are so trifling and insignificant as to be of little service. The surgeon who has the care of the hospital at Boston writes me that his sick are in great want and that he is not in a situation to procure them any relief. At Albany the only article of stores is about 60 Gallons of Vinegar and the sick suffer extremely at times, for want of Provisions. The other hospitals are in a similar situation. Duty and Humanity, therefore, induce me to press the Necessity of attending to the Estimate of stores and medicines given in to the Medical Committee and request that measures may be taken to enable the Purveyor to procure supplies.

I am sensible of the difficulties and Embarrassments of Congress, but am also sensible unless some speedy and effectual measures are taken to relieve the sick, a number of the valuable soldiers in the American Army will perish through want of necessaries, [who] would soon be serving their Country in the Field, could they be supplied.

After having mentioned the state of our Hospitals I am directed by the Gentlemen of the Department to acquaint you of their Distress, for want of pay and request that some pay should be advanced to them, not having received any for these two last years. This has occasioned the Resignation of sundry very valuable officers and though the others are anxious to continue to serve their country, yet their necessities are such, that it will be impossible for many of them to continue unless they can receive some supply.

The officers of the Department have also directed me to apply to Congress on their behalf and to request that their depreciation may be made up to them; they have suffered equally with the officers of the Line, & apprehend they are equally entitled to their depreciation of pay. Should Congress think proper to put them on a footing with their Brother Officers in this respect, it would have a happy effect, & would relieve a Number of men who have suffered in Common with the rest of the Army from the depreciation of our Currency.

I have also to request that the Hospital Officers should be entitled to receive their letters free from the expense of postage, as well as the officers of the Line. The propriety of this will be evident when I mention that returns are to be sent from every part of the Continent to me as Director, and the Expense of Postage would nearly swallow up the whole of my Pay.

Before I conclude, I would suggest to Congress that we have several vacancies for Hospital Physicians & Surgeons which have been occasioned by resignations, and that in Case we should have an active Campaign the department may suffer for want of a proper Number of assistants. The Eldest Mates are qualified to fill those places, and if they could be appointed by Congress, with propriety, it would have a tendency to promote the good of the service. We have also several vacancies for regimental surgeons, there is no Mode pointed out at present for appointing them. They have heretofore been appointed sometimes by the state to which the regiment belonged, sometimes by the Colonels, sometimes by the Director General, and sometimes by the Physician & Surgeon General to the army. Great Confusion and inconvenience has arisen from this Mode and I would submit it [to] Congress whether or not some One Person should not be directed to appoint regimental surgeons in Case of Vacancies.

Should Congress wish any further or more particular information on this subject I shall be ready to furnish it, and would be obliged to your Excellency to have the Matter taken up as soon as possible, that the distresses of the Hospitals may be relieved, and that I may be enabled to return to the Army as neither my Finances nor my Duty may permit me to remain long in this City.

I have the honor to be with the greatest respect and Esteem your Excellency's Most Obedient and very humble servant.

John Cochran D. M. H.

To James Tilton

Philadelphia June 3d 1781

Sir—

I arrived at this place some days ago, in order to transact some matters relative to the Medical Department, and have so far succeeded as to be able to obtain favourable reports from the Board of War to Congress, all of which will be considered in a few Days. The report for making up the Depreciation of our Pay, has been twice read & will have a third reading tomorrow, when I hope it will be finally determined. The Medical Committee is dissolved and the Board of War transacts our Business, until the Financier takes us up.

As it is probable we may soon take the Field, in which Case your services may be wanted, I would therefore request your Attendance at or near the Vicinity of Head Quarters to be in readiness to attend to any Duty which may be assigned to you.

I am

Sir

Your most Obedient and very humble servant

J. Cochran D. M. H.

To Thomas Marshall

New Windsor [c. June 30, 1781]

Dear Sir

I received your Favor of the 10th of May only a few Days ago at my Quarters at New Windsor on my return from Philada. where I was informed you had quit the service, but am happy to find that you still look upon yourself as belonging to the Department. You were numbered among the Mates of the Hospital in the return of the officers delivered to me on my appointment to the Directorship, in which capacity I suppose you will act, until it may please Congress to promote you to a superior station when Vacancies happen, agreeable to your standing & merit for which you may depend on my Interest. It has been represented to me that Medical aid is much wanting in Virginia; I could therefore wish you would lose no time in repairing to that Quarter & join the Hospital now under the inspection of Doctor Willson and there remain until further orders.

I thank you for your kind Congratulations on the honor conferred on me, as Director of the Military Hospitals, by my country. I wish you Health & Success and am

Dear Sir

Your most obedient & very humble servant

J. Cochran

To John Warren

New Windsor June 30th 1781

Dear Sir

* I received your Favor of the 22d of May on my return from Philadelphia where I have been for four weeks attending Congress, in order to obtain some relief for our Department and found every good disposition in that Body to attend to my requisitions, as much as possible, but little more was in their Power than to make fair Promises and grant Warrants on exhausted Treasuries, but I have the most flattering hopes that the Case will soon be altered, and we shall be in happy Circumstances—Much is expected from the actions of Mr. Morris, the Financier. His promises are large and I make no doubt he will fulfil them.

* I must sincerely pity your situation & the Distressed state of the sick in the Hospital under your care.

* While in Philadelphia I obtained Warrants on the different Treasuries of Virginia, Pennsylvania and New York for the sum of 16,116 Dollars in specie or other Money equivalent for three Months pay to be advanced the officers of the Department and A Warrant on the Public Treasury for upwards of 12,000 D[s]. to be put into the hands of the Purveyor for the purpose of purchasing necessary stores for the Hospitals. These different sums will be paid out of the first Money that comes to hand. I also obtained an Act for making up the depreciation on our pay in the same manner as it is made up to officers of the Line, that is to say, Congress have recommended it to the different state[s] to make up the depreciation to the officers of the state to which they belong, this act only extends to such officers as are now in service, tho' there is no intention to exclude any deranged officer who has faithfully discharged his Duty. I suppose Congress will send authenticated Copies of this act to each of the states.

I have accepted the resignation of Dr. Porter on the 25th of June, which will bring him within the Limits of the depreciation Act, and save him much trouble. I have enclosed a Warrant to Dr. Cheever and have ordered that his pay shall commence from the date of the New arrangement in justice to him as he has been doing Duty from that Period.

* You will be particular in forwarding your returns monthly. You may always send them by Post as all Letters to and from me are post free; this I accomplished when in Philadelphia though I had not Interest to obtain the Like for the Department in General, which was my desire. I labored hard for the purpose.

* Before we procure our Commissions, it is necessary we should take the Oath to the States, such as we took under the old arrangement, it becomes proper on every new appointment or promotion. You will therefore take the Oath yourself and cause the like to be done by all your officers down to the Ward Master, either before a General Officer or a justice of the peace & inclose me a duplicate, which I shall forward to the Board of War and demand your Commission.

I am Dear Sir
with the greatest respect & Esteem,
Dear Sir,
Your most obedient & very humble servant
J. Cochran D. M. H.

mem.
The paragraphs marked * were sent to Doctor Townsend with what is annexed on the next page.

To DAVID TOWNSEND, with what [is] marked thus * of the foregoing for Dr. Warren

No promotions were made in the Hospital Department when I left Town. There was no objection to our friend Young's rejoining us, and I have all the reason in the World to hope he is appointed before this time. The only demur in my Mind is that great Bodies move slow. Should Doctor Young's Appointment take place, it is more than probable that you will not both be wanted in Albany, In that Case I hope to see you in the Field, or in some of the fixed Hospitals, which ever of the two will be most agreeable to yourself and where you can render the most essential service to your Country. You will be the best judge when you can be spared, consequently you need wait for no other invitation from me, whenever that Period arrives.

I flatter myself this will be a more active Campaign than perhaps any since the commencement of the War. If you see my son, give my Love to him and give him some of your pious advice. You will oblige me much in enquiring of his Tutor how he comes on and acquaint me in your next. He has been hitherto much neglected, which causes me more Anxiety than perhaps I otherwise might have. I forgot to inform you that you must keep a duplicate of your Oath and send me the other that I may forward it to the Board. There is a resolve of Congress ordering this to be done and that the Director shall see this order complied with

I am Dear Sir

Your most obedient and very humble servant

John Cochran D.M.H.

To Philip Turner

New Windsor June 30th 1781

Dear Sir

I was favored with yours of the 1st of June a few days after my return from Philadelphia, & shall communicate that part of the contents respecting your resignation to the Board of War—the Medical Committee being dissolved—and recommend it to the Board to communicate your intentions to the Congress. I equally regret with the rest of your Friends the loss of a gentleman, who so early distinguish[ed] himself in the Cause of his country and would still be happy in contributing to the Completion of that Glorious Work of the redemption of his fellow Citizens and himself from the Iron Teeth of Tyranny. But the depravity of human Nature is such that, the most exalted Character cannot escape the malevolence of the designing and crafty. How far these Miscreants may have prevailed in banishing you from the Service in which your Endeavors were unwearied in the Cause of Liberty, I know not, but this I know that I would rather behold you resting on a Bed of Roses than contribute to your disquiet in the smallest degree. I wish you Health & every kind Domestic Happiness in your returning to the station of a private Citizen.

I lately obtained an Act of Congress for making up the depreciation of Pay to the Medical Department; the Act recommends us to States to which we belong in the same mannaer with similar Acts respecting the Line of the Army and only extends to those in service at the time the Act passed which was between the 11 & 25 Instant. I shall take care that you come within the Limits of this Act, which may save you much trouble in being able to come at your just Demands.

I am,

Dear Sir, with much esteem and regard,

Your most Obedient and very humble servant

J. C.

To the Board of War

New Windsor July 4th 1781

Gentlemen

When I left Philadelphia I hoped that the Vacancies of Hospital Physicians and surgeons would have been filled up, but I am sorry to be informed by Doctor Treat that nothing has yet been done, which must be attended with very disagreeable Circumstances.

Doctor Turner an Hospital Physician & surgeon, has presented me with his resignation which he begs may [be] accepted, as he has retired to private Practice; and not hearing from Doctor Tilton, an officer of the same Rank, who is now, I suppose, in the State of Delaware, tho' I have ordered him to join the Army, I take it for granted he means also to resign. These resignations will leave us only eight Hospital Physicians & surgeons out of fifteen established by Congress, one of whom is necessarily employed in Boston, one in Philadelphia and one at the Yellow Springs, so that there will remain only five to do the whole Duty of the Hospitals of the Army, a number very inadequate to the service.

The four eldest mates which I recommended to Congress are very uneasy, & unless promoted, I have too much reason to believe will leave the service very soon, which together with four other mates who have resigned since my arrival in Camp will deprive us of a great part of our medical aid. I could wish to have Doctor Young and the four eldest mates whom I recommended to Congress to fill the vacancies, after which [a] regimental surgeon of approved abilities may fill the vacancy occasioned by the resignation of Dr. Turner and if Doctor Tilton should not serve, there will be room for another promotion.

I am altogether averse to any regular succession of Promotion of Physicians and surgeons, in the Hospital Department, for the situation of Medical Gentlemen in our service is very different from other services. The medical officers in the former have been picked up as occasion required, many of whom not the best qualified (to say no worse of them), while those of the latter undergo a strict examination and [are] in general every very way qualified, and I would further observe—particularly in the British service—there is no regular succession; but such are generally promoted in the Hospital Department as are most capable & attentive whether from among the Regimental surgeons or the Hospital Mates. The four eldest Mates, whose names are here enclosed have served as junior surgeons under the old Hospital arrangement from its first establishment, which puts them on a footing with the Regimental surgeon[s] and accepted of Mates places with a View of Promotion. I hope the Honorable Board of War will make such representations to Congress as they may judge most expedient to accomplish an End, which will conduce greatly to the good of the service and the preservation of many a good soldier.

I conceived it my Duty to make this representation and if not attended to, I cannot be supposed to be answerable for the Consequences.

I am Gentlemen
With respect & esteem
Yours &c

John Cochran D. M. H.

To Thomas Bond, Jr.

New Windsor July 5th 1781

Dear Sir

The first salutation I had from his Excellency, on my arrival at Head Quarters was "Doctor, you are a great stranger here," which seemd to convey an Oblique Hint that I might have been there much sooner. I parried the Thrust as well as I could and I flatter myself I have got over it pretty well. I wish I could have stayed a few Days longer in Philadelphia in order, if possible, to have got the Vacancies in the Hospital Department filled up, the neglect of which will be attended with bad Consequences. I have wrote to the Board of War and have given them my sentiments very fully on the impropriety of any regular succession of promotion in the Medical Line. Doctor Turner, the Eastern Hospital Physician and surgeon has presented me with his resignation, which I have reported to the Board of War, and as I have heard nothing of Doctor Tilton, I take it for granted he means to play the same Game; I am confident he is too *upright* a man to take pay and absent himself from Duty when the Troops are all in the Field and so much of the season expended. There will be room enough for individuals in Congress to introduce their favorites.

If you should be fortunate enough to receive any pay on my Account, as I suppose it will be paper, I pray you to exchange it for me into the solid, if it will not give you too much trouble, for the other will be of little present use to me. The state of New York has refused the Warrant in your favor, drawn by Congress and have refused to comply with the requisition of Congress for making up the Depreciation to the officers of the Medical Line. They are most certainly an execrable set of sons of Bitches. A New Assembly is called which may probably think better of the Matter & do justice.

The Army is chiefly at the White Plains, French and American, & from every appearance the time is at no great distance, when the Lads at New York may get a warming; if you should be suffícently in Blast you cannot help taking a peep at us when we come to operate seriously.

For God's sake, endeavor us send us some stores, and Dressings, Lint and Lancets. The Hospitals are ordered to be established at Robison's House, the Barracks at West point and the Artillery Huts near New Windsor; Fishkill Hospital is to be broken up. Ledyard will sure and be ready to receive your Instructions. The most ready conveyance for stores both for this place and the Army will be by Kings Ferry. Boats or sloops are almost constantly plying between that and this place. Stores for the Army should be sent in the same Waggons across Kings Ferry, for none can be expected to transport them from that place. I expect by this Dr. Treat is on his way up and I shall set out for the Army in a few days and continue in the Field this Campaign at the request of the Commander in Chief.

I am Dear Sir,

Your most obedient and very humble servant

John Cochran D. M. H.

To Udney Hay

New Windsor July 10th 1781

Dear Sir

The Military Hospitals for the present are established at Robison's House, the Barracks at West Point and the Artillery Huts near this place, and will require a constant supply of fresh Provisions which I fear will not be furnished unless some other method is adopted than by drawing from the Army as they are brought in from the States, therefore would it not be in your way as Agent for this State to give orders to your Deputies in the Neighbourhood of these Hospitals to furnish the supplies of fresh Meat. Perhaps this may be requesting a matter out of your way and inconsistent with your Duty, please to inform me what you can or cannot do towards supplying us that the Sick and wounded may not suffer. Small meats would suit us best, especially during the warm weather, for I do not apprehend that at each of those places we shall be able to consume a whole carcass before it will be spoiled, besides the other is more suitable for the patients. It is impossible to ascertain the number of sick and wounded to be provided for but there is room at the above places for between 6 or 700 and should the Number increase more room must be provided. If we had between 12 & 20 Milk Cows it would be a great saving and vastly more beneficial to the Sick. You will oblige me in directing a Line in answer to me at head Quarters.

I am Your most obedient and very humble servant

[J.C.]

To Charles McKnight

Camp near Dobbs Ferry, July 18th 1781

Dear Charles—

I received your Favor, intended for me at Philadelphia, yesterday on this Ground, Consequently nothing done respecting the order of Dr. Shippen to Doctor Ledyard. I left for you the Bottle of Varnish you wrote for, at Captn. Mitchell's, Newburgh which please send for. Should we come to operate seriously against New York, which may be the case in a short time, it is more than probable your services may be wanted a while in the Field, especially if there should be a prospect of many wounded.

Your instruments will be necessary, as the Flying Hospital is badly provided with Capital Ones. I wish you to hold yourself in readiness for the above purpose. At any rate, I think your stay in the Field will not be very long. I hope by this time the Hospital is removed from Fishkill to the Artillery Huts, for we shall soon be obliged to send the sick of the Army thither.

Please to order all the officers of the Hospitals in your Vicinity to take the Oath, as formerly prescribed by Congress. It becomes necessary on every new appointment [that] a Duplicate should be sent to me, which I am to forward to the Board of War, & Doctor Ledyard is to take the Oath prescribed to those who have Money passing through their Hands or have the purchasing of any Articles for public use. I am with compliments to Mrs. McKnight and Family,

Dear Sir,

Your most Obedient and very humble servant

John Cochran

To Malachi Treat

Camp near Dobbs Ferry, July 18th 1781

Dear Sir

On my arrival in Camp, two Days ago, I was favored with yours of the 9th instant by Dr. Craik and am sorry for your situation, as well as that of the whole Department, on account of Cash. I hope Mr. Morris will give us some relief soon; he has wrote me for a very particular return of the Medical Department, which I will send him, as soon as I can come at my papers which are at New Windsor.

The assembly of New York would do nothing in the affair of Depreciation, pretending for excuse, that they did not know who were meant by the officers of the Medical Department. This was nothing but a mere shuffle. A New House may think otherwise of this matter and I hope for the sake of human Nature they may.

I had a Letter from Doctor Tilton of the fourth instant, informing me that he only waited a few Days, to settle some accounts, and then would take the shortest route to find me in Camp; surely by the way of the Delaware state, would be rather taking a circuituous route.

I have been uneasy about the Marquis's situation. Had Willson and Jenifer been promoted, then they would have gone on with more spirit and Dignity. Should Cornwallis take it into his head to shift his ground from Virginia to New York, which is not unlikely, the assistance there already would be sufficient, but as that may not be the case, then would not your repairing thither with as much Velocity as possible, be attended with good effects? You must endeavor to raise the Wind by some means or other, to enable you to proceed. Perhaps Mr. Morris may be able to assist you. I look upon it as a matter of much indifference whether we receive any money on our late warrents, unless they are paid in hard money or exchanged immediately, as paper can be of no use to us.

I cannot inform you what is intended against New York or what prospect there is of our succeeding against it this Campaign, but if my own opinion was to take place, I think you may go to Virginia, and after seeing matters put into a proper train there, you will have time enough, to return to perform the purposes you hinted to, to me.

The Enemy have some ships of Force as far as some Miles above Tarrytown which impedes us much in getting our stores and supplies down the river. They burned a large House last night on the West Side of the river nearly opposite to where they lay.

I hope to hear from you by the return of the Post and that you are ready to proceed on your way for Virginia. Wishing you Health and Happiness with my most respectful Compliments to my Friends the Marquis, General Wayne, and every honest fellow of my Acquaintance.

I am,
My dear Sir
Your most obedient and very humble servant,
J. Cochran

To Robert Morris

Camp near Dobbs Ferry July 26th 1781

Sir

Agreeable to your request, I herewith transmit you a Return of the Medical Department, as established by an act of Congress on the 30th of September, by which you will find there are six Vancancies of Hospital Physicians & Surgeons, occasioned by the resignations of Doctors Scott, Bloomfield, Hagan, Jackson and Turner and the promotion of Doctor Burnet, which vacancies, I have solicited Congress to fill up for some time past, the omission of which may turn out very detrimental to the service, for should we have an active Campaign, the number of Hospital Physicians and Surgeons would be very inadequate to the service.

It appears by different reports from the Board of War and others, sent by the Board to his Excellency the Commander in Chief for his opinion, that Congress wish to fall on some mode of a regular Succession of Promotion in the Medical Line according to Seniority which would in my opinion, be attended with the worst of consequences, for in our service we have been obliged to employ such as we could pick up, many of whom were not of the best qualified—to say no worse of them—particularly in the regimental Line, and that these Characters should be promoted according to their seniority to places in the Hospital Department where Gentlemen of the first Medical Abilities are required, would have very disagreeable effects. In the British service where every medical Officer of whatever Rank undergoes a strict examination before his appointment, there is no regular succession of Promotion but they are promoted to seniorities in the Hospital (a station similar to our Hospital Physicians & Surgeons) according to Merit, whether from the Line of Regimental Surgeons or Hospital Mates.

You have been informed, as I am told, that there is no need for filling up these vacancies and that the Department is sufficently extensive as it now stands. Every Gentleman now with me who are acquainted with the circumstances of the department, join with me in [the] Opinion that you have been imposed on. It is true if we could retain in service the Eldest Mates who are qualified to fill the Vacancies, & who have acted in the Character of Junior Surgeons in the old Hospital arrangement of April 1777 from its first establishment and submitted to the degradation of Mates, rather than leave the service, where they had a prospect of promotion, there would be no ocassion for new appointments, for promotion would add nothing to their Medical Abilities. These Gentlemen are very uneasy and are every day soliciting to quit the service. The whole Hospital is conducted by Mates in Virginia for want of Hospital Physicians and Surgeons to send to that Quarter. I have lately ordered a chief Hospital Physician to repair thither.

You will see by the return in what manner the Gentlemen of the Department are disposed of, & tho in some of the Hospitals they are not overburthened with duty, yet 10 days may give them full employ, and perhaps more than they can execute.

I thought it my duty to give you this information, that in case of any ill consequences attended the delay of filling the Vacancies to the full establishment made by Congress September, 1780 that no reflection should be cast on me.

Several Mates have resigned whose places are chiefly filled agreeable to the plan for conducting the Hospital Department.

There are in some of the distant Hospitals Stewards, Ward Masters, Matrons, &c. [for] which I have been obliged to leave blanks for their names, as I have no return specifying them.

If it is necessary to insert the names of the Nurses, Orderly Men, Waggoners, &c. employed in the Hospital service, it shall be done, but it will require time as the Hospitals are scattered at a distance from each other.

I have also sent you a return of the principle officers of the Southern Department. The inferior Officers have not yet been returned to me.

I do not find there is a probability of our receiving any money on the warrants I obtained when in Philadelphia for the use of the Department, either on account of Pay for the officers or to procure necessaries for the sick, for the want of which the sick suffer and we are much embarrassed. For God's sake help us as soon as you can. Most of our officers have not received one shilling of pay in upwards of two years.

I am
Sir
With every sentiment of respect & Esteem
Your most obedient &
very humble servant
John Cochran D. M. Hospls.

To Thomas Bond, Jr.

Campt near Dobbs Ferry July 26th 1781

Dear Sir

I received your favor of the 17th Instant and am sorry that there is no probability of our receiving money on the warrants obtained for the use of our Department, the want of which you may reasonably suppose has a bad effect, both with respect to the officers and the poor suffering soldiers who deserve a better fate; I cannot find that it will answer any end for me to write to the Board on that subject. What can they do or what can any Body in the present state of our Finances do; I have wrote to Mr. Morris and have transmited him a return of the Department agreeable to his orders and have mentioned the affair of pay &c to him, requesting every assistance in his power as soon as possible. I believe our first relief must be from that Quarter. Should we obtain the money for the Warrants in paper, it would be of little use to many, unless changed into hard money, which perhaps might not be so easily done.

I have sent the return from Mr. Morris to you which after perusing please to seal and send him. I have left sundry blanks in it for you to fill up, I mean only of yours and Cra[i]gie's people; Have the Assistant Apothecaries rations? What is the pay of Root and Wainwright, Prudden and Caldwell? Williams a Ration & Leake Hunt Clk. to Ledyard? You will please to fill up the Blank for the Young Man of Sharp DeLaney, Esquire, I lost the memorandum. When you settled these peoples pay and Rations &c, please to transmit a memorandum of it to me that I may enter it in my book in case I should be called on for a return in future.

I herewith enclose you an estimate of Medicines &c for the Campaign, it is probable many of the articles are on hand, therefore regard will be had to that matter—Bark, Salts and Tartar Emetic will be very soon wanted most. (Could you not by Advertisement be able to procure a Quantity of old linen from the good Ladies of your City. I was obliged after the last Skirmish when fifty men were wounded to give every sheet I had in the world but two to make Lint &c.) I dread the thoughts of an action when we have it not in our power to relieve the distresses of the unfortunate.

The Bulk of the Army with his Excellency at their Head went to Kings Bridge where we continued 48 hours to take a survey of the Enemy's works which was done very effectually from every point. This Business was performed on Sunday & Monday last.

I am Dear Sir
Your most Obedient and
very humble servant
John Cochran D. M. H.

To Isaac Ledyard

Camp Pickskill August 2d 1781

Dear Sir

Upon enquiry yesterday of Doctor Eustis, I find that Mr. De La Mater did not go after the stores at New Windsor and the reason assigned for his Neglect was, that being an Executor of the estate of Doctor Foster, he thought it a Matter of too delicate a nature for him, thus circumstanced, to proceed in. This Business, by some means or other, has been postponed too long, therefore I am of opinion you had better proceed with as much Dispatch as possible and endeavor to procure the stores in the hands of the Hookers and forward them on the Camp, as they are much wanted, the sick accumulating very fast. You will take with you the letter from General Washington & my order, with the letter to the Quarter Master and all the papers necessary. They were inclosed to you in the Letter I wrote you from Camp sometime ago by Mr. Hunt. I would advise you to appropriate as much of the 300 dollars in your hands for Hospital use, as will be sufficient to bear your Expenses only, on that service. If you should have any Directions from Doctor Bond, contrary to the above respecting the money, I will settle it with him or replace the same, so that you may incur no censure.

I am your most obedient, &c.

John Cochran, D. M. H.

To Andrew Craigie

Camp near Dobbs Ferry Aug. 14th 1781

Sir

I was favoured with yours of the 6th inst. and am sorry that I was not understood respecting the list of medicines sent you sometime ago. Drs. Craik, Latimer and myself made out an estimate of such medicines, instruments, &c as we judged might be wanted for the campaign, without paying any regard to what you might compound or had on hand, and in my letter to Dr. Bond I thought I was sufficiently expressive in desiring him to pay attention to that matter; therefore had you given credit on the back of my estimate for such medicines as were on hand and you could compound, the business, no doubt, would have been transacted without the least difficulty, and that was our intention at the time the estimate was made out.

I have enclosed the list you sent me, to complete the former. The quantity of Bark I have doubled, not thinking 500 sufficient and it must have been a mistake in transcribing.

You have put down no penis syringes nor large ones, both of which are much wanted. It is probable you have a quantity on hand. Do not by any means neglect the lint &c, which I wrote so pressingly to Doctr. Bond for. Should we have an action before a supply arrives our situation will be very disagreeable indeed; and we know not how soon that will take place. Pocket instruments are more wanted than anything. I have had a conference with Mr. Morris respecting the medical arrangement, and I do not apprehend any material alterations will be made. I flatter myself some people near Head Quarters will have something to say on the subject, which may counteract the selfish design of restless spirits: I believe his Excellency will be consulted, for the first time, on this occasion, and I think I know something about his sentiments. I shall do my endeavor to prevent a ridiculous system or arrangement from taking place. Nothing will be done soon, if ever, if Congressional wheels move as slow as usual.

We have no news in this quarter. Nothing from the West Indies. No French Fleet. Farewell. Compliments to all friends, & believe me,

Dear Sir,

Your most obedient & very humble servant

John Cochran Director Mility. Hospls.

P.S. I hope you will soon have it in your power to fulfill your promise of writing us with a pretty little assortment of medicines &c. &c.

An estimate of Medicines &c wanting for the present Campaign

August 14th 1781

lbs. 50	Argent. Viv:	lbs. 200	Cera flav:
20	Calom: ppt:	12	Magnes alb:
20	G. Guaiac:	1	Ol. Pulig:
40	—Camph:	ozs. 6	Caust. Lun:
20	—Ammoniac	lbs. 200	Flor: Sulph:
6	—Myrrh:	500	Sulph: Viv:
10	Merc. corros. Sub:	2	Vit: Alb:
3	Precip. alb:	2	Vit: Cerul:
5	Praecip. rub:	20	Aloes Tinc.
50	Ol. Vitriol:	12	Pins
500	Sal. Nit:	10	Gross Phials
100	Rad. Jalap:	6	Do. Gallipots
100	Gum. Arabic	100	lbs. Lint
25	Rad. Gentian:	200	lbs. Tow
10	Scill. Sicc:	50	Ream Wrapping paper
100	Lith. Aur:	20	Do writing paper
10	Sponge	12	lbs. Orig. Oris
10	Ipec: c Bol: sine opio:	30	Gallons Ol. Lini
50	Sapo: Castil:	20	Gross Corks
50	Rad: Serpent: Virg:	12	Mattresses 6 wool, 6 hair
1	Flor: Benzoin	6	Sets Amputating Instruments
6	Cort: Cinam:	6	Dozen penis syringes
10	Nux Moschat:		
1000	Sal: Cathart:		
10	Ther: Androm:		

This estimate was sent to Andrew Craigie, Esq. Apothy. to the Hospitals to compleat a former estimate sent him together with what he had on hand.

Staff &c of his Brittanic Majesty's Hospitals at New York, Rhode Island and their dependencies in North America, December 16th 1778

1 Physician & Inspector
1 Chief Surgeon and Purveyor
1 Physician extra & Purveyor
3 Physicians
12 Surgeons some of whom are field Inspectors, Deputy Purveyors, &c.
8 Apothecaries—the same
39 Established Mates
32 Supernumerary ditto
11 clerks
1 Chaplain
1 Deputy ditto
1 Cutler

111 Total

Besides Stewards, Ward Masters, Matrons, Nurses, & Orderly Men.

The British Hospital staff under the command of Sir Henry Clinton has been considerably augmented, since the date of the above list, in physicians and supernumerary Mates.

There is an Hospital staff in Canada exclusive of the above, and the General Hospital for the Hessian Corps in his Brittanic Majesty's service in North America consists of

1 Physician
2 Grand Surgeons
6 Surgeons
3 Apothecaries
1 Chaplain

Number of Mates unknown

The French Troops now under the command of his Excellency General Washington have an Hospital Staff nearly corresponding with the British as to numbers and the grade of their officers.

Aug.[t] 14th 1781

List of the Hospital Staff of the Army of the United States of America, exclusive of Georgia, North & South Carolina as established by Congress Sept. 30th, 1780

1 Director
1 Chief Physician and Surgeon to the Army
3 Chief Physicians and Surgeons to the Hospitals

1	Purveyor
1	Apothecary
15	Hospital Physicians and Surgeons
20	Established Mates
2	Supernumerary ditto
1	Assistant Purveyor
1	Assistant Apothecary
2	Apothecary's Mates
3	Storekeepers
3	Clerks
54	Total

Besides Stewards, Ward Masters, Matrons, Nurses & Orderly Men. The Apothecary, Assistant Apothecary and Mates ought not to be included in the above list, in taking a comparative view between the number of Officers employed in the Hospital of the United States, and those in other services, particularly the British for in the former, the Apothecary, Assistants and Mates, purchase and compound the medicines for the use of the Army and Hospitals and are never employed in any other capacity; while in the latter the medicines are all compounded at Surgeons Hall and sent to the different Armies. In the British service the Surgeon and Apothecary are distinct and separate professions; while in the American they are concentrated in one, and are denominated Hospital Physicians and Surgeons a grade equal to the British Surgeon and Apothecary. The Surgeons attend and prescribe for the surgical and the Apothecaries in some measure do the duty of Physicians in attending and prescribing for the Physical Patients only. Further remark that the Purveyor, Deputy Purveyor, Assistants, &c. are included in the number of their superior medical Officers, acting in both capacities as occasion may require, which gives a balance of four superior medical officers in their favor. The British have forty nine Mates more than are employed in the American Hospitals. Their other officers, [I] suppose, nearly the same with each other. Aug. 14th 1781

The preceding lists were delivered to Robert Morris Esq.y[e] Financier in order to enable him to form some judgement of the present Medical Arrangement of the Hospital of the United States, this 14th day of August 1781

[John Cochran Director Military Hospitals]

To Bodo Otto

Camp near Dobbs Ferry, August 19th 1781

Dear Sir

I was favoured with yours of the 7th instant inclosing the return of the sick and wounded for July, but do not recollect receiving that for June, if I have received it, it must be mislaid, therefore I should be glad [if] you would send me a Copy of it when you send the return for August. Please also at the time you transmit the returns of the sick and wounded, to inclose a return of the officers of the department, Matrons, Nurses, Orderly Men and every person employed, beginning with yourself, Mentioning the names of each, their pay and rations of Provisions and Forage; this is to be done monthly. These things are demanded of me by the Financier which obliges me to be very particular with the Gentlemen who superintend the Hospitals.

I fear there is but little prospect of obtaining Money on the different warrents I procured in Philadelphia. Mr. Morris the Superintendent of Finance, has been at Head Quarters & promises soon to furnish some pay in Specie for the officers of our Department and has already furnished a sum for purchasing Stores, paying the Matrons, Nurses, & orderlies, part of which I suppose will be sent to you.

I received the oath of Frederick Wendt, he must also take the Oath of Office a Copy which I here enclose, your Steward must take both Oaths, and you and your Son must take the same that Wendt sent me. If you have done this already they are not come to hand, and this order is to be complied with immediately as I am called on for these Oaths by the Board of War, to send them, otherwise I shall be reported to Congress.

I am Dear Sir

Your very humble servant

John Cochran D. M. H.

As you may have taken these Oaths before, perhaps you think it needless to repeat them, that is not the Case, for every Officer takes the Oaths on every new appointment. Yours &c.

To J. Nitchie

Head Quarters Peekskill August 25th 1781

Sir

I received your favor by Mr. Vredenburgh, and am much surprised with Doctor Shippen's continuing you as assistant Commissary in the Hospital Department, under the new arrangement, as the plan admits of no such officer, nor did I know on my appointment, that you were in the Hospital employ, as no return has ever been made of you to me, among the other Officers of the Department.

I am sorry you have been so long kept out of your Pay, and that you have not been able to keep your Family from starving but on Credit. Your situation is like many others in our service, for I have not received one shilling of pay in 23 months and there [are] few among us who have been in better circumstances.

I cannot tell you what you are to do, for as you have not been on my Roll, you have not been returned to the Board of War; of course I cannot consider you an officer of the hospital. You ought to settle your accounts as soon as you receive Money to discharge them, but when that will be, I know not. Doctor Bond will be able to give you the best information in what manner and with whom your accounts are to be settled. At the time you request[ed] a certificate entitling you to your Depreciation, you forgot to mention your Pay per month or Day, which is necessary as well as your time of service; otherwise the one will be useless unles the other is specified When you furnish me with Both, I will send you the proper Certificate.

Mr. Vredenburgh says you request an Order to receive your Rations. Surely you cannot suppose me capable of giving an order for Provisions to a person considered to be out of service.

If I can assist you in anything consistent with my Duty, I will do so with Pleasure.

I am,

Sir,

Your very humble servant,

J. Cochran D. M. H.

To the Board of War

Head Quarters East side of Hudsons River
August 29th 1781

Gentlemen

I herewith send you a return of the officers of the Hospital Department of the United States, of the 1st of August 1781, with a Return of the sick and wounded in the Army, under the immediate command of his Excellency Genl. Washington & the Military Hospitals to the eastward of Virginia, for the month of May; the returns for the Hospitals in the other States are not come to hand. All the returns to the last of April which I have been possessed of, were made to the Medical Committee & I suppose are among their papers. The confused state of the Department at the time of my being appointed to the Directorship, has prevented me from complying with the requisitions of the Board of War, in their letters of the first of July & August, but I flatter myself I shall be able to transmit monthly returns in future with accuracy.

You will also receive the oaths of allegience of such of the officers of the Hospital Department as I have been able to procure; the delinquents are in the inclosed list, with the reasons for the deficiencies. The officers pray that their Commissions may be made out and transmitted to me. Those entitled to Commissions agreeable to the plan for conducting the Hospitals, as established by Congress Sept. 30th 1780 are, the Director, Chief Hospital Physicians, the Chief Physicians and Surgeons of the Army, Physicians & Surgeons, Purveyor, Apothecary, Assistant Purveyor, & Assistant Apothecary.

I have been obliged to call the Hospital Physicians and Surgeons from the Hospital at Albany, where by the last months return, there were 75 patients, to attend in the Army on the east side of Hudsons River, & entrust the Albany Hospl. to the care of one Mate, the other two destined for that service being unavoidably detached to the frontiers of the State of New York. The sick therefore will suffer through want of medical aid.

Colonel Willet, who commands on the frontiers has applied for a Hospl. Physician and Surgeon to be sent to that quarter. The detached State of the Army & the smallness of the number of our officers, occasioned by so many resignations & the want of the vacancies being supplied, prevents me from complying with his request.

Doctor Marshall, one of our most valuable Mates, has resigned within a few days, which will be followed by serveral others, who have been long in service, & acted some years in the superior capacity under the old arrangement, & accepted of Mates Stations with an expectation of promotion. A favourable opportunity offered to retain these gentlemen in service, by promoting them to the present vacancies, but it appears as if Congress had forgot that either Hospitals, sick or wounded had any existance. I am confident their places cannot be supplied with their equals, if close attentions, long experience and a capacity to do business have any weight in the scale. If we take a comparative view of the numbers of medical officers in our service, and that of the British & French in this Country, it will be found that, the two latter have double our establishment, supposing it compleated to its full number. I hope I may not be thought troublesome in offering so much on this subject; let my duty, the good of the service & the welfare of the soldiery plead my excuse.

I have the honor to be,
Gentlemen,
With esteem and respect,
your most obedient & most humble servant
John Cochran, Direct. Mily. Hospls.

P.S. Our Army, 'Till within a few weeks has been remarkably healthy, but Dysenteries, Intermittent and remittent fevers, with a few Putrid Cases, begin to prevail.

To Thomas Bond, Jr.

Head Quarters East side of Hudsons River—Sept. 1st 1781

Dear Sir

Inclosed I send you a letter for the Board of War containing a return of the officers of the Hospital Department & such of the oaths of allegiance as I have been able to procure. It is amazing how indolent some of the officers have been in complying with the Act of Congress and my repeated orders to take the oaths. In consequence of this neglect, I have reported them to the Board of War, and if any evil attends it to themselves be it. I have sent them a list of those officers in Philadelphia who have not sworn, and informed them that you would see the order complied with and hand them the oaths with the others, which I beg you will take the trouble to perform.

General Sullivan left in the hands of Colonel Webb, five hundred dollars, which he said was for Hospl. use, & desired it might be given to my order. The money is now in the hands of the Asst. Purveyor, but as no letter accompanied it he is at a loss to know for what particular purpose it was intended. He says he has wrote you on the subject, please to give him an answer by the first Post, if no opportunity offers sooner, for the money is much wanted to purchase necessaries for the sick, and to pay Matrons, Nurses, &c. I hope you will jog Mr. Morris's memory about some pay for the officers of the department, when he has it in his power. Colonel Laurens who passed through camp last night on his way to Philadelphia has put us in great spirits from the supply of money and everything else requisite, arrived in Boston from our good and generous ally, in consequence of which, I hope we shall soon be in high *Blast*. Pleast to write me a line by every Post giving me all the news you hear from the Army under General Washington and the Fleet &c. until the particular service he is on is over, and you will oblige me much.

Compliments to all friends, and believe me

Dear Sir,

Your most obedient and most humble serv't.

John Cochran D. M. H.

Philadelphia
Barnabas Binney Hospl. Ph. and Surg.
John Cowell Mate
Thomas Bond Purveyor
Andrew Craigie Apothy.
Andw. Caldwell }
Thos. Prudden } Mates Apothy.
Edward Williams Clk to Purveyor
Wm. Haskell Storekeeper
James James Clk to Magazine
Jacob Parker Steward

If the above Gentlemen have not taken the proper oaths, you will please to order it to be done and deliver the same to the Board of War with those I send. J. Cochran D. M. H.

To David Townsend

Head Quarters East Side Hudsons River
September 1st 1781

Dear Sir

I was much surprised when Doctor Eustis informed me that you expected to meet me at Robinson's house, if I made any such promise it escaped my memory; & in consequence of your intention to go to Boston this day, I made a push to come here last night.

I have signed the certificate for the officers of the department entitled to depreciation, and wish you success.

I wrote to Doctor Warren the 30th of June to send me the oaths of allegiance of the officers of the Hospital at Boston, which I have not received. You will oblige me in obtaining and forwarding them by the Post at soon as you arrive in Boston. I want the returns for June, July & August and at the same time they send the returns of the sick &c let me have the returns of the officers, matrons, orderly men, & nurses with their pay pr. day or month, rations, &c & names of every person employed in the Hospital. This must be done monthly, accompanying every return of the sick &c. Let this be a standing rule

& punctually observed, which please to communicate in writing to the person superintending the Hospital at Boston. I hope poor Warren is recovered. I am Dear Sir,

Your most obedient & most humble servt.

John Cochran D. M. H.

To Jabez Campfield

Camp Picks Kill Sept. 3d 1781

Dear Sir—

I Rec'd both your Favours of the 25th and 31st Ultimo and can only recommend it to you to attend the patients sent you by Doctor Latimer and such others as he may send which I think it is probable he will from the Route General Washington has taken, until they are either Recovered or in a situation to be removed to this camp, from whence we can easily send them to some of the Hospitals on the River.

I have not heard from Colonel Sheldon, since your appointment, which I am surprised at, Perhaps he thinks I am gone on with General Washington, surely Mr. Trumbull, the General's Secretary, would not be mistaken, for he went to Danbury where his Father and the Council were assembled and on his way thither I met him and Begged his Interest in promising the Appointment, on his return He informed me you were appointed and Desired me to write to you. The Regiment lays somewhere near North Castle, you had Better come to this ground and take the advantage of some Escort, as it will be unsafe to travel that Route alone, on account of the Cow Boys, who are very Troublesome.

Compliments to Mrs. Campfield and Son and believe me

Dear Sir,

Your most Obedient and very humble servant

John Cochran D. M. H.

To Leake Hunt

Camp at Peekskill Sept. 3d 1781,

Sir

Please to issue to John Vredenburgh, ward master of the Flying Hospital, twenty woolen shirts, sixty yards of Baize of Different colours and One hundred pounds of best Brown sugar for the use of the Flying Hospital, he will receipt to you for the Same.

John Cochran Directr Mili'y Hospitals.

To the Superintending Surgeon At the North Windsor Huts Hospital

September 5th 1781

Sir

In future, when the returns of the sick and wounded are made out, let there be also a Return made of all the officers of the Hospital Department doing Duty at the Windsor Huts, matrons, Nurses, orderly Men, Bakers, Waggoners, &c. if employed by the Hospital, with their Names, Pay rations of Provisions & Forage signed by the superintending surgeon and delivered to the Director.

Your humble servant

John Cochran D. M. H.

N. B. The same orders have [been] sent to the Hospitals at Albany and Boston

To the Board of War

Camp Peekskill September 7th 1781

Gentlemen

In my last of the 29th Ultimo, I omitted the return of the sick and wounded in the Hospital for May as mentioned. I sent such of the oaths of allegiance &c of the officers of the Medical Department as have come to hand.

This will be delivered by Doctor Young, a deranged surgeon, whom I recommended to Congress to fill one of the Vacancies of Hospital Physician & surgeon.

If merit and long services have any weight, he will meet with no obstruction.

I have the Honor to be,
Gentlemen,
Your most obedient & very humble servant
John Cochran D. M. H.

To John Witherspoon

New Windsor, Sept. 11th 1781

Sir

This will be delivered to you by the Revd. Mr. Plumb, who was, at an early Period appointed Chaplain to the General Hospital in the Northern Department and has continued to officiate in that Capacity, until this time. When the new arrangement of the Hospital Department took place in September last he wrote to the Director to be informed whether the Chaplains were continued or not, but receiving no Answer he took it for granted that he was not deranged, which induced him to continue in the service, without further inquiry. As soon as I become acquainted with his Circumstances, I informed him that I did not apprehend he was considered as an officer in the Department. He now waits on Congress to solicit a settlement of his Depreciation &c to endeavor to obtain some recompence for his service, since the New arrangement took place.

I have not had the Pleasure of being acquainted with this young Gentleman, but all the officers of the Hospital with whom I have conversed, and others who knew him well, agree, that he attended to the Duties of his Profession with great Assiduity, and that his moral Character was irreproachable. I flatter myself he will meet with that encouragement from you, to which, his merit appears to entitle him.

I am, Sir,

Your most obedient and very humble servt.

John Cochran D. M. H.

To the Board of War

Camp Peekskill September 26th 1781

Gentlemen

I here inclose you a return of the officers of the Hospital Department for the first of September 1781, also a Return of the sick and wounded in the Hospitals and Army for the months of June, July and August, by which you will perceive they have increased considerably in the last Month and have continued to increase in the month of September. The three Months men and new Levies compose the chief part of the sick in the Army and Hospital. I fear they will suffer for want of proper supplies as the Purveyor writes me he has none on hand. I have furnished him with an estimate of such Articles as are most immediately wanted for the Hospitals on the North River, which I beg he may be enabled to procure with all possible Dispatch.

I have also inclosed the oaths of Allegiance and office of such of the officers of the Hospital Department as I have been able to procure, which nearly completes the Whole.

I am, Gentlemen,

Your most obedient and very humble servant

John Cochran D. M. H.

To Thomas Bond, Jr.

Camp Peekskill October 1st 1781

Dear Sir

I was favored with yours of the 11th ultimo, not before this Day, it had been wandering about Fishkill for a considerable time. No Letter accompanied the money with Sullivan and the subsequent One respecting it, went I believe into New York, so that we may soon expect a New Edition of Tommy Bond, from Jamy Rivington. Ledyard is gone to New London, where he sustained the Loss of an uncle, & Brother killed and another Brother taken by that most infamous of all Vagabonds, Arnold. The Money is in the hands of Mr. De La Mater his Clk, to whom I gave your letter for Ledyard. I had a Letter this Day from Warren at Boston, who writes most piteously an account of his extreme sufferings. He cannot receive any Patients into his Hospital for want of Necessaries. I shall speak to De La Mater, and if [there is] nothing contradictory in your letter as to the appropriation, I will send one Hundred Dollars to Warren.

I had a letter from Doctor Otto at Yellow Springs, complaining of the want of Clothing for his Patients and that he had applied to you and you referred him to me for an order to supply him. This is a Matter which I am totally unacquainted with, but if you have any Clothing and there is a propriety in my giving an Order, you will supply him with what Quantity may be necessary to relieve the wants of his Patients, but I imagine such an Order would come with more propriety from the Board of War.

I have inclosed to the Board of War a Return of the sick and wounded, for the months of June, July and August, and have wrote them that I have furnished you with an estimate of such Articles [as] are most immediately wanted for the Hospitals on the Hudson, (as it appears from your Letter that those to the southward are pretty well supplied) requesting them to enable you to send us a speedy supply. Our stores are chiefly exhausted and the sick are increasing every day, tho I must say the Army in general is healthy. The 3 months men &

new Levies compose the greater part of our sick. The stores you sent last came very safe except the sugar, which sustained some considerable Loss from rain on the River in open Boats, owing to its being in boxes instead of Casks. King supports a good character and I do not apprehend the stores were troubled by him, or perhaps any one else. I did not taste the wine, but in general heard that it was very good. I tasted some of the Wine sent [last] Winter a few Days ago at the flying Hospital and it was agreed that the last sent was of a better quality than the former, which I thought very good, and was happy to see the good effect of it on three poor putrid fellows who must inevitably have perished without it. As far as I know, no fault would be found with the Quality of any of the stores sent at that time. There were some Complaints about the Tea, but I had it tried by some very good Judges and they agreed that it was very good.

By a Letter to Ledyard from the Hookers at Windsor, Connecticut, who had Charge of the stores there, [they] say that they had sent some to Boston for the use of the Hospital, some to Doctor Turner, some delivered to the Executors of Doctor Foster to pay public Debts and some were sold to pay the Hookers their Demand for Storage, &c, pay being [for] public officers employed by Foster. Thus are they accounted for.

I fear all has not been well respecting these said stores and I think a very particular enquiry ought to be made into this matter on the settlement of Foster's accounts.

I am,

Dear Sir,

Your most obedient and very humble servant

John Cochran

Estimate of Articles which are immediately wanted in the Hospitals on the North River, October, 1781 accompanying my letter to the Purveyor of this Date.

Viz.

3 Quarter Casks Wine

4 Barrels of Rum

1500 Sugar in Light Barrels

6 Barrels Molasses

4 Tierces Rice
100 Wt. of Tea
500 Wt. of Coffee
500 Blankets }
500 bed sacks } or an order on the Clothier
200 shirts }
500 sheets }
10 Lbs. Spices of different kinds

John Cochran D. M. H.

To Goodwin Wilson and Daniel Jenifer

Camp Peekskill October 8th 1781

Gentlemen

I have the pleasure to inclose you an Act of Congress of the 20th Ultimo handed to me a few days since by the President, desiring me to convey it to you, appointing you Hospital Physicians and surgeons, of which give me leave to congratulate you both in the warmest Manner. The President, at the same time, informs me that they made these Promotions merely at my Instigation, with reluctance, conceiving that there were a sufficiency of medical officers in our Department already. Some evil minded Persons have been too busy with Congress, in retarding your Promotion, and had nearly succeeded in preventing it altogether. I wish you Health and every happiness you can wish and are capable of enjoying.

I am, Gentlemen,

Your most obedient and very humble servant

J. Cochran D. M. H.

To Thomas McKean

Camp Peekskill October 9th 1781

Sir

I was honored with your Favor of the 25th Ultimo, inclosing an Act of Congress of the 20th, promoting the Gentlemen recommended by

The Schuyler-Hamilton House in Morristown, New Jersey. Originally the home of Dr. Jabez Campfield (1738–1821), a Revolutionary surgeon, it was occupied from 1779 to 1780 by Dr. John Cochran and his family. The Philip Schuylers and their daughter Betsey (the future Mrs. Alexander Hamilton) also stayed there briefly during the same period

Photograph from the collection of the Morristown Township Library

me to the Vacancies of Hospital Physicians and Surgeons, for which Indulgence and the Honor conferred on me, in attending to my request you will please to return to Congress my warmest acknowledgements; but I am sorry this measure was entered into with reluctance, from a supposition that the department was already furnished with a sufficient Number of officers of the different Ranks. Could we have retained the Mates, who have been lately promoted, or have procured others of like Capacity and equally acquainted with the particular Duty of Hospitals, to serve as Mates, I should agree with Congress as to the sufficency of Officers of different Ranks, for it is of little consequence to the Service, by what appellation an officer is styled (a change of which can add nothing to his medical abilities), provided they will serve, but that was not the case with these gentlemen, who have done the Duty of Junior Surgeons, with the utmost attention, ever since the Hospital Arrangement in April 1777, until the new one of September 1780 took place. When the Grade of junior Surgeons being abolished, they submitted to become Mates, with a Prospect of Promotion in their turns, and felt themselves so much hurt by its being delayed that they urged a Dismission from Service in order to retire to private Life, where they had a Prospect of providing better for themselves.

With all humble submission, it cannot be supposed that Congress is so minutely acquainted with the medical Establishment requisite for this vast extent of Country, as they could wish. Therefore [they] must depend on Information, and I have too much reason to fear their Information, in this Instance, may have originated with those who had their own Whims more in view than the Honor of Congress, the Good of the service or the country they pretend to serve.

If we take a view of the Hospital Establishments, in other Services, they will be found to exceed ours in the number of superior and by far the numbers in inferior Officers.

The British Establishment under the command of Sir Henry Clinton in the year 1778 consisted of 111 officers besides an extensive establishment for the Hessian Corps. The French Establishment under his Excellency General Washington is very numerous and the pay of their superior Officers (if my Information is right) is from 180 to 200 Dollars per Month, and the grades of the officers of the whole of the above are nearly similar to that of the Hospitals of the United States. They have their Directors, Physicians, Inspectors, chief Surgeons, grand surgeons, Physicians, surgeons, Apothecaries who in some Measure do the Duty of Physicians, mates, Purveyors, Field Inspectors, Clerks &c. Surely the American soldiery are not less worthy the attention of the Public, than that of other Nations.

You will pardon me for taking so much of your Excellency's time in giving you this Information, which I conceived to be my Duty, lest some New fangled system should be offered to Congress by men of restless spirits, which would subject us to many inconveniences from such a Variety of Alterations, amendments, and new Creations of arrangements rendering us at the same time to the Ridicule of the Whole World.

Before I conclude, permit me, Sir, to suggest that while we are endeavoring to provide for the Care of the Body should we not pay some Attention to the Comfort of the souls [of] our sick soldiery in our Hospitals by appointing a Chaplain to perform that Duty; the Brigade Chaplains either find it inconvenient, or have not an inclination to officiate in that capacity.

It is customary to have a Chaplain to the Hospitals of other Nations, to whom we would not wish to yield in point of Christianity.

I have the Honor to be with the utmost respect and Esteem

Your Excellency's most obedient and very humble servant

John Cochran D. M. H.

To James Craik

Camp Peek's Kill Oct. 10th 1781

Dear Craik

Nothing new has occurred in this Quarter Worthy of your Notice since your Departure, I have been mostly with the Army, which is encamped on the hills at and about this place, save about 1000 Troops which are constantly kept between Pines Bridge and the Plains, the Cow Boys are the only troublesome Neighbors we have to combat with. Sir Harry has been busy embarking his troops; sometime I believe he is as much puzzled at this present as he has been at any period whatever. Reports say he is embarking again but for what purpose is all Conjecture. Digby is arrived at N. Y. with 3 ships of the Line and some Frigates, with him came one of the Royal Whelps from Great Britain, the Address from the Gov. & Council with his Answer you will see in the Publick papers. A Young Lad who came out of N.Y. some Days ago being examined before Genl. Heath was asked if he saw the Young Prince, He answered yes; he saw many go to look at him and he thought he might as well see him as the rest, he was asked what he was like and what he thought of him, he said he expected to have seen something more in him than other people but was Disappointed, excepting his being the ugliest person he ever saw, with a very large Nose, his eyes resembling those of a Wall eyed Horse and his legs all of a thickness from his Knees to his Ankles, but that he had a fine Gold Coat, a pretty representative this Fellow will make to cause a Rebellion to Sink at his Approach. I think from the description given of him he is much better calculated to Cause an Abortion in the Fair Sex than to Quell a Rebellion.

We are waiting with Vast Anxiety to hear of your success to the Southward; We are big with Hopes and expect soon to have a happy delivery, We have favourable reports from Greene, pray God they may be true and let the same Prayer be Continued that the troubles of our enemies may accumulate every Hour, and may their Head never cease to Ache, as much as yours has done after a Drunken Frolick.

Congress has at length promoted the five Gentlemen I have recommended, I inclose you a letter to Willson & Junifer, with their Appointments which the President desires me to forward and Informs me at the same time that it was done with reluctance, and merely as it were on my account, Congress conceiving that there were Officers sufficient in the Hospls. of Different Ranks, this has given occasion to my Writing my sentiments on the subject of our Department and I have not failed to represent in the most ridiculous point of View, those restless Spirits who are plaguing Congress with Wild schemes of Alterations, Amendments, New Creations of Arrangements, and what not, having the executions of their Whims more at Heart than the Honor of Congress, the good of the Service and the Country they pretend to serve. I am informed that they now have it in Contemplation to Dismiss all the Chiefs and they are to retire on the Half Pay Alloted some time ago. Nay, it is further said that they thought Hospitals very injurious to the service, that the sick would be better taken care of with the Regiments than in Hospitals, since more Men died in the latter than with the Former. Young's Observations to some of the Members who were making these Wise Remarks was that he thought it would in future be the Height of Folly for any Man to Venture in Bed, since it was well known that more people died in Bed than in any other Situation. It appears that if there were neither Feasibility, Stability or even the smallest glimmering Point of Certainty on this Side the Grave. If Mr. Morris has given into Congress the Report of the Philadelphia Triumvirate, on our Department without the Concurrence of the Commander in Chief and the Heads of the Department, he has acted an Unjustifiable part and forfeited his Word to me. Make my most respectful Compliments to our Common Friend, his

Excellency, if you find a Convenient Opportunity and the Family with the Gentlemen with you, particularly to Latimer and Treat, and tell the latter that I received his Favour of 24 ult. and thank him, I would write him, but have nothing more to say than what is here contained which you may shew him if you think proper, with the Hint, that as I am none of your black and White men I beg he will excuse me from Writing.

It is said that the Troops at New York have some glorious Disorder among them, a thousand times worse than the Fever of Last Year in Philadelphia which caused so many of the Faculty to smile at 10 Yard Distance as you approach them.

Compliments to Mrs. Craik and your good Family,

John Cochran D. M. H.

To John Warren

Camp Peekskill October 20th 1781

Dear Sir

I received yours of the 19th of September with the return, since when Doctor Townshend has returned and informs me that the Prospect for depreciation is not as bad as you apprehended. Doctor Eustis is now in Philadelphia transacting some Business on Account of his unfortunate Brothers and as Doctor Townshend has given him information respecting the state of Affairs with the Boston Legislature, I make no Doubt he will endeavor to do something with Congress on the Subject. I hope to be able to set out for Philadelphia where some matters relating to the Department call me in a few Days, when I shall not fail to do all in my Power to bring the Disease to a favourable Crisis.

The following is a copy of the Instructions sent me from the War Office, which I received yesterday.

War Office Oct. 10th, 1781

Sir

It appears to us that the Hospitals at the Yellow Springs Albany and Boston should be immediately broke up, as the Number of Patients are not sufficient to warrant the Expense. We have ordered all the patients at Yellow Springs to be sent to the Hospital at Philadelphia and you will please to give Directions, as to all the officers at that Hospital, whose services being no longer necessary there, they may be more usefully employed else where. The Patients at Boston and Albany had better be boarded at private Houses, or removed to some other Hospital where they can be taken Care of without the expense attending their present situation. The Patients being removed from Boston and Albany Hospitals, you will discharge all unnecessary officers or Persons employed therein and give orders for the employment of the officers necessary to be retained in the Department at places where their services are most Necessary.

We have the Honor to be Your Obedient servants

Richard Peters

BY ORDER

Doctor John Cochran Director of the Mil'y Hospitals.

Thus endeth the Orders of the Board of War. In consequence of which, you will board out the Patients in the Boston Hospital, at Private Houses (but who is to pay for their Board and who is to attend them afterwards, I know not, as the above orders of the Board leave me and all mankind perfectly in the dark) but if you find this impracticable you will send the Patients to the Hospital at the New Windsor Huts on the West Side of the Hudson River as being the nearest; where they can be taken care of at a less expense than in their present situation. In what manner the expense of Transporting them two hundred miles is to be defrayed, I am as much at a loss to discover as in the former. When this piece of service is performed, (which is the most easy thing in the world sit[t]ing at the Board of War) you will discharge from the service of the Hospital, the Steward, Ward Master, Matrons, Nurses and every kind of person in public employ under you in Hospital service and hold yourself and mate in readiness to attend in such places, where your services may be required.

I leave you to make your own comments on the above orders. I have made mine and am

Your most obedient and very humble servant

John Cochran D. M. H.

To Bodo Otto

Peekskill Camp October 20th 1781

Dear Sir

I Have been honored with advices from the Board of War, informing me of their Intentions to break up the Hospitals at Yellow Springs, Albany and Boston, in Consequence of this they further inform me that they have ordered all the Patients at Yellow Springs Hospital to be removed to the Hospital [at] Philadelphia and desire me to give Directions as to all the officers at that Hospital whose services being no longer necessary at that place, they may be more usefully employed elsewhere. As no New Hospitals are likely to be opened this Season I cannot warrant the continuing in pay the Inferior Officers of the Yellow Springs Hospital. You will therefore discharge the Steward, Ward Master, Matrons, Nurses and every Person in the Hospital employ under you, giving them certificates of their services that they may be entitled to recompence for the same. You will cause them to deliver up all the Hospital Utensils and Furniture of every kind, and deposit them in some safe place in order that they may be disposed of in whatever manner the service may most require; at the same time furnishing me with a List of the same. You will also hold yourself in readiness to repair to some other Hospital where your services are most wanted, but where that will be, I cannot at present form any Judgement. Let the above order extend to your son, who is a Mate. These are new manoeuvers which I am ignorant of, not having been consulted on the Subject. Perhaps they are all for the best, but that does not appear so to me at present

I am

Your most Obedient and very humble servant,

John Cochran D. M. H.

To Richard Peters

Camp Peekskill October 20th 1781

Sir

I was honored with your Favor of the 10th by Order of the Board of War, and in conformity to the Instructions therein contained I have given orders to Doctor Otto superintending, Hospital Physician & Fredk. Otto, Mate in the Hospital, both at Yellow Springs, to hold themselves in readiness to join any of the Hospitals where their services may be most required, and as it is not probable any New Hospitals may be opened this season, I have ordered him to discharge all the inferior Officers and others in the Hospital Employ under him, their services not being immediately wanted else where. In doing which I hope I have the approbation of the Board of War.

I have wrote to Doctor Warren, the superintending Hospital Physician and surgeon at Boston, to board out his Patients in private Houses, but if he finds that impracticable, to send them to the Huts Hospital at New Windsor on the West side Hudson's River, being the nearest Hospital which is only the distance of two hundred Miles, and may be as impracticable as the former Mode of disposing of them in private Houses, especially at this season of the Year, and after he has performed this service he has orders to discharge all inferior Officers in the Hospital Employ under him, and to break up the Hospital at Boston, and hold himself in readiness with his mate to attend where his services may be most wanted.

In my Opinion before this Matter can be carried into execution it will be neccessary to deposit in the Hands of some suitable person to be appointed for the purpose a sum of money to defray the expense of boarding out the Patients from time to time or transporting them to Hospitals at a distance. I do not apprehend you will be able to prevail on any Person to take the above task on him without a reward, and in all probability the expense attending a Physician to be employed in a town, to prescribe for and visit the Patients far remote from each other and the medicines to be expended on this occasion will amount to a greater sum than is expended in the present Mode. However Necessary an Hospital at Boston may be at this Period I do not pretend to say, but while the invalid Corps (having neither surgeon or mate if my information is right) was quartered there and the Continental ships (we are pretty well rid of them now) resorted thither and frequent exchanges of Prisoners, generally in a very low condition took place there, and a number of recruits for the continental Army made that a place of rendevous, besides a number of sick in Prison Ships, I humbly conceive an Hospital was necessarily established there, and upon these Principles I ordered it to be continued by the Approbation of the Commander in Chief.

Congress enacted the 23d of May, 1780 on the application of Governor Trumbull that a suitable House should be taken at or near the Port of New London for the accommodation of such sick American Prisoners as should from time to time be exchanged and landed in that Neighborhood, and that One Senior surgeon or Physician and a suitable Number of Mates should be occassionally employed therein. This Hospital I broke up and assigned my reasons to Congress for so doing, which were approved. If an Hospital was necessary at that place for the reception of exchanged Prisoners only, how much more so at Boston, where so many concurring Circumstances made it proper.

Before I proceed to give any Directions towards breaking up the Albany Hospital I must consult General Heath, for, as the service is circumstanced at Present it seems inpracticable, there being I suppose at this time not less than 3000 Troops in the Neighbourhood of that Place, and it is but a few Days since I applied to General Heath to permit me to send 200 sick to that Hospital, being a large spacious Building belonging to the Public, capable of accommodating in the best Manner five hundred Patients, but was refused on account of an expected visit from the Enemy; and as Albany has a very extensive Frontier liable to the incursions of the Enemy every Moment, and there being a considerable standing Force continually kept up in that Quarter, I think an Hospital absolutely necessary to be continued in that Place. Let us examine the Expense. Part of the summer that Hospital was under the care of a Mate only, the Hospital Physician & Surgeon attending there being necessarily called to do Duty with the

Army on the east side of Hudson's River, and the other two mates destined for that station were detached to the Frontier, a steward, Ward master and a few nurses are all that were employed, besides the medical officers, in that Hospital. Moreover where Troops are there ought always to be a Detachment of the General Hospital, a neglect of which having some Times taken Place in our service has occasioned the Loss of many a good soldier.

In the month of May 4 patients were admitted, 9 discharged, remained 60. In June 38 admitted, 7 discharged, 89 remained. In July 20 admitted, 32 discharged, remained 76. In August 19 discharged, remained 46, including soldiers wives and Children some of whom were Patients and others objects who could not assist themselves. I am pretty confident private Lodgings could not be procured in Albany without a very great Expense and the Money paid Weekly, for none but the most indigent will take in sick, and they must be paid at short periods, and [I doubt] whether in performing this service you would not be obliged to employ Persons necessary to transact the different Duties requisite at a great expanse than at present. In my Opinion it will admit of no comparison.

At this present we are much distressed for covering for our sick. Barns and out Houses [are] proper in the summer [but] are now rendered useless and the sick have been accumulating these six weeks, so that there are not less than 200 with the Army who are proper Objects for the Hospital, which cannot be received for want of room, which must preclude the Idea of sending the sick from Albany to any other Hospitals.

I hope the above state of matters will be satisfactory and I shall wait the further commands of the Board of War.

I have the Honor to be with much respect,

Sir,

Your most Obedient and very humble servant

John Cochran D. M. H.

To Barnabas Binney

Camp Peekskill October 22nd 1781

Dear Sir

I received your favor of the 16th Instant, and am much at a Loss to conceive on what Principles the Board of War mean to break up the Hospitals at Yellow Springs, Boston & Albany, for by their Instructions to me it is impossible to effect the two latter unless at a most enormous expense, for if board cannot be procured at Boston, which it certainly cannot without money to pay for it, which they have not got, then the Patients are to be sent to another Hospital, the nearest being upwards of two hundred miles. Ridiculous as this may appear, I have ordered Warren to put it into Execution, as I am determined to obey my superiors. I have given no directions about the Albany Hospital, and have assigned my reasons to the Board of War and shall await their further instructions. If Oeconomy is the object these Gentry have in view it will appear evident to any Person with half an Eye that they are saving on the small and expending on the large scale; a Fault but too prevalent among the great Ones, proceeding from a Want of better Information and a too great a Proneness to listen to the idle Whims of those who have their own Interest more in View than the Honor of Congress, the good of the service, or the Country they pretend to serve. I know not who is at the bottom of all these Evolutions, for be assured they are new to me. If we take a View of the different Metamorphoses of our poor Medical Department it will give us the most genuine Picture of the Instability of all things here below. I have wrote my sentiments to the Board of War very fully on the subject, but fear to little purpose. I know no reason why you should be removed from Philadelphia to make way for another, for suppose the Board of War had taken it into their heads to break up the Hospital at Philadelphia and send the Patients to Yellow Springs, as they have done heretofore & which may be the case again tomorrow, & surely it would not be supposed that you would take the Place of Dr. Otto. Besides I have wrote him to hold himself in readiness to join any other Hospital where his services may be most wanted. I fear we have some evil Counsellors who are endeavouring to lead us astray, for astray we are going as fast as the Devil can drive us.

I proposed seeing my Friends in Philadelphia in a Fortnight, but the indisposition of Mrs. Cochran will I fear deprive me of that Pleasure.

Compliments to Mrs. Binney, & believe me, Dear Sir, your most obedient and very humble servant,

J. Cochran, D. M. H.

To John Warren

Camp Peekskill October 22nd 1781

Dear Sir

I was favored with yours inclosing the return for September previous to which I had wrote you viz. on the 20th Instant to execute certain matters respecting the Boston Hospital agreeable to my instructions from the Board of War, which I know you have it not in you to perform; that is neither your fault or mine; therefore it is to be supposed you will stand fast where you are until the Board of War either revoke the Decree, or enable you to execute their orders, by depositing a sum of money, which I do not believe they have got, in hands of some person, to be employed for the purpose of boarding out the Patients, and a Physician to attend them, or furnish money to defray the expense of a ridiculous Transportation to a Hospital of upwards of two hundred Miles.

In May, 1780 Congress Ordered the Director, at the request of Governor Trumbull to take a suitable House at or near the port of New London for the accommodation of such sick American Prisoners as might be exchanged and landed in that Neighbourhood and one senior Surgeon, or a Physician and a suitable Number of Mates to attend therein occasionally. Surely if an Hospital was necessary at that Place for the Accommodation of a few American prisoners only, how more necessary an Hospital at Boston, where such a variety of Circumstances combine to make it proper. I imagine you had better wait on Governor Hancock and inform him of these Evolutions. Perhaps a few Lines from him on the subject might have a tendency to set these Misguided People in the right road. I fear their information is bad and they are too attentive to any Puppy who will tell them that there is Oeconomy in the scheme, for we are going to do everything by Oeconomy. I love oeconomy but hate starvation.

The Letters you allude to in your last, from yourself and Doctor Cheever containing certain queries, never came to Hand, otherwise you may depend I should not have treated them with neglect. I proposed setting out in a few days for Philad. in order to transact some Business for the Department, but the particular Circumstances in my Family will prevent me for a time, if not this season.

Compliments to Mrs. Warren and believe me,

Dear Doctor

Your most obedient and

very humble servant

John Cochran D. M. H.

To Joseph Young

New Windsor October 22d 1781

Dear Sir

I received Orders from the Board of War of the 10 instant to break up the Hospitals at Yellow Springs, Boston and Albany. The former they have been pleased to give me no trouble about by ordering the Patients all to Philadelphia. Their scheme with the two latter is to board out the Patients in private Houses or send them to some other Hospitals and to discharge all useless officers and to order those necessary to be retained to some other Place where their service may be most wanted, by which you see they have made no provision for paying for the board, or for the Person to transact this Business, and they are altogether silent in what manner the Patients are to be taken care of after they are in Lodgings, for they positively ordered me to send away, either by dismission or removal, all the officers. I have ordered Warren at Boston to execute this order, but I am too sensible it is out of his Power. I have remonstrated on the Affair of the Albany Hospital and propose waiting the further orders of the Board of War, by the advise of Genl. Heath. I fear the Board of War is badly advised on this subject and they are but too prone to listen to the idle whims of a lot of Puppies who, in order to engratiate themselves with their futile schemes of Oeconomy, will lead us astray. You will please enquire at what Price you can board out the Patients, if it can be done at all, and form some Judgement as to the Expense of that mode and the Present.

In your calculation you will observe to make an allowance for the Persons necessary to perform the different duties, as all the officers of the Medical Department are to be removed in Order to expose the contrivers and advisors of this wild chimerical Evolution. The Patients cannot be removed to any of the Hospitals on this river for they are full and 200 sick in Camp for want of coverings.

I want the return for September, which please send me by the Post, as yours is the only one wanting to compleat my general return to the Board of War.

I think you had better make a representation of this matter to some of the General Officers in your Quarter that they may write to the Board of War to make such an establishment of an Hospital as will be sufficient for the preservation of their Troops.

I intended to have set out next week for Philadelphia but the indisposition of Mrs. Cochran I fear will prevent. She has had an Intermittent for a fortnight, which has proved somewhat obstinate, and has reduced her very low. She is now taking the Bark which I hope will have a proper Effect.

Compliments to all Friends and believe me

Dear Sir

Your most obedt. servt.

John Cochran D. M. H.

To Thomas Bond, Jr.

December 4th 1781, at Philadelphia.

Sir

Herewith you will receive an Estimate of stores and Cash wanted for the immediate use of the Hospitals. I desire you will lose no time in procuring them as we have now 2000 sick, and they are increasing in this Quarter fast. There are upwards of 300 in this Hospital, near 100 of which have the small pox by inoculation and in the Natural Way, many at Trenton and [at] a large Hospital Dr. Latimer has gone off this Day to open at Wilmington. I require that you furnish them with Bedding, Utensils, &c. I presume this Estimate will serve for 3 months. Your stores have been conveyed to the Hospitals in better order, of Better Quality than heretofore, and I highly Approve of your employing a sober man always to attend them. As Rice is scarce I have omitted it on this Estimate in hopes that the stewards will be able to substitute Indian Meal in place thereof.

I am Your very humble servant

J. Cochran D. M. H.

To Robert Morris

Philadelphia December 31st 1781

Sir

On representation of the Distresses of the Officers of the Medical and Hospital Department to Congress on May last, I obtained Warrants for 3 months pay on different States, none of which have been or are likely to be paid and having received Letters from different Quarters from the said officers imploring relief, as they can no longer subsist under their present Circumstances; they have at the same time requested me to solicit that 3 Months pay may be allowed them, which I hope will not be thought an unreasonable Request when few or none of them have received any Pay in upwards of two years.

I have consulted the secretary at War on the propriety of this measure, who desired that I would lay the Matter before you this Evening, when a meeting was to be held by some of the superior Officers to determine on certain Points relative to public Measures.

I have the Honor to be with much respect,

Sir,

Your most Obedient and very humble servant

John Cochran D. M. H.

To James Tilton

Philadelphia January 1st 1781 [1782]

Sir

The inclosed is a copy of a letter of complaint against the officers of the Hospital at Williamsburgh which will appear by the contents. It was handed to me a few days since by his Excellency, requesting me to enquire into the cause of the complaints and whether they really did exist or not, and to make report to him; it therefore becomes your duty, as well for the sake of the Department as your own Character to clear up these aspersions. I have inquired of Doctor Treat about the money which Mentges alludes to, and he informs me that a part of it was left in the hands of Doctor Jenifer for the purpose of purchasing Necessaries for the sick, and the remainder had been appropriated to the like purposes. Col. Mentges by his letter appears to be very desirous of carrying his command with a high hand over the Medical Gentry, and to have mistaken vastly the Nature of his Duty. However, if he saw Neglect and Abuses it certainly was his business to report them, but not before an application to you to have them remedied.

You will oblige me much in letting me hear from you by the first opportunity. You will direct to me at the Purveyors, and order him (if I should not be here) to open it.

You will also send me the monthly returns of the Hospital at Williamsburg, with the names of the Officers and ranks serving with you. No returns of your Hospital have come to hand since its establishment and the Secretary of War is very particular in this Matter.

Doctor Treat informs me that He appointed some additional Mates, which you will please to discharge if the service no longer requires their Assistance, giving them Certificates of their Services, as there is no money to pay them. I wish your returns may be made out from the first establishment of the Hospital at Williamsburg to the first of this month and you will please to inform Doctor Wilson that it is my request that he would do the same for it is by the returns only that we can account for the expenditures of Medicines, Stores and provisions. I have not been favoured with any returns from him in a long time.

Our department has been about to undergo great and various changes by Congress for several months last past, but we remain still in Statu quo principally owing [I] apprehend to a vast variety of whimsical Systems which have been offered to Congress, and every one having his favorite to serve, or rather a favorite system to adopt, has led them into very great confusion. After the whole of last week spent in arranging the Department, on Saturday night it *was* just as *it was*. I think some alteration might take place for the better, but I do not apprehend any very essential alteration will be made.

I wrote yesterday to the Financier representing the distressed circumstances of the Medical officers for want of pay and implored relief in the Premises but have not yet heard the result of my application. Had it not been for the damned new Arrangement we should have had pay some time ago.

You will please to present my Compliments with those of the season to the Gentlemen with you, and believe me,

Sir,

Your most Obedient and very humble Servant

John Cochran D. M. H.

P.S. Since writing the above I have been favored with Jenifer's return to the Month of November. He will make them out from that time.

Copy of a letter from Col. Mentges, Superintending Officer in Virginia to His Excellency, Genl. Washington dated

Williamsburg November 29th, 1781

Sir

Your Excellency is acquainted [with] my having the superintending of the Hospitals in this State. I shall beg to give your Excellency a detail of the distresses of the Hospital. There are no more than three articles of Medicine in the store to cure all Diseases. No kind of Vegetables procured altho' Doctor Treat received two hundred pounds to that purpose. The irregular mode of drawing provision hath caused the greatest complaints of the sick and [they] have been really neglected on that account, as it lays entirely with the Surgeons to draw what quantity they please and are to no person accountable but to the Purveyor General. I have observed that as a great quantity of provisions were drawn as for the number of sick would require in full rations, but what becomes of it I do not know, it lays between the Surgeon and the Steward of the Hospital; likewise all the other Hospital Stores.

I beg to inform your Excellency the Idea I had of my appointment as Superintending officer was this, that I had to correct the Abuses and Neglects committed in the Hospital Department, to call them to an account and bring delinquents to punishment, but this power is not invested in me and only lays with the Purveyor. I must then see a number of brave men being put into the Grave, and I believe on that amount I would be exceeding glad to have your Excellency's perticular instructions where your Excellency may rely will be punctually attended to. Signed Mentges

To Joseph Morgan

Philadelphia January 20th 1782

Sir

I received your Favor of the 12th of December and would have answered it, but expected to have been at Morristown before this time.

In answer to a letter of Quarter Master Forman wherein he proposed to let you work for yourself when we had no employ for you and when we wanted instruments repaired or new ones made, that you should perform that Business and keep an Account of it, for which you should be paid. I acquainted him that I approved of his Plan and expected that you considered yourself in that situation and no longer in the Public service.

I expect to see you at Morristown in a Week or two when I will settle the matter between you and the Quarter Master and let you know on what footing you stand. Our Department is in the most distressed circumstances you can imagine for want of money.

I am Your humble servant,

J. Cochran

To Isaac Ledyard

New Windsor February 2d 1782

Sir

You will order Mr. Johonnot, the Assistant Apothecary, to take such Quantity of the Medicines lately arrived from France as will be necessary for supplying the Hospitals and regimental sick on the North River for the present, and the Whole of the remainder you will forward to Philadelphia with all possible dispatch to Doctor Bond, Purveyor. In order to enable you to perform this Duty you will apply to the Quarter Master for Carriages to transport them, and if he cannot find a careful Person to take Charge of them, you will provide One for that Purpose, so that no Waste may be sustained. You will also order Mr. Johonnot to send a List of Such Medicines as he may retain to Doctor Craigie, the Apothecary, so that they may be compared with the Original Invoices. You will also desire him to furnish the Apothecary with a List of such Mediciines as he may have on hand of the old stock.

I am,

Your very humble servant

John Cochran D. M. H.

To John Warren

Manor of Livingston February 22d 1782

Dear Sir

A few weeks ago in Philadelphia I was favored with yours of a late Date, and as I could not describe your situation in more striking Terms than you had I shewed your Letter to the Secretary at War and the Financier. The former said he was going to Boston and would enquire into the Circumstances of your hospital, and the latter suggested that there was an impropriety in supporting a general Hospital at Boston, offering for his reasons that we had few or no Continental ships of War and there was no Occasion for an Hospital on account of the recruits for the State of Massachusetts, and that he would write to the secretary at War to enquire particularly into the Matter. He further alleged that the Prisoners were chiefly of a private Nature being Captured by private ship[s] of War and did [not] come under the denomination of Public characters, and that the Exchange was entirely confined to the state, and that they ought to be supported by the state, and that he would most certainly endeavour to break up the hospital. Should this be the Case, I apprehend your situation will be some what difficult, for you see by the new regulation the Department is much reduced in numbers, consequently every Person will be called out to do Duty Wherever their services may be wanted. Perhaps it would be attended with very disagreeable consequences for you to leave Boston the ensuing Campaign, therefore had you not better retire on the 20 dollars per Month for Life as stipulated by Congress the 17th of January 1781, for should you in a future Day be reduced to the necessity of resigning rather than make certain sacrifices, you will give up every prospect of future Emoluments for your past services.

I only give you this Hint to put you on your guard and not from any desire to part with you in order to make Way for others; be assured such views are far remote from me, and you are among the last of the Department that I would wish to part with. You will best know the Circumstances of the Hospital at your Place, and will take your Measures accordingly. As near as I can recollect Doctor Bond informed me that he had sent one or two hundred dollars for the use of your hospital last fall, but by whom I do not know. I shall return to New Windsor in a few weeks where I shall continue until we take the Field, where I shall be glad to be favored with a Line.

Your &c &c

J. C.

To Thomas Bond, Jr.

Albany March 17th 1782

Dear Sir

Your Favor of the 26th Ultimo came to hand yesterday, and I am sorry that Mr. Morris will not advance any more money for the Hospital use until he receives an Estimate for the Whole Year, which is impossible to be made unless we are acquainted with the Number of the troops to be employed and the nature of the service, as well as with Articles of stores are to be furnished by the Contractors and Whether he intends by that Estimate to include the Wages of the officers of the Hospital which you are to pay, with the Matrons, Nurses, &c. or only the stores, Medicines and incidental Charges, until this is ascertained Nothing can be done with precision.

When the last Demand was made on Mr Morris we received no more than 1000 out of 4000 Dollars, which was intended for the purpose of defraying incidental Charges, paying Matrons & Nurses & procuring for the Apothecary such Articles as he required to enable him to Compound and prepare Medicines &c. If he has forgot these Circumstances let him turn to your Letter and his own Reason will convince him that he ought to comply with the Requisition without waiting for a General Estimate for a Whole Year.

As you are better acquainted with the Hospital Consumption and will sooner become acquainted with the Number of Troops to be employed &c, than I shall, I wish you would furnish me with a sketch of an Estimate for the Year at the same time that you send me the return of the Stores &c, on hand; this agreeable to Mr. Morris's Idea of what is to be comprehended in that Estimate, and this can best be done by adverting to the last Year's consumption, supposing the Hospitals had been fully supplied. Not having the New Hospital arrangement by me this Moment, I do not exactly recollect whether a Board is necessary or not to determine the Estimate, but I rather think it is. If so, no such Board can be called but by the approbation of the Commander in Chief; this will require time.

As soon as I hear he is come to Windsor, where I am informed he is expected, I shall go down and settle all Matters relative to this Business with as much Expedition as possible. In the meantime I have wrote to Mr. Morris, agreeable to your request shewing him the absolute necessity of his supplying the Hospital with small sums until the Estimates can be furnished.

I came here three Weeks ago to settle my Boys at school and to endeavour to dispose of some of my property for theirs and my subsistence. I hope the paymaster General is possessed of the Notes which Mr. Morris proposed putting into his hands for the two Months pay for the officers of the Army, and that my draught on him in your Favor has been duly honored, so that your Chimney piece may no longer remind you of the 21st of March.

I propose being at Trenton the first of May to settle my depreciation, when it is probable I may visit you in Philadelphia.

I am, Dear Sir,

Your most obedt. and very humble servt.

John Cochran

To Robert Morris

Albany March 17th 1782

Sir

I am informed by the Purveyor of the Hospital that he waited on you in order to be supplied with money to defray the contingent Expenses of the Hospitals, but could obtain none until an Estimate was made of the Expenses for one Year, which cannot be done until I see the Commander in Chief, which will require some time. The Last time I waited on you about Money Matters I presented you with a Letter from the Purveyor (at my desire) requesting 4000 Dollars for the purpose of procuring an immediate supply for the Hospitals and furnishing the Apothecary with such Articles of his Department as were necessary to enable him to compound and prepare Medicines &c. for the ensuing Campaign, which if not attended to in due season may produce disappointments and probably incur a very considerable additional Expense, a Circumstance to be avoided as much as possible. You will please to recollect that you did not find it convenient to advance more than 1000 dollars of the above requisition, I therefore wish you would be so obliging as to furnish him with the remaining 3000 Dollars or such sum as may be necessary to supply the more pressing Demands of the Department so that the sick may not suffer and that we may be enabled to discharge our Duty with credit and propriety. The proper Estimate shall be laid before you as soon as possible.

I have the Honor to be with respect and Esteem,

Sir, your most obedt. & hum. st.

John Cochran D. M. H.

To William Shepherd

Murderer's Creek April 16th 1782

Dear Sir

I am informed that the Surgeon of your Regiment is about to resign and retire into private life; if so, it highly behooves you to endeavour to have his Place filled with a person well qualified to execute that Important Trust and as I would always wish to see Persons promoted who are already in service, in preference to new Hands, you will give me leave to recommend to your particular Notice the Bearer, Dr. Shute, who for several Years has done the Duty of Mate in the Hospital under my immediate Command. I appointed him last Campaign to the surgeoncy of Colonel Hamilton's Corps on expedition against Cornwallis, where he acquired great Applause; and after the Campaign was over he succeeded to the Charge of a very considerable Hospital at the head of Elk, where he discharged his Duty with great propriety. I am confident you will find none of superior and few of equal Abilities with this Young Gentleman, and it will give me great Pleasure to hear that [you] may be able to Obtain the Appointment for him. I am the more solicitous in this Affair from being too sensible of its importance, and I make no doubt you will exert yourself in carrying a Matter into Execution where so much depends on the Event.

I am with Esteem

Dear Sir

Your very humble servant

John Cochran

To John M. Scott

New Windsor April 21st 1782

Dear Sir

The Legislature of the State of New York have, at their last session, passed an Act for making up the depreciation of pay to the Officers of the Hospital and Medical Department belonging to that State, agreeable to the recommendation of Congress. The Commission for settling with the Officers aforesaid is unwilling and absolutely refuses to grant depreciation to any Others than those Commissioned by Congress except the Mates without an Explanation of the Act, ascertaining who were the officers intended by the recommendation. Under the Old Arrangement the Commissary of the Hospitals, who officiated as Stewards only, and on the present Establishment the Stewards, Clerks, Storekeepers, and Ward Masters are all Warrant Officers as well as the Mates, and are entitled to their depreciation equally with the Director or any other Officer serving the United States, and it appears that this was the Intention of Congress. I therefore beg you will move for an Explanation of the above Act and transmit the same to me at Head Quarters by the first Opportunity, by which you will relieve some Worthy Characters, whose Families are suffering &c.

Dear Sir,

Your very humble servant

John Cochran

To Thomas Bond, Jr.

New Windsor, Connecticut, May 1st 1782

Dear Sir

I had a letter from Dr. Willson a few Days since by your desire, acknowledging the Receipt of mine from Albany wherein he urges my coming to Philadelphia to assist in adjusting some Matters relative to the Department. I only wait for the arrival [of] Craik to set out, but I wish my presence could be dispensed with for I am most heartily tired of *shuling* my way so often to that place without one shilling in my Pocket. When the Commander in Chief was consulted about my going to Philadelphia. He asked what Business I had there again. He was told, to give in an Estimate of Stores &c, for the Campaign, He replied as that was to be done in Writing, He could not conceive why I could not Write as Well here as there.

Mr. Morris's letter to you of the 19th of February which is herein inclosed appears to be a pretty tight one. So He will submit the Estimates to the Inspection of professional Men; and pray What then? What have we to do with those Professional Men or What have they to do with us? Are not we sworn to do our Duty according to the best of our Knowledge and skill? His position appears to me the most laughable Finance I ever heard of. I have consulted the General on the Estimate and after some conversation on the subject He desired that I should form one similar to the Hospital Consumption of last Year. I informed him that the Hospitals in general were not altogether as well supplied as I could have wished; then said he, add the deficiencies, as this is the only Rule by Which we can be governed at present. I suppose it will be no difficult task for you to find out the Consumption of last Year, therefore you will oblige me in preparing one by the time I arrive in Philadelphia. A General Order has been issued to all the regimental Surgeons to make a return of the medicines and Instruments on hand, which is not yet complied with. The Whole cannot be got in any reasonable time on Account of the scattered Condition of the Troops. I know they have few or no Medicines, their sick are suffering and require a very speedy supply, which beg may be attended to.

Craigie writes me that sundry new alterations are proposed in our Department by the Secretary at War; with all my heart, if they are for the better, but I have my doubts about the matter. Compliments to all Friends and believe me most sincerely

dear Sir

Your most obt. &c

John Cochran

To James Tilton

Philadelphia, May 4th 1782

Dear Sir

I was favored with yours of February from Williamsburg inclosing the Correspondence between you and Col. Mentges, which was presented to the Commander in Chief and gave satisfaction; I was also favored with yours from Philadelphia last Month, informing me of your going to Dover to inoculate some Recruits, which I suppose is perfectly right.

When I wrote that I expected little or no Alterations would take place in the Hospital Department it was in Consequence of Certain Plans and Alterations being before them, and after one whole Week being spent in discussing the Point, they refered it to a Committee, which induced me to suppose nothing would be done in less than Six Months. I am happy that the Alterations in the Department have met with your approbation and I am of opinion with you that more might be made to Advantage, but the Experiment is dangerous, for if they would stop when they have done what is right we should be less embarrassed.

When I received your last I was in hopes I should have been able to grant you the Indulgence you promised yourself of a considerable Recess from Business; but I have it in Charge from the Commander in Chief to call in all Gentlemen of the Department; I am also ordered to open an Hospital at Cumberland Old Court House, being the place of Rendezvous for the Recruits of three Regiments now raising in the State, and the Route to and from Carolina; and as all the Gentlemen have already repaired to the Northward, except Docts. Binney and Treat who are employed at this Place, the former to be stationed here and latter having Matters of the last Importance to induce him to serve in York State. You will please to repair to this Town as soon as possible, in order to get in readiness whatever may be proper and necessary for the purpose of establishing a small Hospital at the before mentioned Place, of which you will please to take the Charge. This Duty I hope will be perfectly agreeable to you, and that you will pass your time in a manner altogether to your own Satisfaction.

I am of Opinion that one Hospital Mate will be sufficient for this Service, the Regimental Surgeons and Mates belonging to the Virginia Troops now raising ought to give the necessary assistance. You will give the proper Instructions to them for that purpose.

I am Dear Sir

Your most obedient and humble servant

J. Cochran

[RESOLVES OF CONGRESS]

In Congress January 17th 1781 Whereas in the Plan for conducting the Hospital Department passed in Congress the 30th day of September last, no proper establishment is provided for the Officers of the American staff, after their Dismission from Public service, which considering the Custom of other Nations and the like Provision made for the officers of the Army after the conclusion of the War, they appear to have claim to: For remedy whereof and also for amending several parts of the above mentioned plan.

RESOLVED that all officers in the Hospital Department and Medical staff herein After Mentioned who shall continue in service to the End of the War or be reduced before that time as supernumeraries, shall be entitled to and receive during Life in lieu of half pay the following Allowance Viz. The Director of Hospitals equal to half pay of a Lieut. Colonel, Chief Physicians and surgeons of the Army and Hospital Physicians and surgeons, Purveyor, Apothecary and regimental surgeons each equal to the half pay of a Captain. That there be allowed to the Purveyor, apothecary and assistant Purveyor each Forage for one Horse. That the Power given in the aforementioned Plan, to the chief Physician and surgeon of the Army to remove Regimental surgeon and mates, in case of absence without Leave, shall in future extend no further than a power of suspension until such Delinquent shall be reported to a proper Officer for bring[ing] him to trial by a Court Martial.

That the Apothecary may deliver Medicines, Instruments and dressing and other articles of his Department to the Hospitals on Orders in Writing from a Physician and surgeon having the care of any particular Hospital, where the Director and one of the Chief Physicians and Surgeons shall not be present to give the same. That the Power given to the Director and Chief Hospital Physician with respect to the appointment of Matrons, Nurses and other Persons, necessary for the regular Management of the Hospitals be extended to each of the Physicians and Surgeons of the Hospital, in Absence of the Director and Chief Hospital Physicians and Surgeons.

Charles Thomson Secy.

By the United States in Congress March 27th 1781

The United States in Congress assembled proceeded to the Election of a Deputy Purveyor of the Hospital for the southern Army and the Ballots being taken and counted Doctor Nathan Brownson was elected, he having been previously nominated by Mr. Adams.

Extract from the minutes Charles Thomson Secy.

By the United States in Congress May 12th 1781

According to the Order of the Day the House proceeded to the Election of Officers of the Hospital Department for the southern Army and the Ballots being taken

Doctor David Oliphant was elected deputy Director, Peter Fayssoux, chief Physician of the Hospital, James Brown, chief Physician of the Army. Robert Johnson, William Read, hospital Physicians, having been previously The report of the Medical Committee was taken into consideration, Whereat resolved—

That all officers of the Medical Department appointed under the Directorship of Doctor Oliphant, who are now in Captivity in South

Carolina and Georgia and have the charge of the sick prisoners in those states, be continued in their respective Offices as heretofore and be considered as vested with the same Powers and be entitled to the same Privileges and Emoluments as they had and enjoyed before their Captivity, to extend no further than to the Troops and the Hospitals now within the Enemy's Lines.

Extract from the Minutes Charles Thomson Secy.

By the United States in Congress assembled June 11th, 1781

RESOLVED

That the Resolution of the 28th of December 1779, be extended to the Director of the Hospital so that all Letters to and from him be free.

Extracts from the Minutes George Bond. Depy Secy.

By the United States in Congress Assembled. September 20th, 1781

RESOLVED

That the present Vacancies of Hospital Physicians and Surgeons be filled up by the senior Surgeons of the Hospitals lately deranged, the eldest hospital Mates, or Regimental Surgeons, as shall be recommended by the Director and Chief Physician and Surgeon of the Army.

That all future vacancies of Hospital Pyns. and Surgeons be filled by the eldest Regimental Surgeons and hospital Mates, who shall be reckoned of equal Grades, who shall upon Examination be found qualified and obtain a certificate of recommendation from the Director and chief Phyn. and Surgeon of the Army, or of the deputy Director and chief Physician in a separate Department.

That the Persons requisite to fill the higher Grades in the hospital and Medical departments be appointed from time to time, by Congress according to Merit and Abilities.

That all surgeons to Regiments or Corps not belonging to the Line of any particular state, be nominated by the Director of the Hospitals and the chief Physician and surgeon of the Army, subject to the approbation of the Commander in Chief, and shall be equally entitled to promotion to Hospital Physicians and Surgeons with the Regimental Surgeons of state Lines.

On the Recommendation of the Director approved by the Board RESOLVED

That Doctor Joseph Young, a deranged Senior Surgeon and Doctor Goodwin Willson, Daniel Junifer, Samuel Edmison & George Campbell eldest surgeons Mates, be promoted to the Rank of Hospital Physicians and surgeons to fill the Vacancies occasioned by the Resignations of Doctors Bloomfield, Scott, Hagan & Jackson and the Promotion of Doctor Burnet.

On the Recommendation of the Deputy Director Approved of the Board of War.

RESOLVED, that Doctors Thomas, Tudor, Tucker and Vickars be appointed Physicians and Surgeons in the Hospital for the southern Department.

That Daniel Smith be appointed Depy. Purveyor and John Carne Assistant Apothecary in the southern Department Sept. 22, 1781 Ordered That no appointment be made of Mates to supply the Places of those promated in the General Hospital by the Resolution of the 20th until the further order of Congress

Extracts from the Minutes Chas. Thompson

Return of the Military Hospitals and sick in the Army [c. April, 1781]

Hospitals	Admitted	Discharged	Dead	Deserted	Putrid fever	Bilious do	Inflam^{y} do	Intermit^{t} do	Dysentery	Diarrhoea	Rheumatic	Venereal	Wounded	Lame	Convalescent	Ulcered	Remaining	
Yellow Springs weekly return	7	1					1			2	8	5	6	5	12	12	50	February 1781
Philadelphia B sent to Yellow Springs 2	31	19			16			8	1	1	3	10		17	5	8	50	
Boston—weekly	9	7	1				11	3			1	4		5	13		37	March 1781
Fishkill	7	11					2				3	4	2	3	15		25	
Philadelphia B.	31	18	1		11		1	8	2		3	7		14	10		56	
Yellow Springs weekly	5	9						1		1	6	3	7	6	8	12	44	
Chesterfield weekly	1	26						5		1	2		17	5	25		55	
Army &c.						3	1	7		8	18	14	4	43	38		288	
Morris Town		4		1			3	1			2	2	5		6		19	
Philadelphia G^{l}					11	1	5	15	1	5					36	2	78	

Return of the Military Hospitals and sick in the Army for May 1781

Hospitals	Admitted	Discharged	Dead	Deserted	Convalescent	Wounded	Ulcers	Fevers: Inflammat.	Fevers: Intermittent	Fevers: Bilious or Putrid	Fevers: Nervous	Dysentery	Diarrhoea	Venereal	Rheumatic	Various Chronic	Casual Hurts	Small Pox	Total Remaining	Soldiers wives & children	Total	
Albany	4	9	-	-	8	4	3	1	3	-	1	1	2	3	8	9	1	-	33	27	60	
Fish Kill	16	5	-	1	11	4	3	-	-	-	-	-	-	6	2	1	-	3	30	11	41	
Robinson's House	44	29	1	-	8	6	2	4	-	4	3	1	-	16	5	7	5	-	61	2	63	
Yellow Springs	6	11	-	1	4	5	11	1	1	-	-	-	2	2	4	4	-	-	34	1	35	
Morristown	"	"	"	"	2	5	-	1						1	1	3			13	7	22	2 sick officers
Flying Hospital of the Army	-	-	-	-	19	1		8	16	3	-	7	5	8	10	18	41	6	142	-	142	
Boston	9	7			13	"	"	11	3					4	1		5		37		37	
	79	61	1	2	65	25	19	26	23	7	4	9	9	40	31	42	62	8	390	40	400	

Sent a copy of the above to the Board of War   John Cochran D. M. H.
September 8th 1781

Return of the Military Hospitals and sick in the Army—for June 1781

Hospitals	Admitted	Discharged	Dead	Deserted	Convalescent	Wounded	Ulcers	Fevers: Inflammat	Intermitt.	Bilious or Putrid	Nervous	Dysentery	Diarrhoea	Venereal	Rheumatism	Various Chronics	Casual Hurts	Small Pox	Total Remaining	Women & Children	Total	
Albany	38	7	-	-	3	3	3	1	6	-	-	3	1	5	8	25	4	2	64	25	89	
Fish Kill	13	1	1	-	5	-	1	1	-	-	-	-	3	4	2	10	5	1	32	10	42	
Robinson's house	80	25	3	5	16	6	5	8		11	3	6	2	13	8	11	12	6	107	3	110	
Flying Hospital	-	5	-	-	31	3		16	29	12	6	5	12	9	26	12	56	1	218	-	-	
Yellow Springs	10	10			4								1	2	6	20			32		32	
Boston																						
Morristown Hosp. broke up		4	1		2	3								1		2			8	7	17	-2 sick officers
	141	52	5	5	61	15	9	26	35	23	9	14	19	34	50	80	77	10	461	45	508	

The above is exclusive of the Hospitals in Virginia and to the southward from whence there are no returns John Cochran D. M.H.

Sent the above to ye Board of War—September 26th 1781

Return of the Military Hospitals and sick in the Army for July 1781

Hospitals	Admitted	Discharged	Dead	Deserted	Fevers: Convalescents	Wounded	Ulcers	Inflamm.	Interm.	Bilious or putrid	Nervous	Dysentery	Diarrhoea	Venereal	Rheumatism	Various Chronic	Casual Hurts	Small Pox	Total	Women & Children	Total	
Albany	20	32	1	3	7	6	5	1	3			1	1	5	6	16	1	-	52	24	76	
New Windsor Huts	40	11	-	-	9	4	13	1	4				5	9	12	11	-	-	68	28	96	
Yellow Springs	-	2	-	-	2	4	11	-	-				1	2	6	3	-		30		30	
Philadelphia	13	48	1	1	-	-	1	-	1	1	1		-	1	-	3	-		8		8	
Flying Hospitals	-	-	5	-	-	41	-	-	-	-			-	-	-	-	-		41	-	41	Those were wounded
Flying Hospital	-	5	-	-	-	2	-	-	4	12				3	-	5	4		21	-	21	
Robinson's House	75	35	6	-	20	45	-	1	1	7		6	2	8	4	5	14	19	132		132	
	148	133	13	4	38	102	30	3	13	11	1	7	9	28	28	43	19	19	352	52	404	

The above &c. as on the other side
Sent the above to the Board of War
Sept. 26, 1781

John Cochran D. M. H.

Returns of the Military Hospitals & sick in the Army for August 1781

Hospitals	Admitted	Discharged	Dead	Deserted	Convalescent	Wounded	Ulcerous	Fevers: Inflam.	Fevers: Intermit.	Fevers: Bilious or Putrid	Fevers: Nervous	Dysent.	Diarrh.	Venereal	Rheumat.	Various Chronic	Casual Hurts	Total Remaining	Women & Children	Total	
Flying Hospital	119	17	-	-	5	7	14	-	31	27	4	2	-	1	11	9	4	47	4	102	Sent to Genl Hosp[l]
Army East of Hudson R.	-	-	-	-	44	2	25	-	25	34	-	11	38	7	6	15	-	207	-	207	
Albany Hospital	-	19	1	-	1	5	4	1	3			1	-	5	2	5		29	17	46	2 small pox
Yellow Springs	-	4	-	-	3	-	-	-	-	-			1	3	6	15	-	28	-	28	
Philad[a] B Hosp[l]		4	1	-	-	-	1	-	3	4	-	-	-	2	-	5	1	17	-	17	
New Windsor Huts Hosp[l]	98	19	1	1	21	5	8	3	15	1	-	4	13	9	20	27	16	142	35	177	
Robinson's House	134	123	2		13	23	5	3	-	43	-	8	2	17	8	12	8	142	-	142	
Boston Hospital	4	5																23		23	
	355	191	5	2	87	42	57	7	77	109	4	26	54	44	53	98	29	735	56	742	2 small pox

The above &c.

Sent the above to the Board of War Sept. 26th, 1781   John Cochran D. M. H.

Returns of the Military Hospitals & sick in the Army for September 1781

Hospitals	Admitted	Discharged	Dead	Deserted	Convalescent	Wounds	Ulcers	Fevers: Inflamat.	Fevers: Intermit.	Fevers: Bilious or Putrid	Fevers: Nervous	Dysentery	Diarrhoea	Venereal	Rheumatic	Various Chronic	Casual Hurts	Total Remaining	Women & Children
Philad[a] Brit: Prisoners																		60	Various diseases
with American Army																		12	chiefly Chronic Cases
ditto Barracks Hosp!							1		6	3		1		8		1	2	22	
Garrison of West Point									17			75			23	20	coughs	135	3 months men
ditto West Point						6			24			26		14	15			85	regular Troops
Williamsburgh Hosp! Virginia Sept. 25th	Various cases																	250	Sick soldiers wives & Children + 6 officers
New Windsor Huts	143	80	3	2	17	6	6	2	22	65		18	4	13	19	17	11	200←	23 Total 229
Yellow Springs	1	1			1	2	8						2	2	4	7		26	1 soldier's Wife
Robison's House	123	122	8		20	15	3	1		54		13	4	9	5	7	7	138	
Boston Hospital					1	3	1			2		2			1	10	2	22	
Albany Hospital	18	4	1		2	5	4		5	3		6	7	1	7			40	18 Women & Children
Hanover Virginia																			

Sent the above to the Board of War

Return of the Sick & Wounded in the Military Hospitals & in the Army for the month of October 1781

Hospitals &c.	Admitted	Discharged	Dead	Deserted	Convalescent	Wounds	Ulcers	Fevers: Inflamat.	Intermitt	B & Putrid	Nervous & Remittent	Dysentery	Diarrhoea	Venereal	Rheumatic	Casual Hurts	Various Chronics	Women & children patients	Small pox	Sent to G. Hosp.	Officers sick & wounded	Total Remaining
Albany Hospital	29	15	2	Various Diseases																		84
Flying Hospital East of Hudson	84	24	4		2	3		2	4	13		1		3	1		6	3		49		44
Williamsburg Hospital		25	10	3	54	59			109	3		43	20	8	11	16	3					326
Hanover Virginia		No accurate return but supposed to be about																				212
Flying Hospital & sick in ye camp Yorktown			6		147			25	209	12	14	71	103	21	17	13	14					646
Robison's House Hosp.^l	45	69	4		24	12	2	4		34		6	2	10	3	6	5					108
Philadelphia Hospital	126	43			10	12	10	9			7		4	13	8		9		3			85
British Prisoners at ditto	73	11	2		9	2	5	17	2		5		10		3		5		2			60
New Windsor Huts	Return miscarried but suppose the sick to amount to																					250
Total	355	187	28	3	252	88	17	57	324	62	26	121	139	55	43	35	42	3	5	49		1815

N.B. The sick of the Army to ye Eastward of Hudson River & the Garrison of West Point are not included in the above return.

John Cochran

Return of the sick & wounded &c. in the Military Hospitals & Army
for the month of November 1781

Hospitals	Admitted	Discharged	Dead	Deserted	Convalescent	Wounds	Ulcers	Fevers: Inflamty. fever	Intermitt.	Bilious or Putrid	Nervous or Remit.	Dysentery	Diarrhoea	Venereal	Rheumatism	Various Chronic	Casual Hurts	Women Patients	Children	Sent to G. Hosp.[1]	Total remaining	
Albany	15	29		1	12	13	5	3	3	1			2	1	3	6	8	6	15		54	
Flying Hosp[1] & Army	17	24	2				Various diseases													35	44	
Williamsburg	12	128	23	1	38	49		5	10	1		49			11						186	23 Small pox
Philadelphia	316	124	18	4	18	30	10	43	9		28		40	11	10	52					314	63 ditto inc. British prisoners 48
Trenton	90	14	4		19			10	7				9	1		3					72	23 ditto
Honover Virginia				on the first of November there were in this Hospital																	114	
New Windsor Huts	134	88	4		17	9	20	17	20	24	4	18	7	17	37	30	5	19	14		264	6 officers sick & wounded
Boston-no return																						
Total	584	407	51	6	104	101	35	78	49	26	32	67	58	30	61	91	13	25	29	35	1048	

N.B. The sick of the Army to the Eastward of the Hudson River & the Garrison of West Point are not included in the above return. John Cochran D. M.H.

A return of the sick & wounded in the Military Hospitals & Army for the month of December 1781

								Fevers															
Hospitals	Admitted	Discharged	Died	Deserted	Convalescent	Wounded	Ulcers	Inflam.y	Intermi. & Remit.	Bilious or Putrid	Nervous	Dysentery	Diarrhoea	Venereal	Rheumatism	Various Chronics	Casual hurts	Small Pox	Women patients and children	Orderlies	Nurses	Total Remaining	
Philadelphia Hosp.	133	188	39		12	13	6	27	5				18	8	6	24		48				167	
Ditto British Prisoners	7	10	1	1	2		2	14					1	2	1	19		2				43	
Wilmington	105	47	23		12						11	1	1					5		3	2	35	
Head of Elk	118	60	20		small pox—dysentery—Diarrhora & putrid bilious Fevers																	38	
Trenton	18	43	11	2	8			10	6				3			1		6		4		38	
Boston	17	13	3			7	6		8	Fevers		5			6	6						38	
Hanover Virginia	10	23	1	2	6				13				4	6	3							32	
New Windsor Huts	55	50	13	1	27	1	29	23	27	6	3	19	17	19	17	13	5		25			239	8 wounded officers & waiters
Williamsburg Hosp[1]	14	71	20	3	0	24	Various diseases					50										74	
Albany	13	6			16	1	12			1		1		4		5			15		4	63	4 Sick & Wounded officers with waiters
Total	490	557	131	9	83	46	55	74	59	7	14	26	44	39	33	68	5	61	40	7	6	767	

Not a Bene None of the sick belonging to Army are included in the above Return

John Cochran

A Return of the sick & wounded in the Military Hospitals & Army for the month of January 1782

Hospitals &c.	Admitted	Discharged	Dead	Deserted	Convalescent	Wounded	Ulcers	Fevers: Inflam^y	Fevers: Inter^t & Remit.	Fevers: Bilious or Putrid	Fevers: Nervous	Dysentery	Diarrhoea	Venereal	Rheumatism	Various Chronic	Casual Hurts	Small Pox	Women Patients & children	Officers, sick & wounded	Sent to New Windsor	Total Remaining	
Albany	12	2		1	14	5	4	2				1		8	1	9			21	4		69	
New Windsor Huts	27	69	7	4	20	2	20	25	19	8		13	9	11	12	13	2		26	7		187	
Philadelphia	111	94	24		21	9	7	16	41				13	3	10	12		14				146	
Ditto British Prisoners	17	12	1	1																		36	
Williamsburgh	19	22	11			19																55	36 sick
West Point	54	16	7			~~2~~		~~8~~	~~10~~	~~20~~		~~3~~			~~6~~	~~4~~			~~Various Causes~~		22	9	Various Diseases
	240	215	50	6	55	35	31	43	60	8		14	22	22	23	34	2	14	47	11	22	502	

N.B. The army sick are not included in the above and the returns for the Head of Elk, Wilmington, and Trenton miscarried.

John Cochran D.M.H.

A return of the sick & wounded in the Military Hospitals & Army for the month of February 1782

Hospitals &c	Admitted	Discharged	Dead	Deserted	Convalescent	Wounded	Ulcers	Fevers: Inflam^{y}	Fevers: Inter^{t}&Remit.	Fevers: Bilious or put^{d}	Fevers: Nervous	Dysentery	Diarrhoea	Venereal	Rheumatism	Various Chronic	Casual Hurts	Small Pox	Women & Children Patients	Officers, sick&c.	Sent to G.Hosp^{l}	Total Remaining	Total
Boston	2	2	1																			28	
Philadelphia	54	66	10	2	29	6	3	27	23				3	6	7	13		5				122	
ditto British Prisoners	17	21		1																		31	
New Windsor Huts	33	44	5	1	18	3	16	17	15	10		7	5	16	15	13	1		20	4		160	
Army at West Point	1143	851	39		19	6		7	16	40		10		15	15	13		1002			8	245	~~1143~~
Army E.side Hudsons River					180	1		11	18	19		2	17	2	17	29	45	216				557	~~557~~
ditto Inoculated	1177	926	35															1177				216	~~1177~~
ditto natural	38	12	23															38				3	~~38~~
	2464	1022	113	4	246	16	19	62	72	69		19	25	39	54	68	46	2438	20	4	8	1362	

N.B. The sick of the Army on the Delaware, New Jersey, North of Albany, or the Cavalry, are not included in the above return.

J. Cochran

A Return of the Sick & Wounded in the Military Hospitals & Army for the month of March 1782

Hospitals &c.	Admitted	Discharged	Dead	Deserted	Convalescent	Wounded	Ulcers	Fevers: Inflam^{y}	Fevers: Inter^{t} & Remit	Fevers: Bilious & Putrid	Fevers: Nervous	Dysentery	Diarrhoea	Venereal	Rheumatism	Various Chronic	Casual Hurts	Small Pox	Women Patients & Children	Officers sick & w^{d}	Sent to Gen^{l}Hosp^{l}	Total Remaining
Boston	1	12	3																			31
New Windsor Hutts	44	22	1		26	5	8	5	9	16		2	6	22	18	19	18		23	6		183
West Point	11		1																		7	3
Army at West Point			8		30	9		22	23	42		5		13	21			180			15	345
Army E. Side Hudsons River					171	1		16	16	26		3	20	4	16	25	34	35				367
Philadelphia	31	56	6	2	1	1	3	16			6	3			8	8		5	15	8		94
Albany miscarried																						

Sent the above to ye. Secretary at War

A Return of the sick & wounded in the Military Hospitals & Army under the immediate command of his Excellency General Washington for April 1782

Hospitals	Admitted	Discharged	Dead	Deserted	Convalescent	Wounded	Ulcers	Inflam^{y} Fever	Intermit. & Remit ditto	Bilious & putrid ditto	Nervous	Dysentery	Diarrhoea	Venereal	Rheumatism	Various Chronic	Casual Hurts	Small Pox	Women patients & children	Officers & Waiters	Sent to G. Hospital	Total remaining	
Albany		2			3	1	7	2						5	1	7			23	1		50	4 nurses
Boston	Various diseases chiefly chronic																					20	
New Windsor Huts	79	72	3	3	30	3	6	11	15	5		5	8	27	13	19	11		13	4		170	12 nurses & 7Corp.[1] guards at ye Huts.
Philadelphia	74	36	6	4	6	9	9	11	41	5	1	2	11	12	6	9	1	10	7	7		134	
British Pris^{ns} in ditto	Various diseases																					73	

N.B. None of the sick of the Army are included in the above Return.

A Return of the sick & wounded of the Army & Hospitals under the immediate command of his Excellency General Washington for the Month of May 1782

Hospitals	Admitted	Discharged	Dead	Deserted	Convalescent	Wounded	Ulcers	Inflam.y Fever	Intermit & remit.	Bilious & putrid ditto	Nervous	Dysentery	Diarrhoea	Venereal	Rheumatism	Various chronic	Casual Hurts	Small pox	Women patients & children	Officers sick & Witers	Sent to ye Genl. Hospl.	Ruptures	Total Remaining.	
New Windsor Huts	40	41	4	2	40	3	6	7	15	6		2	4	26	13	12	13		25	4			176	8 nurses and Corp.[1] guards
Albany	1	8			6	3	7	1						5	1	6			16				45	4 nurses
New Hampshire Hutts Small Pox	90	64	3															90					23	
Army					68	3		1	79	3		4	12	17	26	29	122				5	8	370	
Philadelphia	89	87	3	2		2	8		38	1			5	13	1	29		29	5	4			129	
																							743	

Sent the above to ye Secretary at war

A Return of the sick & wounded in the Army & Hospitals under the immediate command of his Excellency General Washington for June 1782

Hospitals	Admitted	Discharged	Dead	Deserted	Convalescent	Wounded	Ulcers	Inflamatory fevers	Intermit & remit. do	Bilious & Putrid	Nervous	Dysentery	Diarrhoea	Venereal	Rheumatism	Various Chronic	Casual Hurts	Small Pox	Women & children patients	Officers sick with waiters	Sent to ye General Hospl.	Total Remaining
New Windsor Huts	122	47	6		27	2	19	19	16	14		15	11	38	26	20	6		19	4		236
Philadelphia	20	51	4	1			1	7		6		10	1	3		18			22	10		68
British Prisoners							Various diseases															70
Army sick				1	124	2		7	134			17	23	27	23	62	139				9	567
Albany Hospital	4	5	1	-	9	2	3		2			1		1	1	6			19			44
New Hampshire Huts	20	23	"	"	"	"	"	"	"	"	"							23	"	"	"	
	140	103	11	2	160	6	23	33	152	20		43	35	69	50	106	145		60	14	9	985

Nota Bene—In making out this Return let the New Hampshire Huts Hospital be included, which is not added in the above return—being inserted after the return was footed.

Sent the above to ye Secretary at War

A return of the sick & wounded in the Army & Hospitals under the Command of his Excellency Gen. Washington for July 1782

Hospitals	Admitted	Discharged	Dead	Deserted	Convalescents	Wounded	Ulcers	Inflamy fevers	Intermitt&remitt. fevers	Bilious & Putrid	Nervous	Dysentery	Diarrhoea	Venereal	Rheumatism	Various chronic	Casual hurts	Small Pox	Women & children Patients	Officers sick wt. waiters	Sent to Genl. Hosp.	Total remaining	
New Windsor Huts	44	47	3		21	2	12	9	34	22		6	13	38	17	30			19	2		225	
Army sick	"	"	"	"	117			15	216	2		41	78	22	26	72	135				15	729	
Albany hospital	7	9	-	1	2	3	6					1		1	1	9			10			43	four nurses & their children
Philadelphia	28	21	5			3	2	3	33	5	6	13	1		8							74	15
Prisoners of War	-	-	-	-	-	Various Diseases																63	

Sent the above to ye Secretary at War.

Return of the sick & wounded in the Army & Hospitals under the command of his Excell. Genl. Washington for Aug. 1782

Hospitals	Admitted	Discharged	Dead	Deserted	Convalescent	Wounded	Ulcers	Inflamy. Fevers	Intermitt. & Remitt. fev.	Putrid & Bilious fev.	Nervous Fev.	Dysentery	Diarrhoea	Leus Venerea	Rheumatism	Various Chronic	Casual hurts	small pox	Women & children patients	Officers sick with waiters	Sent to Gen. Hosp.	Total	
New Windsor Huts	50	74	3	1	32		11	2	17	27		15	14	13	15	24	8		32	3		177	12 Nurses
New Boston Huts	263	43	4		50	4		10	50	41		23		19	7	12						216	
Albany	3	4		1	4	4	4	1	"	"				2	"	7	"	"	25	"		47	
Army			1		127			18	129	90		38	47	23	32	43	150					697	
Philadelphia	62	20	3		12	2			34			1	26			27				6		108	
Prisoners of War						Various diseases																70	

Sent the above to ye Secretary at War

Return of the Sick & Wounded in the Army & Hospitals under the command of his Excell^{y} Gen'l. Washington for Sept. 1782

Hospitals	Admitted	Discharged	Dead	Deserted	Convalescent	Wounded	Ulcers	Inflamat. Fever	Intermit. & Remitt fev.	Putrid & Bilious fevers	Nervous	Dysentery	Diarrhoea	Lues Venerea	Rheumatism	Various Chronic	Casual hurts	Small Pox	Women & Children patients	Officers sick with waiters	Sent to Genl. Hosp.	Total Remaining	
New Boston Huts	63	81	15	4	20	4			40	20		30	20	18	6	3	1		17			179	
Philadelphia Hospital	43	53	3	7		2			20	2		15	10	8	1	3	3	5				69	
British Prisoners							Various diseases															37	
Flying Hosp^{l} & Army	119	16	4		129		87	5	174	63		24	47	17	20	41	14				26	621	
New Windsor Huts	36	60	3	3	29		7	11		17		13	11	12		30	7	-	23	8	-	168	
Albany Hospital	17	6			3	3	6	5	5			2			2	10			11			59	nurses & children 12
	278	216	25	14	181	9	100	21	239	102		84	88	55	29	87	25	5	51	8	26	1133	

[A return for October 1782 was begun, but only the heading was completed]

A Return of the sick & wounded in the Army & hospitals under the Command of his Exy. Genl. Washington November 1782

Hospitals	Admitted	Discharged	Dead	Deserted	Convalescent	Wounded	Ulcers	Inflammatory fevers	Intermit. & remitt fevers	Putrid & bilious ditto	Nervous fever	Dysentery	Diarrhoea	Lues Venera	Rheumatism	Various chronic	Casual hurts & lame	Small pox	Women & children patients	Officers sick wt. waiters	Sent to Genl. Hosp.	Total Remaining	
New Windsor Huts	95	42	6		33		10	33		23		23	14	11	15	26	11		40	4		243	
Albany Hospital	29	38	1		5		6	2	3					3	7	8				5		54	(15 nurses & children included)
New Boston Huts	24	157	4	4	29	3		3	3	9		7	1	9	7	8	6					85	
Army sick					89	4	38	20	38	34		19	25	20	44	75	170					576	
Philadelphia	33	47	3		13	7	8	3	4			3	6	7		8	5	13	27	11		84	
British Prisoners at ditto					various diseases																	39	
																						1081	

A Return of the sick & wounded in the Army & Hospitals under the Command of his Excellency Gen'l. Washington for December 1782

Hospitals	Admitted	discharged	dead	deserted	convalescent	wounded	Ulcers	Inflamatory fever	Intermitt & remit ditto	Putrid & Bilious ditto	Nervous	Dysentery	Diarrhoea	Lues Venerea	Rheumatism	Various chronic	Casual hurts & lame	Small Pox	Women & children patients	Officers sick & waiters	Sent to ye General [Hosp.]	Total Remaining
New Boston Huts Hosp.	6	56	1		13	2		3	1	2		1	1	2	4	3	2					34
New Windsor Huts Hosp.	49	59	6		61		16	33		8		11	11	21	27				49	4		241
Small Pox Hosp.	33	19	14															33				000
Army sick					73		22	35	21	26		9	26	31	45	89	170					547
Philad. Hospital	34	35			7	6	2	3	4			7	3	12		11	3	14	18	11		71
British Prisoners ditto	various diseases																					39
Albany Hospital	Return in the Post Office—I suppose, & no money to redeem it.																					932

NAMES	RANK	DATES OF COMMIS:^{s}	EVENTS
Wm. Shippen	Director	Oct. 6, '80	Resigned Dr. Cochran appointed Jan. 17, 1781
John Cochran	C.ph & Sg. Ar.	do	
Jas. Craik	C.Hosp^{l} phn.	do	Appointed in Dr. Cochran's room
Mal.^{y} Treat	do	do	
Ch^{s} McKnight	do	do	
Thos Bond	Purveyor	do	
[Isaac] Ledyard	Ass^{t} Purv^{r}	do	
And^{w} Craigie	Apoth^{y}	do	
[Wm.] Johonett	Asst. Apoth.	do	
Jas. Tilton	H. p. & Surg^{n}	7th	
Saml. Adams	do	do	
Dav. Townsend	do	do	
H^{y} Latimer	do	do	
Francis Hagan	do	do	resigned
Phil. Turner	do	do	
Wm. Burnet	do	do	promoted in the room of Dr. Craik removed
John Warren	do	do	
Moses Scott	do	do	resigned
David Jackson	do	do	ditto
Bodo Otto	do	do	
Moses Bloomfield	do	do	resigned
Wm. Eustis	do	do	
George Draper	do	do	
Barn^{s} Binney	do	do	
Josiah Root	Asst. Apothy.		
And^{w} Caldwell	ditto		
Thos Prudden	ditto		
Goodwin Willson	Asst. Purveyor		
Goodwin Willson	Mate		
Daniel Junifer	ditto		
Samuel Edmiston	ditto		
Geo. Campbell	ditto		
John Cowell	ditto		

NAMES	RANK	DATES OF COMMIS:S	EVENTS
Fredk. Otto	ditto		
Jonathan Morris	ditto		resigned the 17 of June 1781
Ebenezer Stockton	ditto		
John Duffield	ditto		
Henry Moore	ditto		
John G. Wright	ditto		
Joseph Bartlett	ditto		resignation accepted June 19th, 1781
Wm. Vinal	ditto		ditto reported by Dr. Eustis, see his letter May 14, 1781 Dr. Vinal resigd. July 20, 1781
Wm. I. Smith	ditto		
John Coventry	ditto		
Danl. Shute	ditto		
Jacob T. Egberts	ditto		
Samuel Woodruff	ditto		
George Stevenson	ditto		
Abijah Cheever	ditto		
Stephen Graham	ditto		
Thos. Waring	ditto		
Jonathan Porter	ditto		resignation accepted 25th June 81
————————	ditto additional		Virginia, Name unknown, lived with Sharpe Delany, Esq.
E. Cogswell	ditto additional		
Wm. Hassall	Storekeeper		Ph.
James James	Clk. Magazine		Ph.
Jacob Parker	Steward		Ph.
Minne Voorhees	Storekeeper		F. H.
Edward Williams	Purveyor & Clk.		Phila.
[Leake] Hunt	Asst. ditto Clk.		Fish Kill
John Brown	Steward		Artillery H. Hosp.
John Forbes	Ward Master		ditto
Mary Lake	Matron		ditto
Richard Lake	Wagoner		ditto

A Return of the Officers &c. in the Genl. Hospital of the United States, Exclusive of Georgia and South and North Carolina July 23d 1781

Names	Rank	Pay pr Month or day	Rations per Day	Rations of Forage	Where Stationed &c
John Cochran	Director	150 Dol^{s} per month	2 Rations 1 for servant	2	Headquarters
James Craik	C.Phy^{n} & Surg^{n} to ye Army	140 Dol^{s} pr do	2	2 one two Horse Wagon	With the Army
Malachy Treat	C.Phy^{n} & Surg^{n} to ye Hosp.	140 Dol^{s} pr do	2	2	Philadelphia ordered to Virginia
Charles McKnight	C. do & do	140 pr do	2	2	Hospital-New Windsor Huts
William Burnet	C. do & do	140 pr do	2	2	Hospital-Robison's House
Thomas Bond	Purveyor	130 pr do		1	Philadelphia
Andrew Cragie	Apothecary	130 pr do		1	Philadelphia
Isaac Ledyard	Asst. Purveyor	75 pr do			Fishkill
[William] Johonett	Asst. Apothecary	75 pr do			Fishkill
Josiah Root	Asst. Do	50 pr do	1		Albany
Franc^{s} Wainwright	Do Do	50 Ditto	1		Fishkill
James Tilton	Hosp^{l} phys^{n} & Surg^{n}	120 per Do	1	1	on his way to join the Army
Samuel Adams	Do Do	120 per Do	1	1	Hosp^{l} New Windsor Huts
David Townsend	Do Do	120 per Do	1	1	Hosp^{l} Albany
Henry Latimer	Do Do	120 per Do	1	1	F. Hosp^{l} Army
Francis Hagan	Hosp^{l} Surg^{n} & phys^{n}	120 per Do	1	1	Resigned
Phil. Turner	Do Do	120 per Do	1	1	Do
William Burnet	Do Do	120 per Do	1	1	Promoted to C.phys.& surg. to Hosp^{l}

A Return of the Officers &c. in the Genl. Hospital of the United States, Exclusive of Georgia and South and North Carolina July 23d 1781

Names	Rank	Pay pr Month or day	Rations per Day	Rations of Forage	Where Stationed &c
John Warren	Do Do	120 per Do	1	1	Hosp! Boston
Moses Scott	Do Do	120 per Do	1	1	Resigned
David Jackson	P. & surg. to ye Hosp.	120 Dols. per Mo.	1	1	Resigned
Bodo Otto	Do Do	120	1	1	Hosp! Yellow Springs
Moses Bloomfield	Do Do	120	1	1	Resigned
William Eustis	Do Do	120	1	1	Hosp! Robison's House
George Draper	Do Do	120	1	1	Flying Hosp! with the Army
Barn^s Binney	Do Do	120	1	1	Philadelphis, attending the sick in genl. &c.
Goodwin Wilson	Mate	50	1		Virginia Asst. to Purveyor
Dan! Jenifer	Do	50	1		Virginia
Sam! Edmiston	Do	50	1		Garrison—West Point
George Campbell		50	1		Flying Hosp! with the Army
John Cowell	Do	50	1		Philadelphia. attending Goal
Fred^k Otto	Do	50	1		Hospital Yellow Springs
Jon^a Morris	Do	50	1		Resigned June 17th 1781
Eben^r Stockton	Do	50	1		Hosp! New Windsor Huts
John Duffield	Do	50 Dol^s per Month	1		Small pox Hosp^l near West Point
Henry Moore	Do	50	1		Hosp! Robison's House
John G. Wright	Do	50	1		Hosp! New Windsor Huts
Joseph Bartlet	Do	50	1		Resigned June 19, 1781
Wm. Vinal	Do	50	1		Do July 20th, 1781

Wm. P. Smith	Do	50	1	Hosp. Albany
John Coventry	Mate	50 Dols.pr month	1	Hosp.l New Windsor Huts
Daniel Shute	Do	50 pr Do	1	F.Hosp.l with the Army
Jacob V. Egberts	Do	50 pr Do	1	Hosp.l at Albany
Samuel Woodruff	Do	50 pr Do	1	Do at Do
George Stevenson	Do	50 pr Do	1	Hosp. New Windsor Huts
Abijah Cheever	Do	50 pr Do	1	Hosp. at Boston
Thomas Waring	Do	50 pr Do	1	Hosp. New Windsor Huts
Thomas Marshall	Do	50 pr Do	1	ordered to Virginia—resigned
Jonathan Porter	Do	50 pr Do	1	Resigned June 25, 1781
Stephen Graham	Do	50 pr Do	1	Hosp. New Windsor Huts
Michael Detrick	Do	50 pr Do	1	Virginia
Wm. Cogswell	Additional Mate	50 pr Do	1	Hospital Robison's House
And.w Caldwell	Asst. to ye Apoth.y	50 pr Do	1	Philadelphia
Thomas Prudan	Do to Do	50 ditto	1	Philadelphia
John DeLaMater	Clk. to Asst. Purvey.r	2 d.rs per day		Fish Kill
Edward Williams	Clk. to Purveyor	2 d.rs per day		Philadelphia
Leake Hunt	Storekeeper	2 do pr Do		Fish Kill
Minne Voorhees	Storekeeper	2 do pr Do	1	Flying Hospital with the Army
Wm. Hascall	Do	2 do pr Do		Philadelphia
James James	Clk. Magazine	30 do per month		do
Jacob Parker	Steward	35 pr Do	1	do
John Brown	Do	35 pr Do	1	Hosp.l New Windsor Huts
James Lamb	Do	35 pr Do	1	Hosp.l at Albany

A Return of the Officers &c. in the Genl. Hospital of the United States, Exclusive of Georgia and South and North Carolina July 23d 1781

Names	Rank	Pay pr Month or day	Rations per Day	Rations of Forage	Where Stationed &c
John Scott	Do	35 pr Do	1		Hosp[l] Windsor Huts
Thomas White	Do	35 pr Do	1		Hosp[l] Robison's House
Alex McCaraher	Do	35 pr Do	1		Hosp[l] Yellow Springs
Thomas Wallcut	Do	35 pr Do	1		Hosp[l] at Boston
Dan[l] Henry	Ward Master	35 pr Do	1		Hosp[l] Danbury ordered to Fish Kill
Charles Couch	Steward	35 pr Do	1		Hosp[l] Virginia
William Duncan	Ward Master	25 pr Do	1		Hosp[l] Albany
John Vredenburgh	do	25 pr Do	1		Hosp. Morris Town Huts
John Forbis	do	25 Dollars per month	1		Hosp. New Windsor Huts
Jonas Dix	do	25 do pr do	1		Hosp. Robison's House
Fred[k] Wendt	do	25 do pr do	1		Hosp. Yellow Springs
[name scratched out]	do	25 do pr do	1		Hosp. at Boston
George Edmiston	do	25 do pr do	1		Virginia
Sarah Ray	Matron	Half dollar per day	1		Hosp. Albany
Mary Lake	do	do	1		Hosp. New Windsor Huts
Nardy	do	do	1		Hosp. Robison's House
Catherine Wendt	do	do	1		Yellow Springs
Elizabeth Sickles	do	do	1		Flying Hospital with the Army
[no name]	do	do	1		Hosp[l] at Boston
Mary Parker	do	do	1		Philadelphia

N.B. There are employed at present about thirty nurses in the different Hospitals, a number of Orderly men being soldiers, some artificers, and wagoners. As the sick and wounded accumulate so as to fill the Hospitals already established or to require new ones to be opened, more stewards, ward masters, matrons, nurses & orderly men &c. must be occasionally employed, nurses 2/ per day, rations per day 1/, orderly men if soldiers 1/ per day, rations per day 1/, orderly men not being soldiers 2/ per day, rations per day 1/.

Sent a return of the above to the Board of War Aug. 1, 1781

John Cochran

A Return of the Medical Officers &c in the Southern Department of the United States of America July 23, 1781

Names	Rank	Pay per month or day	Rations per Day	Rations of Forage	Where Stationed &c.
David Oliphant	Deputy Director				South Carolina
Peter Fayssoux	C.phy^{n} of the Hosp.	140 Dolls.per month	2	2	do
James Browne	Cphy^{n} of the Army	140 Dolls. do do	2	2	do
Robert Johnston	Hosp^{l} phys^{n}	120 do do	1	1	do
Wm. Reed	do	120 do do	1	1	do
Nathan Brownson	Dept. purveyor				do

N.B. The above is all the returns I am able to make of the Southern Department, having no returns from that Quarter since my appointment. The above I collected from the appointments of Congress. I know not the pay of the Deputy Director or the Deputy Purveyor.

In pencil
By —— Congress—20 Sept. 1781
Doctors Thomas } appd. Physicians & Surgeons for the Southern Dept.
Tudor }
Tucker }
Vickars }
David Smith—Deputy Purveyor
John Crane Asst. Dept. Apothecary.

ADDITIONAL LETTERS OF JOHN COCHRAN

To Richard Peters

New Brunswick
October 6th 1770

Sir

You may remember that when your nephew Doctor Peters was indisposed at this Place, that I administered Sundry Medicines to him; by the advice of Dr. McKean and some of the Physical Gentlemen of New York who were consulted in his Case for which I never received any satisfaction. As you were here at that time and shewed much concern for his situation, I know of no one to whom I can apply but to you; I therefore hope you will excuse me for troubling you at this time. I never took any particular account of the services rendered him, therefore must leave the matter with you.

I am Sir your most obedient humble servant
John Cochran

[Papers of Richard Peters VII, 7, HSP]

To Philip Schuyler

New Brunswick, February 22nd 1776

Dear Sir:

I received your agreeable Favor of the 30th January for which I thank you. The frequent various Accounts of your situation respecting your Health gave much anxiety and I must confess that I am not altogether without my fears on account of your safety. Your spirits I doubt are too much for your Constitution which you would do well to favor as much as the Nature of things will permit, for though in this day of Publick Calamity when our all and that of our Posterity is at stake and calls for the most vigorous execution of every Person in our common Defense, yet those on whom most depends ought to be extremely careful to preserve themselves for the good of their oppressed

Country, you would therefore do well to employ such persons about you as will be able to take off your hands such parts of the Business as can with any degree of propriety be done by another. Congress may have been right in pressing your Continuance in office in such terms as prevented your quitting yet in a private Capacity you might have given great assistance and preserved yourself. I sincerely hope that you may be restored to your health so as to take an active part and that you may acquit yourself in such a manner as to answer the warm Expectations of your Friends in the Publick.

Gitty joins me in Congratulations on the Birth of your Daughter and we are glad to hear that sister Schuyler and the young Linnet are so well.

John Schuyler who entered College after last vacancy not having a Preceptor constantly over him, studying at home and only attending recitation at a particular hour from his youth and vast volatility has become rather idle, I took much pains to keep him industrious but found it in vain as I was much abroad; I therefor[e] thought it best to return him back again to school where a strict Eye is kept over him and he [is] keeping place with his Class which in College reads the same thing, he can take his degree at the same time with the rest and will not be retarded. He is a Boy of excellent natural parts and free from vice in general. I have not been able to hear from Beverly Robison, who I think has not used me well. Mr. Hugh Wallace on whose hands your order on him is, has wrote to him several times but to no purpose.

I hope Peter will do his Duty. We thank you for thinking of him.

Our Love to sister and the Children and believe me most sincerely Dear Sir

Yours very affectionately

John Cochran

[Schuyler Papers, NYPL]

To Thomas McKean

New Brunswick, July 7th 1776

Dear Sir:

The bearer, Lieutenant Woodman of the Twenty-Sixth Regiment, taken prisoner at Ticonderoga last summer, has resided in this town ever since, on his parole. As far as I know he has behaved himself with decency respecting publick matters; nor do I find he has ever been charged with taking part either with one side or the other. He has made a [new start] in this town, and is at present employed in repairing it. He is married to a daughter of Mr. Legrange of this place and has a family of six children, which renders his removal from hence rather distressing; therefore if any indulgence, consistent with the publick safety, can be allowed him, I hope they will not be improperly bestowed. I know your readiness to do acts of humanity, therefore leave the matter of it particularly to your judgment and the publick security.

I am, dear sir, your very obedient, humble servant,

John Cochran

[Force, *American Archives*, 5th series, vol. 1, col. 104]

To Philip Schuyler

Head Quarters Morris Town January 21st 1777

Dear Sir

I received your favor of the 20th ult° a day or two ago. I thank you for your kind offer of Friendship in doing every thing in your Power to promote my Interest but above all for your anxiety for the safety of myself and Family. Gitty and the whole Family I believe are gone to Walters at the Manor where I hope they will have the Pleasure of seeing you which I am sure will add to their Happiness. You will have heard of the favorable turn our Affairs have taken since the 25th of December. I had the Pleasure to see the Garrison of Trenton lay down their Arms and submit Prisoners of War. Never were a set of beings so panic struck since the Creation as the whole Garrisons on the Delaware when they heard of the fate of Trenton. We were equally successful at Princetown and had we that night only 500 light horse to pursue the Enemy to Brunswick I surely believe Amboy Bay would have brought them up. Our men and officers behaved in general with such bravery as would do honor to any Troops in the world. The militia from different parts of the American World are daily coming in. What Number our Army at present consists of is impossible for me to tell or what route we shall take from hence. I have remained with General Washington ever since I wrote you, but on what footing I know not. He has the power from Congress to make what appointments he may think proper for the good of the service as well respecting Hospitals as in any other Department. He sent for me last night and desired I would draw up an Arrangement for the Hospital for the ensuing Campaign which I have done and expect to set out to day for Philadelphia to assist Dr. Shippen in compleating the Plan and having everything put on the best footing. In this arrangement I expect to be provided for genteely as I am sure it is the General's Intention so to do. I would rather be second in Command in that way than first for I find that almost every Person who has been at the head of the Medical Department has been much blamed. Both Morgan and Stringer are dismissed the service and one Potts appointed in Stringer['s] room. Morgan's Place not yet filled up. As you so near us I hope you will pay General Washington a visit, when if I return home from Philadelphia I hope to have the pleasure of seeing you which would afford me real satisfaction. Yesterday a party of our militia fell in with a large foraging party of the Enemy who had 3 field pieces. We drove them, took nine prisoners, 84 Horses chiefly English and upwards of twenty Waggons. In short a day does not pass but that we take Prisoners or Deserters are coming in. Even the new caught Highlanders from the 42nd desert to us. If we will only act with a becoming firmness and Spirit the Day is our own with the smiles of Heaven, nay I am sure the justice of our Cause almost claims the Interest of Heaven.

Love to sister Schuyler and Family and believe me

Dear Sir Yours most affectionately

John Cochran

P.S. I never received the 100 from Robison, you would oblige me greatly in paying it to Gitty as thro' a mistake she went away without that supply of money necessary for the Winter. John Cochran

[Schuyler Papers, NYPL]

To Philip Schuyler

Morristown February 29th 1777

Dear Sir:

The Enemy, supposed to consist chiefly of the reinforcements from Rhode Island, to the amount, it is said, of between 3 and 4 thousand landed at Amboy on Sunday last and marched through Woodbridge into the Country northwest. They had not proceeded far beyond Woodbridge when they were attacked by about 4 or 500 of our advance guards who continued to harrass them on their march for many hours taking every advantage of the ground Woods etc. The enemy were frequently thrown into great Confusion and after many severe skirmishes they retreated to Amboy and were pursued by our Sons of Liberty within a half mile of that Place. General Vaughan who commanded at Amboy ordered the Troops to make a stand on some advantageous Ground near the Town and encamp for that Night but to no purpose..The loss they sustained is very uncertain. The Prisoners we took that Day were seven and they took as much pain to carry off their Dead as we Indians did, notwithstanding which many were found on the fields. The Inhabitants who were spectators of the action, say the Enemy's Loss was considerable and the Deserters say some 2 to 300 others from 4 to 500 killed and wounded. They barbarously killed two of the Peasants on their way, for not immediately assisting with Teams to carry off the killed and wounded. These poor unfortunate wretches were of the numbers who had taken protection from General Howe. This with many reiterated acts of inhumanity has greatly exasperated the Inhabitants who are coming in by the hundreds, giving up their protection and taking the oath to the state. Their intention in coming out is very uncertain; some think they were only a foraging party, while others are of the opinion that they intended establishing a Post some distance in the country in order to give them a greater scope. They are greatly distressed for Forage and have only salt provisions both for men and officers. There are few of their imported horses remaining either for their Waggons or troop and those miserably poor. I do not think they can stay in the state they are in till the grass. We are under no apprehension of an attack from them in this Quarter nor do I think they will gain Philadelphia this season, should they attempt it we are in a very good situation to play them a trick. Our army is in fine spirits and pretty healthy unless that the smallpox is and has been troublesome. We have now under inoculation about 300 and as one set gets out we take in another and so on till we inoculate the whole of our regular Troops. We frequently pick up straggling fellows from the Enemy and Deserters to our different Posts since General Washington's arrival in this town amounts to near 30 per week one week with another. The very sentries often come off. Since Christmas the Enemy must have suffered, at least 3,000, in New Jersey killed, disabled by wounds and prisoners. This I know to be a fact from the best intelligence. Col. Neilson of New Brunswick surprised and took prisoners near seventy of our Cousin Cortlandt Skinner's regiment with a Major Stockton of Princetown at their Head, one of the most abandoned scoundrels on Earth. This happened about a fortnight ago.

There is nothing yet fixed respecting myself. A new general arrangement for the whole Continental Hospital is expected to take place very shortly. The General only waits for the approbation of Congress before He carries the plan into Execution. The arrangement was given him by Doctor Shippen and myself for which purpose I was sent by the General to Philadelphia. I expect to hold some Place worth my while. I even had an aversion for a Directorship for many Reasons but should have no Objection to a Rank which would intitle me to the same Emoluments. Should I go to the northward, in all probability I would be farther from my Family than being with General Washington. I know little of Doctor Potts, but sure I am that such a Trust would require a man of Temper and Skill in his Profession. The moment any thing is settled for me I shall not fail to acquaint you therewith.

I am much distressed about my two absent Boys. I fear they are not kept to school which will be a very great loss of time if they are not. I doubt not but that my very good Friends will do every thing in their Power to make the time as agreeable to Gitty as her present situation will admit of. I thank you for the money given her. I believe I forgot to inform you that I am pretty certain Mr. Hugh Wallace to whom I assigned your draught on Mr. Robison never received the money.

I shall always be happy to have a Line from you when Season permits and if there is any particular of which you would chuse to be informed you may command me provided always that you excuse this informal paper. Better I have not nor can I procure it at present.

Love to Mrs. Schuyler and the Family and all Friends and believe me Dear Sir

most sincerely and affectionately yours

John Cochran

[Ely Autograph Collection, NJHS]

To Alexander Mitchell

Head Quarters Morristown April 26th 1777

Dear Sir:

I have been long looking for an opportunity of writing to you & have had actually two Letters by me which I could not forward. I had a Letter a few Days ago from Mrs. Cochran, she & the Children are very well with all her Friends with whom she is exceeding happy. She frequently writes me and as often begs her Love to you & my sister acknowledging her Gratitude for your great attention to her & Family. A Gentleman of the name of Carter will call in all probability for my Chair; Let him have it: the Harness belonging to the Chair is newer & more substantial then the sulky.

Congress have appointed me Physician & Surgeon General to the Army in the Middle Department & director of a flying Hospital at 5 Dollars a day & six Rations consequently I must be continually in the Field with the army. This will effectually prevent me from seeing my Family in some time or visiting any of my particular Friends.

You will oblige me much in forwarding to me the following Books which I shall want; Cheseldon's Anatomy both Works, Brooks practice of Physick 2 vol. Alexander's Essays, Whites Surgery, Sharps Surgery, Huxham on Rever, on Air, White on the Nerves.

When or where we shall move from hence will depend on the movements of the Enemy. I shall be glad of a Line when convenient. I shall probably send for my Colt some time hence. Pray keep an Exact account of the Expence both where he was & where he is now. My love to my sister and believe me most affectionately

Dear Sir

Yours &c

John Cochran

If the Books are put up in a little Box or Package and directed to me at headquarters, and sent down to Col. Erwings I may get them from thence by some waggon.

[Ely Autograph Collection, NJHS]

To John Sullivan

Middlebrook July 3rd 1777

Sir

Your Letter of Complaint to General Washington, against the Surgeons of the General Hospital is now before me. You charge us with detaining a Number of Sick, belonging to Colonel Hazen's Regiment, of refusing to receive them into the Hospital, and of sending them away at Nine O'clock at Night through the Rain. Whoever gave you this Information is a Stranger to the Truth, and it would have been well; that you examined a little more particularly into the State of this Matter, before you had lodged your Complaint. At half an Hour after seven O'Clock on Sunday Night Word came from Colonel Hazen's Regiment 25 Sick to be admitted into the Hospital, there was no Return sent with them, nor had I any Place to accomodate them in, at that unseasonable Hour; and had I not returned them to their Regiment, where I presume they had Tents, they must have lain in the open Field and perished.

I ordered the person who came with them, to bring them back in the Morning, with a proper return signed by the surgeon and I would provide Waggons to transport them to the General Hospital. They were not returned to me till late the next Evening, when I ordered the person who had the charge of them to a Barn over the Mountain which I had occupied for the purpose of an hospital, the men suffered from being out at that late Hour, especially as it rained at Times, and the Evening was very damp.

The Sick of Colonel Hazen's and Hall's Regiments were received into the General Hospital yesterday, without an orderly Man or Woman sent with them, to there is a general Order for a proportionable Number of Women from the different Regiments to attend the Sick, when sent to the Hospitals at Black River or Mendham. You may acquaint the Gentlemen Colonels of your Division that I will receive no Sick into the hospital, without a proper Return of the Mens' Names, their Regiment, Companies and Diseases; this is agreeable to General Orders, my Instructions from Congress, the Director General and entirely agreeable to common sense.

The men of Colonel Hall's regiment were not refused admittance into the Hospital, by a certain Doctor Draper; as you set forth, because their were no Orderly Men sent with them; the Doctor only required the Serjeant who came with them to see them to the hospital, and he replied he would be damned if he did. You have pointed out to his Excellency the Regulations of Congress, respecting the Hospital Department and say from such Procedure, little Benefit has been derived to the Army. I know not what your Ideas of Benefits may be, but give me Leave to assure you that I have received into the Hospital 1100 Sick from the different Regiments since my Arrival in Camp and have disposed of them in such a Manner as I have been directed, and I can aver they have been properly taken care of.

You say that Surgeons have no Medicine or proper places to take care of the Sick. The Surgeons to Colonel Hazen's Regiment was at the Opening of the Campaign provided with as complete a Chest, as was ever sent into the Field, and he like an attentive good officer left it behind him this Morning in the Field. I picked it up, and sent it to the Hospital Tents, having no Waggon to bring it on; I hope you will take proper Notice of this Neglect and let the offender be brought to Justice, Sick men may Be taken Care of in Tents untill they can be conveyed to Hospitals, if proper attention is paid to them by their officers or Surgeons.

I am sorry to inform you that your whole Charge is without Foundation, and you must, either have been imposed on yourself or your Intentions must have militated against the Reputation of Gentlemen who, I flatter myself, have paid as much attention to the Duty, of this Department, as any Set of Men in the Army. I would not even except a Major General.

I must insist that you will write to his Excellency, withdraw your Charge, unsay every thing you have said, or I will take the necessary Steps to do myself, and the Gentlemen under my Direction that Justice every honest Man has a Right to expect.

I am Sir your Humble Servant

John Cochran

[George Washington Papers, 4th series, vol. 50, LC]

To Albigence Waldo

Valley Forge, Dec. 31st 1777

I am willing to oblige every Gentlemen of the Faculty, but some of the Boston surgeons have by taking an underhand method of getting furlows, occasion'd a Complaint to be lodg'd with his Excellency who has positively forbid my giving any furlows at present. We shall soon have regimental Hospitals erected, and general Ones to receive the Superabundant Sick from them; if you will tarry till such regulations are made, you will have an honorable furlow, and even now, I will, if you desire it—recommend you to his Excellency for one, but desire you would stay a little while longer, and in the meantime recommend to me some young Surgeon for a Regiment and I will immediately appoint him to a chief Surgeoncy from your recommendation. I shall remember the rascals who have us'd me ill.

[*Pennsylvania Magazine of History and Biography* 21 (1897): 316]

Detail of a watercolor showing the widowed Mrs. Cochran at the age of 84, drawn in 1808 by the Baroness Hyde de Neuville

Courtesy of The New-York Historical Society, New York City

Camp Valley Forge, January 10th 1778

All Regimental Surgeons and Mates who are now absent from the army in the Middle Department without leave from the Commander-in-Chief or Surgeon General of the Army, are required to repair to their respective regiments, by the fifteenth day of February next. Should they not pay attention to this notice, they may depend on being advertised in the public papers as deserters and treated as such.

John Cochran, S.G.

N.B. Regimental Surgeons and Mates, properly qualified to discharge their duties are now wanted.

[*Pennsylvania Packet or the General Advertiser*, January 21, 1778]

General Orders

Valley Forge, January 21st 1778

It being impossible for the Surgeon General of the Flying Camp to make provisions for the sick, unless they are sent to places properly furnished for the purpose, all officers and regimental surgeons are therefore to apply to the Chief Surgeon [Assistant Director] present in Camp and take his directions where to send the sick. A contrary practice has been attended with great inconvenience to the sick and probably has occasioned the death of several men. Many have been sent to hospitals already crowded with patients or to places where no provisions had been made.

[Gibson, pp. 151–52]

To Jonathan Potts

Camp Valley Forge March 22d 1778

Dear Sir:

I Received yours of the 17th inst. with the Articles agreeable to the Invoice, for which we thank you. I sent all the articles to the flying Hospital Store, except the Loaf Sugar and Spirits, to be distributed by our Commissary to the Sick in Camp and the Inoculated Patients, on our Orders agreeable to their wants. I also sent to the Commissary two Barrels of Brown Sugar, Chocolate and wine which I brought in my return Sleigh from Albany. One Quarter cask of wine from Albany was stolen on the way down, at a Committe Mans House where it was thought to be very safe—I thank you for your promise of instruments; they are very much wanted and the sooner you forward on Cutlery, the better. Medicines are much wanted; particularly Camphor of which we have not one particle and Vials—a number of Troops from the Southward are expected in Camp in the course of two or three weeks, are ordered in without taking the smallpox, of consequence will be Inoculated some where near Camp; Molasses in abundance will be expected for the purpose of supplying these People, and the sooner a small supply for present use of this and Rice is forwarded the better. The Gentlemen of the flying Hospital present their best compliments while I am,

Dear Sir

Your very humble Servant

John Cochran, surgeon-general of the Army

[Jonathan Potts Papers, vol. 4, p. 21, HSP]

To James McHenry

Manor Livingston January 29th 1779

Dear Mac:

I arrived here last Saturday from Boston, where I was stationed some time longer than I expected, partly through inclination and partly through the solicitations of the Marquis, who would not part with me until I saw him safe on Board & after staying two nights with him in Nantasket road, I took my leave and suppose he sailed on the 11th instant, the day I left Boston.

I much hoped by this time to have been at Head Quarters with my family & to have spent the remainder of the winter in the very agreeable manner, I began it, but on my arrival at this place, I had the unhappiness to find Mrs. Cochran extremely ill of a most considerable Rheumatism & Fever which have confined her chiefly to her bed for these four weeks, in exceeding great pain. As I have little expectations of her recovery shortly, (if at all) I must necessarily be confined here & wait the event, of which I beg you will acquaint the commander-in-chief; whom God long preserve.

I flatter myself, my absence will be attended with no injury to the service. I suppose there are General Hospitals established near your Quarters for the reception of the regimental sick & Draper will attend to seeing them conveyed thither at proper times and seasons & that the regimental sick are properly supplied with the usual stores, the same as last winter.

I shall be happy in having a few lines from you. Please to make my most respectful compliments to the General and his good Lady Mrs. Washington with the Family & all Friends and believe me most sincerely & affectionately

Dear Mac

Your very hble. servant

John Cochran

Please direct me to the care of Colo. Udney Hay D.Q.M.G. Fishkill

[Henry E. Huntington Library, San Marino, California]

To George Washington

Manor of Livingston March 25th 1779

Dear Sir

I should not trouble your Excellency at this time but am under apprehension that my absence may be attributed, more to a neglect of Duty than any real Cause. When I came to this Place on my Way from Boston to Head Quarters I found Mrs. Cochran so dangerously ill, that I could not possibly leave her but at the utmost risk of her Life, and am sorry to say that her Circumstances are such that I cannot justify myself in abandoning her at present. I hope as the weather grows more mild, she will recover so that I may be able to join the Army, but if my immediate Attendance cannot be dispensed with, I shall be reduced to the disagreeable necessity of resigning my Commission which would give me much Pain for as I have already born a share in the Contest thus far I should be sorry to retire until we see the end of it.

As I would not trouble your Excellency heretofore, I wrote to Dr. McHenry to acquaint you of the Reasons of my being delayed; my silence on that Head I flatter myself will not be construed into a want of respect. You will oblige me infinitely in ordering the Gentlemen of your Family to favor me with a Line.

I am with best Compliments to Mrs. Washington

Dear Sir

Your affectionate and

very humble servant

John Cochran

[George Washington Papers, 4th series, vol. 101, LC]

To James Abeel

Smith's Place, July 12th 1779

Dear Sir:

I most wretchedly forgot when my waggoner Titus Vespasianus passed through Morristown to tell him to call on you for the odd articles I gave Draper the memorandum on you for. As I shall have everything in readiness for my Carriage in a short time, I hope you will forward my request by first safe opportunity; if you should miss my Waggon. A Dissappointment will hurt me more particularly as I want them solely for the accomodation of Mrs. Cochran, who is with me and in tolerable good health. She desires her best Compliments to Mrs. Abeel and Mrs. Neilson who I think is with you. You will please to present mine also.

I am dear Sir

Sincerely your very humble servant

John Cochran

[Peck Collection, The Rhode Island Historical Society, Providence]

To Andrew Craigie

Morristown January 18th 1780

Dear Sir

I wrote you some time ago by Dr. Coventry but he has taken Care to lose your Answer which disappoints me very mush. On the receipt of this I beg you will say again what you said before. I had a Letter some days since from Dr. Latimer informing me that he had left my Watch with you & that I was to give you Instructions what was to be done with it. This Letter lay long in the office before I received it therefore could give no directions about it you will take care of it & the paper of Directions with it, as I have no copy. Col. Clement Biddle will call for the Watch and endeavour to have it repaired.

I have been on the [cussidest] Winter Excursion with Lord Stirling to Staten Island that was ever invented. Many of our men and officers are much frost bit. I wish some of our Gentlemen in Philadelphia who are on severe Duty, had been of the Party, just to have varied the scene a little; perhaps they would have found some difference between Laying a snow Bank and basking in the sunshine of Jollity. We are blessed little obliged to the Lads for any supplies to sweeten the Cup. Coventry informs me you have sent on the chest I thank you for it. Not one ounce of anything has arrived for our comfort since I came to this place. Draper will be the bearer of this & will give you a full account how matters stand with us.

I am Dr Sir with great Trust
your sincere Friend &
Very humble servant
John Cochran

PS I am informed that there is in somewhere, either in the Druggstore or in the possession of Dr. Potts a number of Cases of Pocket Instruments while our surgeons in the Army are dressing with wooden Probes—Pray be kind enough to inform me how that Matter stands. I have been writing for Instruments this twelve months, but to no purpose.

[Andrew Craigie Papers, American Antiquarian Society, Worcester, Massachusetts]

To Jonathan Potts

Morristown, March 18th 1780

Dear Sir

I received your Favor by Dr. Bond and am very sorry for the present situation of the Hospital finances; the stores have all been expended for two weeks past, and not less than 600 Regimental sick and lame, most of whom require some assistance, which being witheld, are languishing and must suffer. I flatter myself you have no blame in this matter, but curse on him or them by whom this evil is produced. The vengeance of an offended Deity must overtake the miscreants sooner or later. It grieves my soul to see the poor, worthy brave fellows pine away for want of a few comforts which they have dearly earned. I shall wait on his Excellency, the Commander-in-Chief and represent our situation, but I am persuaded it can have little effect, for what can he do? He may refer the matter to Congress, they to the Medical Committee, who would probably pow-wow over it for a while, and no more be heard of it. Thus we go before the wind. Compliments of all my friends, and believe me, Dear Sir

Yours very sincerely,

John Cochran

[Jonathan Potts Papers, vol. 4, p. 104, HSP]

To the President of the Medical Committee

Morristown April 11th 1780

Sir

It becomes necessary for me to acquaint the Medical Committee that, as it was probable I should soon be destitute of stores for the regimental sick, I wrote to Doctor Potts the Hospital Purveyor, for a proper supply, in order to prevent the fatal consequences which must ensue from the want of them. I had for answer that he neither had stores on hand or money to purchase any with.

The whole stock was expended on Monday last the usual Day of issuing and then only at half Allowance for the Week and unless a supply should arrive in a few Days the sick must suffer greatly. I am informed, this Day that the General Hospitals in the vicinity of the Camp, are nearly in the same situation respecting stores, so that little relief can be expected from that Quarter.

I hope the above report will induce the Medical Committee to take the most effectual steps to enable the Purveyor to provide the necessary Comforts for the languishing soldiery who merit the utmost attention from that Country, which they have been so bravely defending.

I am
Sir
your most obedient and very
humble servant
John Cochran, S and P
General to the Army

[Papers of the Continental Congress, NA]

To Andrew Craigie

Tappan August 9th 1780

Dear Craigie

For God's sake, send us on a supply of Medicines & dressings, particularly lint otherwise we are ruined. If Cutting does not soon approach & afford us every assistance necessary I will not be silent. I have already represented his and the other gentleman's neglect of duty to the Committee of Congress, who I believe have taken the matter up, and I fancy there will be very sudden rattling among the dry bones. There never was so shameful a piece of conduct.

Fail not to send me the Coc. Indic. We shall open a flying hospital tomorrow, our whole stock of medicines will not hold out 3 weeks, and the regimental surgeons have little or none. Horrid murmurs begin to arise. The Express waits, therefore have only time to add God bless you, do not forget us

yours most sincerely,

John Cochran

Write me by opportunity

[Andrew Craigie Papers, American Antiquarian Society, Worcester, Massachusetts]

To an Unidentified Recipient

Tappan Camp September 4th 1780

Dear Sir

Are you not a Nincumpoopa. Why not send me the Hat & three Pair of shoes as ordered by General Greene; It would have been all clear gain, which is some consideration to a Man who has received neither Pay or subsistence these 15 Months. You were so supple in making the memorandum that I really began to think, there was something more than a Humbug in the case, & I have not yet, altogether made up my Mind, on the subject, but that I may find some reality in your Promise.

Dear Sir your most devoted etc.

John Cochran

[Boston Public Library]

To James Duane

Camp near HackensackBridge
September 9th 1780

Dear Sir

Our Director General is now with us and sets off for Philadelphia tomorrow. He says on his arrival there the Congress mean to take up the medical Department and new arrange the same. No Department wants new modeling more; for whether from a Defect in the officers or in the system or in both, I will not take upon me to determine, but so it is that, I verily believe no Department ever was in such confusion. At this moment there is not a Hospital Surgeon within Forty Miles of our Camp, to take the sick off our hands when the Army moves; though there is scarce a [Corner] of the Continent but that you may find Physicians and Surgeons General, with senior Surgeons, Juniors and Mates [para]ding, all in continental Pay.

The Director tells me an entire new system is to take Place, which will be as near the British Establishment as the nature of our circumstances will admit. He proposes one Director General, six Physicians and Surgeons and 20 Mates. The Purveyor, [Quarter]master etcetera to be taken out of the Physician and Surgeon. I do not dislike the Plan, but as this will reduce the number of the Physicians and Surgeons already in Pay, Congress must determine who are to be retained and who are to be discarded, of which they can be but very incompetent Judges; of course the man who has the most Interest, let his services or medical abilities be what they will, without Interest he must go to the Wall. For your Information I would venture to give you a few Characters which in my Opinion would contribute much to the Honor of the Establishment and the Public weal. For surgeon, I would propose four young Gentlemen, single men, and unconnected with anything but the Army. From such People we may expect constant service. They are Doctor Latimer, Hagan, Tilton and Townshend, who are all doing Duty at this moment and have rendered more essential service to the thirteen United States, than almost all the Hospital surgeons on [the] continent. There are many other valuable Characters in the same Station, who I dare say will not be forgot; I mention these more particularly, because I know they have few Friends in Congress and are little known unless where their Duty leads them.

Doctor Craik at present an ass[istant] deputy Director-General in the Middle Department, has one of the highest places in the New Arrangement, though I much question whether he will be proposed, as [one] of three Physicians. He left a most extensive Practice to jo[in] the Army thro the solicitations of the Commander[-in-Chief] of whom he is the greatest Favorite. It would be ha[rd] handed if that great man should not have the compliment paid him of one single appointment, where the safety of his own Person is concerned; but so it is in this [hard] age that I must fear the Idea will not strike your [own] Body in the same manner it does me.

A Doctor Craigie now doing the Duty of Apothecary-General in Philadelphia ought to be continued at the Head of that Branch in preference to any other person though I [have] my suspicions he will be undermined by a certain P[erson who] shall be nameless at Present for certain reasons.

As to myself I would wish to continue in my present station, and flatter myself, I have as good, if not a better right, to be at the Head of the Physicians than any man on the continent. You know my [own] Services and the sacrifices I have made, consequently it will be needless [again] to enumerate them.

I can rely on your Friendship and am

Dear Sir

Your most obedient and very humble servant

John Cochran

Doctor Craik whom you well know, [and] will have an interview with [before] he leaves Town, He can [tell] you the characters of most of [the] medical gentlemen and I wish, from his impeachability and known Integrity some attention could be paid for [opinions]; The service would be greatly appreciated by [JC]

[James Duane Papers, NYHS]

To James Duane

Camp Totowa Bridge Oct. 20th 1780

Dear Sir:

I was favored with yours of the 22nd of September and the 6th Instant, and give you my warmest Thanks for the attention you paid to my Interest and that of the Gentlemen recommended to your Notice. I hope, it will be the constant Endeavour of each and all of us, to act such a part, as will entitle us to a continuation of your Favor and that of Congress.

The honorable Manner, in which I was elected Chief Physician to the Army, is very flattering and pleasing, and it gives me the highest satisfaction, that my past Conduct has been acceptable.

The Director General does not seem altogether well pleased with me for running him so hard. He charges me with giving him opposition; he is much mistaken, if he thinks I wanted to supplant him, for be assured, I would not exchange stations. I must acknowledge myself rather hasty in my Conjectures respecting t[he] Hospital arrangement; judging from former [times] I had little reason to expect any thing would be done. You may rest perfectly satisfied that no Person or Persons have inflamed me against Congress; my own Feelings, in consequence of what I term Injustice, have been the sole cause of my Discontent. I cannot conceive why such Discrimination between us officers and the L[ine]. Do not surgeons in the Field undergo every sp[ecies] of Fatigue, Hardship and Inconveniency with t[hem], and surely Hospital surgeons run greater risk three to one, by contracting Diseases in attending on the sick. Cutting us off from our half pay in the new arrangement I look upon, to be a very great Hardship and will be attended with bad consequences, and though it should not produce many Resignations, yet Men cannot be brought to do their Duty with that satisfaction and alacrity which could be wished for, and will always create Jealousies. From trifling Matters of this [kind] Congress loses much of their Consequence and our Conf[idence]; however, I am not without hope that on a proper [repres]entation, they will attend to any Defects, which may [be poi]nted out and amend them. I flatter myself that Congress means to make up the Depreciation of our Money; if they do not many of us are most effectually ruined, and I doubt not you will acknowledge that the greatest Injustice will be done us. We desire nothing more than to be put on the same Footing with the Army, or to be placed in that state, which is most conformable to the Custom of other Nations. These I am [sure] you will allow are reasonable requests [gra]nting these, you will discover your Love and affection [of] your officers, and obtain Love for Love, but in adopting a different Line of Conduct, you must expect [curses] instead of Prayers, as a Natural Consequence. Is it not extremely hard for me to part with so much of my property, to officers, for half pay, while I am excluded, who have shared in every Toil with them.

You complain that Congress have not Power, and attribute many of our misfortunes to the indolence of the states. This may be true respecting many Matters but cannot hold good respecting us, for one single Resolve, which may be contained in three Lines, would put us allright, we should be perfectly contented and fully [sa]tisfied and no more reviling would be heard from our Quarters. All would be love and Harmony. [I would] wish for the sake of my Country, Posterity and that honorable Body that, they were near the Divinity, in perfection, for by them we rise or fall.

I had a Letter this Evening from Walter, dated the 6th Inst. at Providence. He had been as far East, as Boston, and proposed returning immediately to his own house; He informs that he coughed but once, which was the fourth Day after setting out on his Journey, by which I conclude he is much better. I wish he could go as far to the southward, even as[far as] Annapolis for the [time].

I am with the most obliging respect and Esteem Dear Sir,
your sincere Friend and very
humble servant

John Cochran

P.S. Doctor Craik begs to present his most respectful compliments.

[James Duane Papers, NYHS]

To Mr. Fisher

New Windsor, December 8th 1780

Sir:

The Boat which brought my Baggage had on Board a Barrel of Peas and another of Flour for Mr. Peter V. B. Livingston which was taken in, at the Manor and intended to be forwarded to him at Baskenridge. Upon inquiring of my servant He informs me that they were not left with my things. I therefore beg you will ask the Boat man what is become of them, and if still on Board please to order them to be left at

Mr. Ellison's, New Windsor, as I have an opportunity of forwarding them in a day or two. You will give me information of this by the return of Dr. Latimer who goes over to Fishkill and much oblige

Your humble servant

John Cochran

[Schuyler Papers, NYPL]

To James Duane

Manor of Livingston December 10th 80

Dear Sir

I arrived at this Place on Sunday week, where I found all well and shall return to Camp in a few Days. I hope before this time all our Hospitals affairs are determined by Congress to the satisfaction of the Department. I am informed that a certain Mr. Wells, one of the Commissioners of Accounts, at Albany is extremely ill of Dropsy, a Disorder which seldom fails to do execution, without the assistance of one of the Faculty, which will produce a Vacancy. Walter is now abroad, and cannot apply himself to you for your Interest in procuring him the Place, therefore I wish to mention this Matter to you, to prevent your engaging your Interest to any other, as I know he is desirous of accepting that office. I am Dear Sir

yours most sincerely,

John Cochran

[James Duane Papers, NYHS]

To John Lamb

New Windsor December 25th 80

Dear Sir

The Bearer Mr. Robi[n]son formerly of Capt. Mott's Company, agreeable to your recommendation, called on the Pay-Master for his Pay, but from certain Excuses is put off. Perhaps these Excuses have a real Foundation, therefore he may have no cause of Complaint for the present.

He further wishes to have some Clothing of which he stands much in Need, being almost naked, this can be procured by an order from you, on which it will be delivered, and waits on you for that purpose. He is teaching a small School within a few Hundred Yards of my Quarters and has the care of one of my Children, I have assured him you will see Justice done him as far as Circumstances of the Times and his situation will admit us.

He requested a Line from me, therefore excuse my indulging him and giving you this trouble.

I am with the Compliments of the season Dear Sir

Yours most sincerely

John Cochran

[NYHS]

To Samuel Webb

New Windsor March 4th 1781

Dear Sir

I was favored with yours of the 28th ultimo this Day, also another of a former Date which, I did not answer, because of no opportunity. The Machine I ordered to be sent to me with all the possible Despatch and I hope to receive it soon.

I have not wrote to the Governor, because I have expected to set out for that place for these 10 Days last past, and shall get under way for it tomorrow morning and you may depend every power of mine shall be exerted to obtain the Desire of Mrs. Banker.

I am sorry for her situation and shall omit no opportunity of rendering her my best services.

Take care of your self and give my Love to Mrs. Webb, my Favorite, Mrs. Banker, and Family and believe me

Dear Sir

Yours most sincerely

John Cochran

[Samuel B. Webb Papers, Yale University]

To the Board of War

June 4th 1781

Gentlemen:

I would recommend Doctor Joseph Young a deranged Senior Surgeon Doctors Goodwin Wilson, Daniel Jenifer, Samuel Edmundson and George Campbell eldest Surgeons Mates in the Hospital to fill the Vacancies as Hospital Physicians and Surgeons in the Hospital Department occasioned by the Resignations of Doctors Bloomfield, Scott, Hagen, Jackson and the promotion of Doctor Burnet.

(agreed to)

I am Gentlemen etc.

John Cochran DMH

[Papers of the Continental Congress, NA]

To Joseph Carleton

Camp near Dobb's Ferry July 18th 1781

Sir

On my arrival in Camp, two Days ago, I was favored with yours, containing a rule of the Board of War for returns to the last of April. The return of the officers of the Medical Department and the sick in the Hospitals have been transmitted to the medical Committee to that Period. I shall furnish monthly returns to the Board of War, of the above regularly, as soon as they come to hand. The scattered and distant situation of the different Hospitals, will prevent me from being so early in my returns as I would wish.

I am

Sir

Your most obedient and vary humble servant

John Cochran D M H

[Beinecke Rare Book and Manuscript Library, Yale University]

To Philip Turner

Camp Peekskill October 22nd 1781

Dear Sir

I was favored with yours, but not in time to answer it by the return of the Post, as I was then at New Windsor, and was obliged to wait until I went to camp to obtain an authentic copy of the Resolves of Congress for Depreciation, which I here inclose, with a certificate of your services, all of which I hope will be satsifactory and enable you to obtain what you are so justly entitled to; for surely if a state can be so far under the influence of Satan as to defraud those who have made the sacrifices which you, and many others of our Department have done to save them; they deserve neither the Protection of Heaven nor the assistance of those upon Earth, but to be bound in everlasting chains, which may God in his infinite Judgement load them with, whenever they attempt it. I heartily wish you success and am dear Sir

Your most humble servant

John Cochran

[*Annals of Medical History* 10 (1928): 15]

January 26th 1782

This is to certify that Dr. Bodo Otto served in the capacity of Senior Surgeon in the Hospital of the United States, in the year 1776, and when the new arrangement took place in April, 1777, he was continued in that position until the subsequent reorganization of October, 1780. He was then elected a Hospital Physician and Surgeon, in which capacity he officiated until January, 1782, when a reduction occurred in the number of officers, and he was deranged.

During the whole of the time, Dr. Bodo Otto acted in the above stations, he discharged his duty with great faithfulness, care and attention. The humanity for which he was distinguished towards the brave American soldiers, claims the thanks of every lover of his country, and the success attending his practice will be a sufficient recommendation of his ability in his profession.

Given under my hand, the 26th day of January, 1782.

John Cochran
Director of the Hospitals

[Gibson, p. 321]

To George Washington

New Windsor 18th May 1782

Sir

In conformity with your Excellency's Request, we have perused the Letter, which was submitted to us, from the Secretary of War, respecting the treatment of the Regimental Sick, of the manner in which they are to be accomodated before they become objects for the General Hospital. We perfectly agree with the Secretary at War, in his observations on the Subject. The mode recommended has been practised in our army these several years, when our Circumstances would admit of it; and nothing was wanting to compleat the System, but the Hospital Tents which could not be obtained, the addition of which, to each Regiment, will be attended with the most salutary Effects.

That the Sick who are thus under the particular Care of their respective regimental Surgeons, may be supplied with Hospital Stores necessary for their various Cases, We are of opinion that a Quantity of Stores should be drawn in bulk from the Contractor (who will not issue in so small Quantities as may be necessary for each Regiment) and deposited in the Store of the Flying Hospital, to be issued by the Steward, agreeable to the order of the Physician of the Army, or next Junior officer, to the Sick and wounded of the Flying Hospital, as well as those in the regimental Hospital Tents. A report is to be made by the regimental Surgeons to the Physician of the Army, of the Number of the sick of each Regiment, of their Names, Diseases and Companies every two Days—that no Deception may be practised, and to enable him to be as accurate as possible, and observe every Species of Oeconomy in the orders for Issues consistent with the good of the Sick.

We would also recommend so soon as the Sick become subjects of the Hospital Tents that one half of their usual rations of Beef and Bread and all their Spirits be deducted, which will in some degree compensate for the expense of the Stores. The Director and Physician are sufficiently empowered to order the necessary Supply of medicines for the use of the Regimental Sick.

We have the Honor to be your Excellency's most obedient and very Humble Servants.

John Cochran D.M.H.
James Craik Physician to the Army
John Latimer Surgeon

[George Washington Papers, 4th series, vol. 198, LC]

To Andrew Craigie

New London June 19th 1782

Dear Sir

Sundry of the Regiments in this Quarter begin to be sickly and the surgeons cannot attend to their Complaints for want of medicines, consequently the Hospitals will become very much crowded, which at this season of the year will be productive of the worst of consequences; you will therefore lose no time in forwarding to the Army such medicines as you have on hand without waiting to complete the whole Estimate, and I wish you could come yourself to give the necessary directions and attend to the replenishing the Regimental Chests which is a very important Matter at this period. The few Chests you have sent are of no use at present as Mr. Root your Mate is not arrived and you requested Doctor Craik that, they should not be delivered until his arrival.

The secretary at War who left us this morning, seeing the absolute necessity, there is for the medicines being with the Army, has promised to see that you are furnished with the means of sending them, even should it be done at his own Expense.

I wish you would inquire of Mr. Williams about my Letter Book, which I forgot in Philadelphia. I want it very much and shall be ruined if it miscarries. Plan to ask Willson about my sword and Carabine. I gave him an order for the morning I left Philadelphia. Cannot you contrive some Day to bring the whole with you?

I am with Compliments to all the Gentlemen of the department and as many others as you please

Dear Sir

Your very humble servant

John Cochran

[Andrew Craigie Papers, American Antiquarian Society, Worcester, Massachusetts]

To George Washington

Fishkill August 6th 1782

Sir

Being called on last spring to form an Estimate of Medicines, Instruments, Stores etc. for the Hospitals of the United States, for one year, I presented the same to the Secretary at War on the 6th of May last, and enforced the compliance with my Requisition in the strongest Terms, but more particular the immediate supply of Doctor Craik's Estimate for the Field (which was included in the general one) a very small part of which has yet been furnished, which will reduce us to very great Difficulties, if some effective means should not be fallen on to give us a sufficient supply, not being provided for the most triffling Incidents.

The Articles now most in Demand, both for the Hospitals and the Field service are

Bed Cases, Pillow Cases, Shirts, Sheets, Blankets, Old Linnen, Lint, Tow, Bandages, Thread, Pins, Ointments, some few Articles of medicine to make up the general assortment and a small sum of money to purchase Vegetables, for the sick and wounded and to defray sundry incidental Charges.

The Hospital now opening at Colonel Jackson's Huts, is destitute of Bed Cases, Pillow Cases, sheets, Blankets and some articles of Furniture.

I cannot learn by any late Regulations in what manner the regimental sick are to be supplied with stores, tho' a scheme had been recommended for that Purpose some time ago and the sick are suffering.

The above is submitted to your Excellency's consideration while I have the honor to be with

Respect and Esteem

Your Excellency's most obedient and very humble servant

John Cochran DMH

[George Washington Papers, 4th series, vol. 203, LC]

To Timothy Pickering

West Point October 15th 1782

I will consider it as a particular favour if you will order the Artifices to make a small bedstead, such a one as was made for General Gates. I am obliged to lie very uncomfortable on three very small [stools] and in consequence of catching a cold have gotten a return of fever.

I am still your very

humble servant

John Cochran

[NA 93, 24126]

To Timothy Pickering

Camp Verplank's Point October 23d 1782

Sir:

Previous to my knowledge of the destination, of the Winter Quarters of the Troops, & presuming at the same time that, Head Quarters would be at Newburgh, as last year, I hired a part of Mr. John Ellison's House, for the accomodation of my Family, which I propose removing there immediately, The Rooms I occupied last Winter are already taken up, by which means I am prevented from going in there, as I wanted. Since contracting with Mr. Ellison for his Rooms I have been informed that, on making your arrangements for Quarters for the Superior Officers, you have allot[t]ed this House for one; I therefore thought proper to give you this Notice, in order to prevent any disappointment to yourself or the Gentleman you intend this Quarter for.

I am

Sir

your humble servant

John Cochran

[NA 93, 24111]

To Timothy Pickering

Newburgh November 2d 1782

Sir

I arrived at this Place last night and cannot find that you have assigned me any Quarters. You will therefore oblige me, as soon as may be, what Provision you have made for me and where, that I may take possession.

I am

Your humble servant

J. C.

[NA 93, 24113]

To Timothy Pickering

New Windsor November 4th 1782

Sir

I was honored with your Favor of yesterday in answer to mine of the first instant relative to Quarters. Such a Favor I believe as has been seldom conferred on the Director of the Military Hospitals by the Quarter Master General of the Army of the United States. What would induce you to treat me with so much illiberality, I am at a loss to conceive. I cannot attribute your conduct to inebriety for I have more than once heard you say, you never had been drunk. Can it proceed from Ignorance of your Profession when you have wrote a whole Book on the military arts. To say you are somewhat near-sighted, is the only Excuse I can make for you, and that is a bad one.

In assigning Quarters your Partiality in Favor of those immediately under your own Inspection is too conspicuous to require any comment, while some of the gentlmen of the Department which I have the Honor to superintend, and one of them the second in command have been cooped up in a small house where the only alleviation to their Misfortune was the want of Fuel, which you in the abundance of your Oeconomical System, withheld from them.

Permit me for a moment to examine a little into this *famous* Production of yours. You say "as you have thought fit to take up Quarters, for yourself I thought it unnecessary to find you any." I fear you have put your Intellects on the wrack and strained your Comprehension beyond all due Bounds to have made this Discovery. Did I not w[rite] on from Verplank's Point that I had hired part of Mr. Ellison's House for my Family, without giving the least intimation of any Provision for myself? Can it be supposed that your having hired a seat for Mrs. Pickering should deprive you of Quarters as a public officer where your Duty called your Attendance? I should think not, and you have taken special care of yourself. Your case and mine are similar and considering the matter in this point of view I demanded Quarters for myself. You further say "This step of yours has struck every Body with whom I have conversed as exceedingly improper, especially as it deprived the General Officer next in Rank to the Commander in chief." The first part of this extraordinary Paragraph gives me no uneasiness for with those with whom you converse mostly I would wish to converse least. Thank God, I am as independent of them as I am of you. Your Frowns and their Frowns, your smiles and their smiles are all suspended in the same Balance and let whichever will predominate, I am most perfectly indifferent. In the latter part you are most criminally mistaken, for I did fairly and of my own accord without the least solicitation make General Gates an offer of the Quarters I had taken for my Family.

You go on further and say, "I and others have been embarrassed and made very uneasy and you have disobliged *one* whom I am persuaded you would not wish to offend." The embarrassments to yourself and others, which are not infrequent are of your own procuring, for had you attended to your Duty when I gave you the earliest Notice I possibly could of my having taken the Quarters, by calling on me, I would have given them up immediately even to an officer of inferior Rank to General Gates, on condition of your procuring suitable Quarters for an officer of my relative Rank in the Army, which I am well persuaded you would have very little inclination to perform. This Piece of your Conduct I attribute more to your Pride than Ignorance.

I wish you had explained yourself and told me who this *one* is whom I have so much disobliged. If you mean General Gates, you have wandered greatly in the Dark for I had the thanks of that Gentleman, conveyed to me yesterday by Colonel Tilghman, for my generously offering him the Quarters, you took no proper steps to procure.

You further mention that "as Mr. Ellison and myself are so well agreed in the case you dare say he will be able to make a shift to accomodate me at his House." I perfectly agree with you in this Instance, that as matters now stand, he will be able to accomodate me at his house extremely well exclusive of the shift which I think you had better reserve for yourself, as it may be up to you in some future Day when you may be called on to make an Arrangement of Quarters for General Officers. I do not wish you any uneasiness about my agreeing or disagreeing with Mr. Ellison. I have never differed with any Person in whose House I have been quartered and cannot help confessing that it gives me some little pain to be obliged to differ even with you.

When you receive this, you will be two Letters in my debt, I forgive the Ballance and this shall close the Correspondence. Should you conceive your Feelings injured by this reply to your scurrility, I am ready to give you any satisfaction you may demand, where Pen, Ink and Paper are not concerned.

I am
Sir
your very humble servant
John Cochran
D.M.H.

[Timothy Pickering Papers, Massachusetts Historical Society]

To Horatio Gates

New Windsor November 8th 1782

Sir

I had a note last night from one of his Excellency's Aids, that, he agreed to my being quartered on the other side of the River, agreeable to a Proposition of my own some days agao, in order that you might be accomodated near your Command, and has given orders to Colonel Pickering to provide me a good House accordingly. I set out immediately for the above purpose and when I have obtained Quarters I will remove my Baggage which I cannot conveniently do, until I have some Place to go into. This probably will not delay you more than this Day, as I shall not lose a moment to accomplish my End.

It is a little unfortunate for us both that, Colonel Pickering was either unacquainted with his Duty or that certain Prejudices prevailed too much, to permit him to execute it.

I am with due respect
Sir your very humble servant
John Cochran

[Horatio Gates Papers, NYHS]

To Henry Knox, West Point

Newburgh January 5th 1783

Dear Sir

I was favored with yours respecting the Brimstone and am exceedingly sorry that it was out of your Power to give us that Assistance which I am sure you wished to do.

Be so obliging as to furnish me with an order on your man at Springfield for one thousand pounds Brimstone and I will try my Interert with our Trusty and well beloved Timothy to get it on from that Quarter. It will at any rate (whether I succeed or not) give me an excellent Pretext to tease him.

I am, on this Piece of tattered Paper, which is the best I have got
Dear Sir

Your very humble servant

John Cochran

[Henry Knox Papers, Massachusetts Historical Society]

To Timothy Pickering

Newburgh February 2nd 1783

The inclosed was handed me yesterday by Lieut. Lee from Captain Mott whose situation for several Years has been very distressing on Account of his Health, few have suffered more or made a greater struggle for life than he has done, & I believe his present circumstances are equally as bad as he paints them. He appears to merit relief but that is out of my Power to afford him, as I know of no provision made for sick or wounded officers, unless they are put into the Hospitals alloted for the privates or they are billeted by the Magistrate. His allowance of Fuel has been too scanty heretofore for an Officer in his situation, being no more than the common allowance for an officer of his rank in Health.

I should suppose the mode by which he can be relived, is only through the Quarter master General, you will therefore give such Directions respecting him as you may judge proper and I will transmit them by the next Post.

I am

Your humble servant

John Cochran D.M.H.

[NA 93, 24258]

To Horatio Gates

Newburgh February 2nd 1783

Dear Sir

I was honored with your Favor of the 9th ultimo, by Post from Boston, relative to my Orders to Doctor Warren of the 3rd of December, to join the Army.

You may recollect, Sir, that I wrote you circumstantially respecting Doctor Warren's situation & my desire of having him drawn out of Boston, especially as the Hospital at that place was broken up, but not being able to succeed, on account of the many obstacles thrown in my way, I referred the whole matter to your Decision. My letter on the subject was dated the 27th of August last, since when I have not heard from the Doctor until the 2nd ultimo, which was in answer to mine of the 3rd of December, wherein he complains of my treating him with some Degree of severity. Surely, when the Doctor received your orders to remain in Boston, for the purposes therein contained, the least he could or ought to have done was to have communicated the contents to me, when he well knew how anxious I was to discharge my Duty and at the same time to give him every imaginable Indulgence but this neglect and inattention brought on me many reflections and a severe reprimand from the commander-in-chief, which produced my letter of the 3rd of December before alluded to.

I believe few are better acquainted with the Doctor's Merits or knew his worth & abilities in a higher point of sight than myself & I flatter myself you will do me the justice to acknowledge that when I had the Pleasure of seeing you last Summer at HeadQuarters I interested myself so much in the Doctor's Favor that I was almost afraid of being charged with impertinence.

Be assured that if I had been made acquainted with your orders to him I should not have given those of a contradictory strain, but would have paid all due deference to your commands.

I hope this relation will be sufficient to evince the rectitude of my conduct toward the Doctor and that my Heart will reserve the favorable impression you are pleased to entertain of it for which accept my heartiest Thanks

I have the honor to be with the most perfect
respect and Esteem
Dear Sir
Your most Obedient &
Very humble servant,
John Cochran

[Medical Center Library, Duke University]

To Philip Schuyler

New Windsor March 9th 1783

Sir

By virtue of an act of the Legislature of the State entitled an Act to enable John Cochran, Esqr. to locate two Thousand Acres of Waste and inappropriated lands within this State, I do hereby locate a Tract of vacant and unappropriated Land on the south side of the Mohawks River adjoining the southeast corner of fifty thousand acres, granted to William Bay and others containing two thousand acres of Land with the usual allowance of highways.

Your humble servant
John Cochran

[Schuyler Papers NYPL]

To John Neilson

Newburgh March 10th 1783

Dear Sir

I was favored with yours of the 5th instant by Mr. Tenbroeck, who at the same time delivered me one hundred pounds Jersey currency in species etcetera, which was a welcome Guest,? and for which I thank you; the Remainder of the New Jersey promission had better remain in statu quo, until aliter ? which probably may be the case when the legislature will levy a Tax for sinking it. This sum will carry me awhile; and enable me to discharge some Debts, which were becoming inconvenient.

I find the old Gentleman has paid the last Tribute to nature, after a well spent Life, may the Turf lay easy on him and I hope he is now enjoying the Felicity of the just and upright. He surely was an honest man and a true Patriot. It will make me happy to hear that you are made better by this.

I am just returned from a three Weeks siege at the Legislature of this State, which, if any thing, exceeded the attack at Trenton. You must know, I had a Claim under the King of Great Britain, upon this State, as a reduced staff officer of the last War for 2,000 acres of unappropriated lands, and have had address enough to obtain an Act for the Location and an order for the Grant. To pay the King's debt was a bitter Pill to many, but so it was that I crammed it down, and the operation was agreeable to my wishes.

Mrs. Cochran is very well as were both my little boys when I heard last from them, she begs to join me in best respects to Mrs. Neilson and hopes most ardently for the Period of Peace, when we may once more enjoy the happy meeting of our Friends.

I am
dear Sir
your most obliged Friend
and very humble servant
John Cochran

The paper is infamous, for this my Cover.

Newburgh March 10th 1783 Received of Colonel John Neilson by the hands of Mr. Cornelius Tenbroeck the sum of One hundred Pounds species, which he has been so obliging as to exchange New Jersey new emission for.

John Cochran

[John Neilson Papers, Rutgers University Library]

To John Lillie

Newburgh March 25th:[17]83

Sir

When I wrote you that the Quantity of sulphur was received, which General Knox gave the order for, I did not know how the matter was circumstanced, until Mr. Wainwright the Apothecary informed me this evening that 4 Boxes of sulphur were received said to contain 2000 pounds. He has issued 3 Boxes, the fourth remaining Box he sends by the Sergeant agreeable to your order.

When I wrote you, I supposed that half of the Quantity sent for would be sufficient to answer our purpose but as it has not, you can have no more of the Fox than the Skin.

I am your very humble Servant

John Cochran

[Massachusetts Historical Society]

To William Eustis

New Windsor Huts, June 24th 1783

Arrangement of the Hospital at New Windsor Huts

William Eustis	}
Samuel Adams	}
	} Surgeons
	}
	}
William Cogswell	}
Joseph Prescott	Mates
	}
John Brown	Steward
Daniel Hendry	Ward Master
Mary Lake	Matron

Sir

It is the order of the commander in chief that the above shall be the establishment of the Hospital, at the New Windsor Huts, for the present. You will there please to take under your Care the Department agreeable to the above List, and inform the other Gentlemen whom you have returned to me as belonging to the New Windsor Hospital that they are to consider themselves as on Furlough agreeable to the resolve of Congress of the 26th of May last and a late General Order.

I am Sir

Your humble servant

John Cochran
D.M.H.

[Massachusetts Historical Society]

To George Washington

Newburgh June 25th 1783

Dear Sir

As the happy Period is arrived which will restore us to the station of private Citizens and produce Separation, I cannot take leave of your Excellency without acknowledging that Obligation I am under to you, for your polite Treatment ever since I had the honor of serving under your Command, and be assured that my Bosom will forever glow with the warmest sentiments of gratitude for your friendly Patronage.

May your Excellency be happy and live long to enjoy the Honors of your hard earned Laurels.

Permit me, Sir, to request a certificate of my Services in the Military Department, which I shall esteem as the highest Favor.

I have the honor to be with the utmost Respect and Esteem

Your Excellency's

most obedient and very humble servant

John Cochran

[George Washington Papers, 4th series, vol. 222, LC]

To John Pierce

New York January 13th 1784

Dear Sir

I was favored with yours of the 4th instant and with Pleasure comply with your request and inclose you a list of such of the Gentlemen of the Hospital Department as are entitled to the Commutation of five years full pay, who have been deranged & come under the resolve of Congress of the 17th January 1781.

When you consult the above Resolve you must judge for yourself whether officers resigning are entitled to Commutation. I am totally ignorant of the Circumstances of Dr. Tillotson's leaving the Hospital as he negotiated that Affair with Congress. The inclosed from Doctor Turner in answer to one of mine ordering him to join the Army immediately will convince you whether he resigned or not—On the receipt of it I referred his Case to the Board of War, but not hearing from the Board & his not complying with my Orders, I was desired by the Commander in Chief to Accept of his Resignation and discontinue him in my returns, which I did and gave him Notice of the same, & he has done no duty since that Period. Doctor Crosby was to all intents & purposes considered in the same point of View with the regimental Surgeons & was a most deserving Officer. He was deranged by a resolve of Congress on a new reform of the Army.

I hope above will be satisfactory and I am

Dear Sir

Yours most sincerely

John Cochran

[NA 93, 4598]

To John Neilson

New York May 4th 1784

Dear Sir

I saw Jacques in town a few Days since and talked over our Money

Affairs and he very generously charged not quite two half Joes, for which I am obliged to him as well as to you for your friendly Offices in this and many other matters *quae nunc reddere longum est*. As I must keep my Jaws wagging while here I wish you would send me a Dozen of your best cured Hams, as soon as convenient and a few Pounds of butter by way of lubricating the Passage, and will remit you the amount by the return of the Boat, if sufficiently in blast and I will send Jacques his half Joe, being the Balance in Debt at the same time.

If you can prevail on that Heaven born son of Vulcan, Tom Northwick to take down the Smoke Jack in my old House and fix the proper Flyers; which are with another set in the Garret and which he took off while the British had Possession of Brunswick and send it to me by Mr. Voorhies you will do me another kindness.

I inclose you, your Receipt for the hapen left in your Hands against Surgery and beg you will send me those I gave for the monies received, which I Suppose is Necessary.

All Friends are well; Compliments to Mrs. Neilson and Family [I am]

Dear Sir

Your sincere Friend and very humble servant

John Cochran

As the new Emission in your Hands, belonging to me, may be troublesome to you, please send it by Mr. Voorhies.

[John Neilson Papers, Rutgers University Library]

To Thomas Riche

Philadelphia June 25th 1784

Sir

On my arrival at this place received a line from you and heartily wish it was in my power to Comply with it—I will Just inform you of my Circumstances my business will but just Support me and my Children—the way I am in. I have some landed property which I have Advertized for Sale on purpose to pay my debts, and as Soon as I can Sell it for Cash am determined to pay all my debts and your[s] Sir will be one of the first.

I am Sir your Humble Servant

John Cochran

[Henry E. Huntington Library, San Marino, California]

To John Pierce

New York July 4th 1784

Dear Sir

When you wrote me some time ago for a return of officers of the Hospital Department who were entitled to Commutation, you mentioned Doctor Tillotson having applied for the same.

I made out the return & forwarded it to you agreeable to your request, and informed you that, Doctor Tillotson having retired from the Service previous to my taking charge of the Department I know nothing of his Pretension, since when, I find that he did not resign as had been alleged, but was deranged by Congress, upon some new Arrangement taking place and altho' the Act for granting certain allowances for half Pay to the medical Department, may have passed subsequent to his retiring from service, yet from the spirit of the act, it appears clearly that the Hospital officers are meant to be put on the same footing both with officers of the Line, therefore I would con[sider] Doctor Tillotson as justly entitled to his Com[mutation]. If upon examining [in]to this Matter & conv[ersing] with him on the subject, who can explain it much better than I can, you should be induced to be of the same opinion with me, I doubt not you will grant him Commutation, should any form Certificate be wanting only point out the Time? and I will furnish it.

When you finally settled my Account there was deducted 100 Dollars which I received from Mr. Robert Morris, some time before, & for which I gave him my Note, I am extremely obliged to Mr. Morris for settling it in that way & shall always esteem it an act of Friendship. I hope you have the Note as your voucher, so that it may not, thro' mistake, come against me in any future Day.

I am Dear Sir your very humble etc.

John Cochran

[NA 93, 29325]

To John Neilson

New York March 31st 1786

Dear Sir

I received your Favor some time ago with £40 exchanged for Paper; your ready compliance with my request claims my acknowledgements; but I cannot stop here for away must go the whole; I have by way of a Venture sent 700 Dollars more and must beg of your Attention to the exchange of that Sum, as soon as possible, if practicable. I have to pay a considerable sum of money on the first of May next and I fear shall be much puzzled to make it up, for a Dollar or a half Joe is almost as rare to be seen at this Moment as a swallow in Winter since the attempt of the Legislature to make Paper money. I owe Peter Nephew of Middle Brook £4/10 New York currency for Butter, which I beg you will pay him out of the Paper when exchanged. I have inclosed you my account for Medicines and attendance etcetera—with a receipt, the amount of which you will please to place to the credit of my account. When at Leisure, I will thank you to furnish me with a state of my account with you that I may know how I stand in These Days of looking out Sharp. If I owe a Butcher or a Baker a Dollar, I am bored without Mercy, however I keep altogether clear with these Gentry. Compliments to Mrs. Neilson and Family and am

Dear Sir

Yours most sincerely

John Cochran

[John Neilson Papers, Rutgers University Library]

To John B. Schuyler

New York, June 26th 1788

Dear Sir

This will be delivered to you by Mr. Dirck Lefferts of this City who is on a Jaunt to the Saratoga Springs for the recovery of his Health, by my recommendation, and intends to remain some time in order to give them a fair chance. If your Father's small house is empty at that place and you will give him an order for the use of it you will confer a Favor on me as well as Mr. Lefferts who is my particular Friend, and I am,

Dear Sir

Yours most affectionately

John Cochran

[Schuyler Papers, NYPL]

To George Washington

New York, May 1st 1789

Dear Sir

Permit me to congratulate you and my Country on your appointment to the Presidency of the United States of America by the unanimous voice of the Citizens. That you may be happy and successful in the discharge of this important Trust, is my most ardent wish.

A reliance on the Benevolence of my Countrymen and Necessity compelled me to make an application, which I should wish I did not stand in need of. A short detail of my present Condition will justify my Request. On the eighth Day of May, 1786, I was appointed by Congress, Receiver of the Continental Quota of Taxes for this State, and Commissioner of the Loan Office for the same, with a Salary of one Thousand Dollars per annum: this with the assistance of my professional service, afforded me a comfortable subsistence for my Family, until Congress by an act of the 23d of March 1787 deprived all the Loan Officers, of their office rent, Clerk and every other charge, except that of Stationery, which from the vast multiplicity of Business transacted in my office, being at the seat of Congress, has left me by no means an adequate compensation for my Trouble.

The Practice of Physic is become no longer an object with me, for my late Indisposition has confined me so long that my Business has fallen into the hands of others and it would be difficult to recover it again, should I ever be able to go through the Drudgery attended on that Profession.

The principal part of my property consists in uncultivated and unproductive Lands. This situation induces me to look up to my Country for a continuation in their service, by holding an Appointment best suited to my Abilities. My appointment under the late Arrangement, being connected with the Collection of the Treasury of this State, such an employment under the new Constitution, would be very agreeable to my Wishes and I have a confidence that I am sufficiently competent to discharge the several Duties of said office with propriety. How far my former services and present situation may entitle me to this request, is best known to your Excellency and with you I leave the issue, persuaded that I shall not be forgotten.

If anything improper in this application has escaped me I trust your Forgiveness.

I have the honor to subscribe myself
Your Excellency's
most obedient and very humble servant
John Cochran

[George Washington Papers, 7th series, vol. 6, LC]

To George Washington

New York July 10th 1789

Sir

I did myself the honor to address your Excellency shortly after your arrival at this Place on the subject of my being continued in the service of my Country, under the new Constitution, without designating any particular office, since when I find that Congress are about to establish three distinct offices, for the Collec[tion] of the Revenue of the Port of New York, viz. A Collector, a naval officer and Surveyor. A nomination to the naval office would be extremely agreeable to me and from the best information, I can obtain, respecting the duties of said office, I flatter myself that I am altogether competent. I am the more induced to make this request as there has been no such office instituted in this state, since the Revolution, therefore there would be no interference with any other Person holding an office under the former Government.

I take it for granted, the Loan Officer will soon be dismissed, which makes me more solicitous to come forward at this Period, in order to have a Chance of securing something more permanent under my present circumstances and advanced stage of life, which render me incapable of pursuing my former occupation.

Permit me the Liberty of herewith inclosing two Certificates, one from the Board of Treasury and the other from Mr. Nourse, the Register, of my Conduct as Commissioner of the Loan Office for the State of New York during my transacting of Business of said office, which I hope will give satisfaction.

I have the honor to subscribe myself
your Excellency's
most obedient and very humble servant
John Cochran

[George Washington Papers, 7th series, vol. 6, LC]

To Philip Schuyler

New York July 3d 1792

Dear Sir

I this moment received a letter from Walter Livingston, whose misfortunes seem to overwhelm him, tho he seems to have as much Fortitude as comes to his Share under such complicated troubles. He has an ardent desire to see you. In a postscript to his letter he writes me thus. There is a particular that General Schuyler can serve me. If he is in town tell him so, if not write him so I lose no time. It is confidential Business. I must either see him, or send him a Letter by a Gentleman. It cannot be trusted to the Post.

Your Sister, who is in the utmost distress, presses her love to you, and begs you to give him every advice in your Power, that it may contribute to assisting him in his difficulties.

I am with Love to Mrs. Schuyler and the Family,

Dear Sir

Yours most affectionately

John Cochran

[Emmet Collection, 6062, NYPL]

To Philip Schuyler

New York July 17th 1792

Dear Sir:

By Captain Marsellis, I send you five hundred Dollars for my son James, which you will please to pay him on Order and I hope in the space of a few weeks to send him the like sum. He appears anxious to purchase a small place in the neighbourhood in order to fix himself in that Country, and I am anxious to assist and see him gratified.

Walter went up to pay his Brother a visit and I hope will continue some time with him, this is a bad Place for a Boy of Walter's disposition to acquire knowledge in his Profession in, where Study and application are necessary for that purpose; I hope James will be useful to him.

A Nesbit from Scotland purposes waiting on you. He comes recommended by Doctor Robison one of the Professors, Edinburgh, as a Person of very mechanical Genius, and particularly excels in constructing Locks for inland Navigation in which Business he has had much experience, by pursuing it, for many Years both in Scotland and in Holland, if my information can be depended on. I hope by conversing with him you will find him worthy your notice and encouragement.

Immediately on receiving yours of the 8th Instant I wrote to Walter Livingston informing him of your readiness to give him your aid, as far as was consistent in extricating him out of his disagreeable situation, this has given your Sister better spirits.

Our Love to Mrs. Schuyler and the family and believe me Dear Sir yours most affectionately

John Cochran

[The New York Academy of Medicine Library]

To George Washington

New York August 1st 1793

Sir

I have been again attacked with a Paralytick Stroke, which had until this period rendered me incapable to discharge the duties of my office. I am now recovering very fast, and the public business is no longer suspended. A very close attention to business for the future will, however, probably be inconsistent with a perfect reestablishment of my health, and prevent me from taking more exercise, and enjoying a mind more free from care. For these reasons I wish to resign, provided the appointment of my son James to this office which I hold would meet with your approbation. With respect to its emoluments, it is the same thing which of us hold it. The same benevolent motives therefore, which governed in appointing me to the office, will I flatter myself, induce the appointment of my son James.

I am with the greatest
respect and gratitude,
your obedient and
Humble Servant

John Cochran

[George Washington Papers, 7th series, vol. 6, LC]

APPENDIX A:

LETTERS TO JOHN COCHRAN

A youthful portrait of Lafayette by Jean-Baptiste Weyler, probably done during Lafayette's return visit to France in 1779

In the possession of the author

Lafayette to John Cochran

St. Jean D'Angely, near Rochefort,
June 10 [1779]

I feel very happy, my dear doctor, in finding an occasion to tell you how heartily I lament our separation. It is, indeed, highly pleasing for me to be under so many obligations to you, because there is no gratitude in the world which can exceed the bounds of my affection for the good doctor Bones—that name I shall ever give you—and I sincerely wish, I even earnestly hope, you will, before long, hear from my own mouth, the ardent love I entertain for America, the respect and affection which bind me to our great General; and the present situation of affairs give me some happy notions of my seeing soon the American shores. That happiness I most ardently wish for.

My health, dear doctor—that very health you have almost brought back from the other world—has been since as strong and hearty as possible. From every one of my countrymen, from the first to the last, a thousand flattering marks of attention have been conferred upon me. I have left Versailles and Paris some days ago, and am for the present with the King's own Regiment of Dragoons, which he gave after my arrival, and some Regiments of Infantry. That station I shall, perhaps, have before long for beginning a more active life and coming nearer our Red friends.

As during my fit of illness the watch I had then was of great use to you for feeling the pulse, I thought such a one might be convenient, which I have entrusted to the Chevalier de la Luzerne, and I beg leave to present you with. I did fancy that adorning it with my heroic friend's picture would make it acceptable.

Be so kind, my dear sir, as to present my respects to your lady, and my best compliments to your brother doctors, and my brother officers of the Army. Tell them how sincerely I love them; how much I desire to join them again. I was in hopes Lts. Howard and Parker had a design to visit France, but I don't hear from them. If any such friend of mine comes to this country I hope their first step will be to renew our acquaintance.

There are no interesting news for the moment, but a general peace in Germany. England makes its best efforts; Spain will, I think, soon join, and poor old England will get a bad stroke this campaign.

Farewell, my dear doctor. Whenever I meet with coursing [howlowing] and drinking, I call again to my mind the happy days we have had in Boston. I hope they will begin before long, and I will tell you myself how sincerely I am, dear doctor,

Your most obedient humble servant

Lafayette

[Proceedings of the NJHS, 4th ser., vol. 5 (1920): 117–18]

George Washington to John Cochran

West Point, 16 August, 1779

Dear Doctor,

I have asked Mrs. Cochran and Mrs. Livingston to dine with me tomorrow; but I am not in honor bound to appraise them of their fare? As I hate deception, even where the imagination only is concerned, I will. It is needless to premise, that my table is large enough to hold the ladies. Of this they had ocular proof yesterday. To say how it is usually covered, is rather more essential; and this shall be the purport of my letter.

Since our arrival at this happy spot, we have had a ham, sometimes a shoulder of bacon, to grace the head of the table; a piece of roast beef adorns the foot; and a dish of beans, or greens, almost imperceptible, decorates the centre. When the cook has a mind to cut a figure, which I presume will be the case tomorrow, we have two beefsteak pies, or dishes of crabs, in addition, one on each side of the centre dish, dividing the space and reducing the distance between dish and dish to about six feet, which without them would be near twelve feet apart. Of late he has had the surprising sagacity to discover, that apples will make pies; and it is a question if, in the violence of his efforts, we do not get one of apples, instead of having both beefsteaks. If the ladies can put up with such entertainment, and will submit to partake of it on plates, once tin but now iron (but because so by the labor of scouring), I shall be happy to see them; and am, dear Doctor, your,

G.W.

[NYHS]

Richard Peters to John Cochran

War Office Octo. 10th 1781

Sir

It appears to us that the Hospitals at the Yellow Springs, Albany & Boston should be immediately broke up as the number of Patients are not sufficient to warrant the expense. We have ordered all the Patients at Yellow Springs to be sent to the Hospital at Philadelphia & you will please to give directions as to all the officers at that Hospital whose services being no longer necessary at that Place, they may be more usefully employed elsewhere. The Patients at Boston & Albany had better be boarded at private Houses or removed to some other Hospital where they can be taken care of without the expense attending their present situation. The Patients being removed from the Albany & Boston Hospitals, you will discharge all unnecessary officers or Persons employed therein & give orders for the Employment of the Officers necessary to be retained in the Department at places where their services are more necessary. We have been favored [with yours] of the 26th ultimo with the papers inclosed. We shall do everything in our power on the subject but you know well that the means of providing the Articles do not lie with us, & we are convinced the Financer has more than [the necessary] Ability to comply with the Demands from all Quarters.

We have the honor to be your very obedt. servant

Richard Peters

[Richard Peters Papers, HSP]

Robert Morris to John Cochran

[Philadelphia] Office of Finance 4. Jan: 1782

Sir,

I have been honored with your Favor of the thirty first of last Month stating the Wants of your Department which it would give me very sincere Pleasure to be able to releive. You must I am sure be sensible that even if the Means were in my Power there would be an Impropriety in paying one Department while the other Departments and the Line of the Army remain unpaid. I am under the Necessity therefore of requesting you to wait until I am in Capacity to make general Payments when your Department will come in for its Proportion and in the Interim the Subsistence allowed to others will be paid to them in Proportion to the several rations they may be entitled to draw.

With great respect I have the Honor to be Sir your most obedient and humble Servant

R[obert] M[orris]

[Robert Morris Papers, LC]

John Pierce to John Cochran

West Point January 5, 1784

Dear Sir:

Many Characters claim the Commutation who have been in your Department, and without any legal information I am unable to do them justice—it will therefore be a public obligation as well as a private one to these Gentlemen, if you will ascertain what Persons deranged in 1781 or 1782 who have been in the Hospital are entitled to this commutation of five years pay.

I have a Letter before me from Doct. Turner who says "among the resignations you will find a number of Doctors which resigned, but not my name among them, I stand fair to hold fast the encouragement of Congress"—I have deferred my answer to him until I can have the pleasure of a line from you—

The settlement of pay & commutation for your Department was closed this Day.

I am with real esteem & friendship
yours

[John Pierce]

Doct. Tillotson has applied, also Doct. Crosbey., if the Latter was considered as a regimental surgeon I think he must be entitled.

[NA 93, 29308]

APPENDIX B:
UNPUBLISHED LETTERS
RELATING TO THE MEDICAL DEPARTMENT

Philip Schuyler to Gouverneur Morris

Albany February 18th 1778

Dear Sir:

Permitt me to Introduce to you the bearer Doctor Stringer a brother sufferer from the envy and malevolence of that selfish set who with such unremitting vigilance and rancour prosecute those who will not be their tools, he has suffered much in his reputation and fortune and I fear that much of it has been occasioned by that Countenance which it was my duty to give him as being a faithful Servant of the public and one whom perhaps would not have been exposed to the Ill treatment he has experienced if It had not been out of resentment to me—permit me to narrate his case. In August 1775 when sickness was spreading thro the army under my command with an alarming rapidity, When no Hospital was provided for by Congress, no medical assistance other than the Surgeons of regiments, when we were totally destitute of Medicines, I Intreated Mr. Stringer to repair to Ticonderoga and afford his assistance, the reasons he gave for refusing the request were so clearly satisfactory that nothing but the highest necessity would satisfy me in repeating the request, at length he was prevailed not only to give up an extensive and beneficial practice and enter Into the public Service, but brought along with him a large Stock of his own medicines. The late Mr. Lynch was well aware that nothing but Continuance in the public Service, with generous appointments would compensate for the Sacrifice the Doctor made, and he accordingly promised both Dr. Stringer and me that he would use his influence to procure him the directorship in this department, Congress conferred It on him soon after Mr. Lynch's return to Philadelphia, and Mr. Stringer discharged the duty of his office with great attention and proper Oeconomy and to the Satisfaction of Every honest man, but unfortunately It was discovered that he was a Yorker, and what was worse he was supposed to have procured the appointment thro me. In 1776 the Army experienced a want of Medicines and now the Cry became loud against him, altho It was by no means his fault, Congress had been applied to in February before, Medicines were promised him from the Eastward but none arrived at length the Complaint was brought Into Congress whether In particular against Dr. Stringer or the whole Medical branch In general I cannot say, the Consequence was an order that enquiry should be made Into the conduct of the directors of the Hospitals, their Surgeons and this order I received on the 12th of January 1777 at Fish kill two days after my return here, I advised the Doctor he must prepare for an Enquiry, which would soon be made, but on that evening (the 28th of January) he received a Dismission from Congress dated the 9th of January, you will please to observe that if I had received the first Order at Albany the Dr. might have been tried, certainly acquitted with honor, . . . and yet, dismissed chagrined as he was to have such a Stigma thrown upon him by the representative body of the united States, he still continued to discharge the duties of his office until his Successor arrived which was late in March. The power of Congress to dismiss one of their Servants without giving him a tryal no one will be hardy enough to contest, but In what the Justice of such dismissions consists I believe none will be able to penetrate; But political necessity and the great Interests of the States may make it necessary to Sacrifice an Individual to the weal of the whole, Granted, but is It necessary to add Insult to the Injury occasioned by necessity, nay is It not Incumbent on every body to Support the accused In all cases until his guilt is proved and can bare assertion be deemed sufficient proof, surely not. However so It is, The Doctor's case is distressing, he cannot Contest without the power of Congress he wishes however for some reparation and that Congress would by some appointment wipe away that Stigma which he is willing to believe was occasioned by the Irresistable force of necessity, I am greatly interested my Dear Sir in seconding his wish, for I am altho unintentionally the cause of his Misfortunes, will you be good enough to Interest Yourself in his or rather In my favor, and procure him If possible the Directorship of this department upon Dr. Pott's resignation. I dare answer for his Conduct under It., he is fully competent to the business and I have the fullest Confidence that the business will be carried on with as much Oeconomy as is possible; I am informed Messrs Chase and Carrol are out at Congress, should they be there when this arrives permitt me to beg that you will shew them this. . . .

Philip Schuyler

[Gouverneur Morris Papers, CUL—Special Collections]

William Shippen, Jr., to Gouverneur Morris

Moor Hall 17. June 1778

My dear Sir

I am importuned by all the sons of Aesculapius to apply to you in their behalf & intreat you to finish the new arrangement of the medical department—much good will arise to and expence be saved for the public by making only one System, & that much in the manner you have before you, a great many useless & ignorant officers will be discharged, men of science will be enlisted & no more employed than are necessary—Many offer now for places, I put them all off till the examination, which should be held immediately—any particular duties of the subordinate officers must be pointed out by the medical triumvirate as necessity requires—Dr. Jones is now at Trenton & I hear intends for camp in a few days.

Your name sake, Mease, Nesbit &c are here anxiously waiting to go into the city & by all accounts we can procure, to morrow will be the day.

I expect in a day or two to send you my general return, have been very busy here these ten days in removing the sick from the army & instituting new hospitals in its rear. Our Army is numerous & in fine order, plentifully supplied with every thing but cloaths—Tents enough arrived to day, for them all.

Cochran, Hutchinson conjure you as their patron & protector to use your great influence in our Behalf—please to present my Compts to Messrs Duer, Banister, RH. Lee etc. Your most obedient

& Humble Servt

W. Shippen, Jr.

[Gouverneur Morris Papers, CUL—Special Collections]

Gouverneur Morris to William Shippen, Jr.

Phila 17th May 1779

Sir:

I had the Honor of yours of the 15th Instant this Morning and confess that I am not a little astonished at the Contents of it. You profess yourself unwilling to derange a System which is now in exceeding good order etc. You have so often & so fully acknowledge the Defects of this System, a System which I cannot but think pregnant with Disorder and Profusion that it is impossible for a Man of my plain understanding to comprehend the Reasons which have so suddenly converted you into an Advocate of it or it into Perfection. But what is most surprizing in the Harmony which untill very lately at least hath certainly not existed but which I now learn from such high Authority prevails throughout. It is very possible that you may suppose the Committee have time to throw away in Attention upon the versatile Projects which the Gentlemen of your Department may from time to time adopt. Permit me to assure you that this is not the Case. Speaking for myself I will avow the same Earnestness to arrange and establish the Medical Department which I have hitherto been impelled by but I neither can not will cooperate in Measures which appear to me pernicious. I am to intreat that you will meet the medical Committee at the State House on Wednesday Afternoon at 6:00 oclock and bring with you such of the medical Gentlemen as are in Town as also the present System and the Form in which Business is conducted under it.

I have the Honor to be
with the greatest Respect
Sir—
your most obedient
&
humble Servant
Gouv Morris

[Gouverneur Morris Papers, CUL—Special Collections]

SELECT BIBLIOGRAPHY

Manuscript Sources

American Antiquarian Society (Worcester, Massachusetts)
  Andrew Craigie Papers
American Philosophical Society (Philadelphia, Pennsylvania)
  Benjamin Franklin Papers
  Feinstone Papers
Chester County Historical Society (West Chester, Pennsylvania)
  Papers of H. F. C. Heagey
  Papers of Harry K. Wilson
Columbia University-Special Collections (New York, New York)
  Gouverneur Morris Papers
Delaware Hall of Records (Dover, Delaware)
  Francis Theodore Tilton typescript, 7 vols., n.d.; "Dr. James Tilton of Delaware 1747–1822."
Historical Society of Pennsylvania (Philadelphia, Pennsylvania)
  Gratz Collection
  Richard Peters Papers
  Jonathan Potts Papers
  Jacob and Isaac Taylor Papers
  Letter Book of James Steele
  Papers of Anthony Wayne
Library of Congress (Washington, D.C.)
  George Washington Papers
  Papers of the American Revolution
Library of the National Society of the Daughters of the American Revolution (Washington, D.C.)
  Orderly Book of William Stewart
Massachusetts Historical Society (Boston, Massachusetts)
  Timothy Pickering Papers
University of Michigan-William L. Clements Library (Ann Arbor, Michigan)
  Papers of Sir Henry Clinton
  James McHenry Papers
National Archives (Washington, D.C.)
  Papers of the Continental Congress
  War Department Collection of Revolutionary War Records—Class 93.
New Jersey Historical Society (Newark, New Jersey)
  Ely Autograph Collection
  Hugh Hughes Letter-Book
  James Parker Papers

New Jersey State Library (Trenton, New Jersey)
  William S. Stryker Collection
New-York Historical Society (New York, New York)
  James Duane Papers
  William Duer Papers
  Horatio Gates Papers
  Livingston Family Papers
New York Public Library (New York, New York)
  Emmet Collection
  Schuyler Papers
Oneida Historical Society (Utica, New York)
  Erastus Clark MS
Presbyterian Historical Society (Philadelphia, Pennsylvania)
  Cochran Family Genealogy
Rutgers University Library-Special Collections (New Brunswick, New Jersey)
  Livingston Papers
  John Neilson Papers
Yale University (New Haven, Connecticut)
  Webb Family Papers

Published Sources

[Abercrombie, James H.] "A Description of the Yellow Springs in Pennsylvania." *The Portfolio*, 3d series, vol. 4 (July 1810): 44–47.

Abstracts of Wills on File in the Surrogate's Office, City of New York. 15 vols. New York: The New-York Historical Society, 1893–1907.

Alden, John R. *General Charles Lee, Traitor or Patriot?* Baton Rouge: Louisiana State University Press, 1951.

Applegate, Howard L. "The American Revolutionary War Hospital Department," and sequels. *Military Medicine* 26 (1961): 296–306, 379–82, 450–53, 551–53, 616–18.

——. "The Medical Administrators of the American Revolutionary Army." *Military Affairs* 25 (1961): 1–10.

——. "The Provincial Medical Departments during the American Revolutionary War." Ph.D. dissertation, Syracuse University, 1962.

Bagg, Mose M. *The Pioneers of Utica.* Utica, N.Y.: Curtiss & Childs, 1877.

Baker, William S. *Itinerary of General Washington from June 15, 1775 to December 23, 1783.* Philadelphia: J. B. Lippincott Co., 1892.

Balch, Thomas, ed. *The Journal of Claude Blanchard, 1780–1783.* Albany, N.Y.: J. Munsell, 1876.

Ballagh, James Curtis, ed. *The Letters of Richard Henry Lee.* 2 vols. New York: The Macmillan Co., 1912–14.

Barclay, Cornelia B. *Our Branch of the Barclays.* New York: Frederick H. Hitchcock, 1915.

Barclay, Sidney, ed. *Personal Recollections of the American Revolution.* New York: Rudd & Carleton, 1859.

Batchelder, Samuel F. "Harvard Hospital Surgeons of 1775." *Harvard Alumni Bulletin* 22 (1920): 501–13.

Baxter, Katherine Schuyler. *A Godchild of Washington: A Picture of the Past.* London and New York: F. T. Neely, 1897.

Bell, Whitford J., Jr. "The Court Martial of William Shippen, Jr." *Journal of the History of Medicine and the Allied Sciences* 19 (1964): 218–39.

——. *John Morgan, Continental Doctor.* Philadelphia: University of Pennsylvania Press, 1965.

Benedict, William H. *New Brunswick in History.* New Brunswick, N.J.: privately printed, 1925.

Biddle, Charles. *Autobiography.* Edited by James S. Biddle. Philadelphia: E. Claxton, 1883.

Biddle, Walter C. "Doctor John Cochran." *Pennsylvania Magazine of History and Biography* 3 (1879): 241–49.

Bill, Alfred Hoyt. *New Jersey and the Revolutionary War.* New Brunswick, N.J.: Rutgers University Press, 1964.

Billias, George, ed. *George Washington's Generals.* New York: William Morrow & Co., 1964.

Biographical Directory of the American Congress, 1744–1961. Washington, D.C.: United States Government Printing Office, 1961.

Blanton, Wyndham B. *Medicine in Virginia in the Eighteenth Century.* Richmond: The William Byrd Press, 1930.

Bolton, Charles K. *The Private Soldier Under Washington.* New York: Charles Scribner's Sons, 1902.

Boudinot, J. J., Jr., ed. *The Life, Public Services, Addresses and Letters of Elias Boudinot.* 2 vols. Boston: Houghton Mifflin, 1896.

Boyd, Thomas A. *Mad Anthony Wayne.* New York: Charles Scribner's Sons, 1929.

[Bradstreet, John.] *An Impartial Account of Lieut. Col. Bradstreet's Expedition to Fort Frontenac.* London: T. Wilcox, 1759.

Brinkerhoff, T. van Wyck. *Historical Sketch and Directory of the Town of Fishkill.* Fishkill Landing, N.Y.: Dean and Spaight, 1866.

Brown, H. E. *The Medical Department of the United States Army.* Washington, D.C.: Surgeon General's Office, 1873.

Brunhouse, Robert L. *The Counter-Revolution in Pennsylvania, 1776–1790.* Harrisburg: Pennsylvania Historical Commission, 1942.

[Buettner, Johann Carl.] *Narrative of Johann Carl Buettner in the American Revolution.* New York: Charles F. Heartman, 1915.

Burke, John. *A Genealogical and Heraldic Dictionary of the Peerage and Baronetage of the United Kingdom.* 101st ed. London: Burke's Peerage Limited, 1956.

Burnett, Edmund C., ed. *Letters of Members of the Continental Congress.* 8 vols. Washington, D.C.: The Carnegie Institute, 1921–36.

Butterfield, L. H., ed. *Letters of Benjamin Rush.* 2 vols. Princeton: Princeton University Press, 1951.

Campbell, John H. *History of the Friendly Sons of St. Patrick and of the Hibernian Society.* Philadelphia: The Hibernian Society, 1892.

Carney, Sidney H. *Some Medical Men in the Revolution.* New York: Society of the Sons of the Revolution, 1899, pp. 193–208.

Chard, Thornton, ed. "Excerpts form the Private Journal of Dr. John Cochran." *New York History* 25 (1944): 360–78.

——. "Illustrations Pertaining to the Life of Doctor John Cochran." *Bulletin of the History of Medicine* 20 (1946): 76–84.

Chastellux, François Jean. *Travels in North America in the Years 1780, 1781 and 1782.* Translated by Howard C. Rice, Jr. 2 vols. Chapel Hill: University of North Carolina Press, 1963.

Clark, J. Henry. *The Medical Men of New Jersey in Essex District from 1666 to 1866.* Newark: privately printed by the author, 1867.

Clarke, Thomas W. "General John Cochran." *New York State Journal of Medicine* 42 (1942): 798–801.

[Cochran, John.] "Biographical Memoir of John Cochran, M.D.," by E. J. Marsh. *New Jersey Medical Reporter* 2 (1849): 25–28.

——. "Biographical Memoir of the late John Cochran." *American Medical and Philosophical Register* 1 (1811): 465–68.

Cochrane, John. "Medical Department of the Revolutionary Army." *Magazine of American History* 12 (1884): 241–60.

Coleman, John M. *Thomas McKean, Forgotten Leader of the Revolution.* Rockaway, N.J.: American Faculty Press [1975].

Corner, Betty C. *William Shippen Jr., Pioneer in American Medical Education.* Philadelphia: American Philosophical Society, 1951.

Corner, George W., ed. *The Autobiography of Benjamin Rush.* Princeton: Princeton University Press, 1948.

Dalley, Joseph W. *Woodbridge and Vicinity.* New Brunswick, N.J.: A. E. Gordon, 1873.

Dangerfield, George. *Chancellor Robert R. Livingston of New York, 1746–1813.* New York: Harcourt, Brace, 1960.

Desmond, Alice Curtis. *Alexander Hamilton's Wife.* New York: Dodd, Mead, & Co., 1952.

Douglas, Robert B., ed. *A French Volunteer of the War of Independence.* New York: J. B. Bouton, 1897.

Duane, William, ed. *Extracts from the Diary of Christopher Marshall.* Albany, N.Y.: J. Munsell, 1877.

Duer, William A. *New York as it was during the Latter Part of the Last Century.* New York: Stanford and Swords, 1849.

Duffy, John. *Epidemics in Colonial America.* Baton Rouge: Louisiana State University Press, 1953.

Duncan, Louis C. *Medical Men in the American Revolution.* Carlisle Barracks: Medical Field Service, 1931.

Duncan, William, ed. *The New-York Directory and Register for the Year 1794.* New York: T. and J. Swords, 1794.

Dunlap, William. *Diary.* Edited by Dorothy C. Barck. 3 vols. New York: The New-York Historical Society, 1930.

Egle, William H. "Minutes of the Board of Property . . . containing Minute Book K." *Pennsylvania Archives,* 3d series, vol. 1 (1894): 25–110.

Farmer, Laurence. "The Early Directors of the Medical Service of the American Revolutionary Army." *Bulletin of the New York Academy of Medicine* 36 (1960): 765–76.

Ferguson, E. James and John Catanzariti, eds. *The Papers of Robert Morris, 1781–1784.* 2 vols. to date. Pittsburgh: University of Pittsburgh Press, 1973–.

Fitzpatrick, John C., ed. *The Writings of George Washington from the Original Manuscript Sources, 1745–1799.* 39 vols. Washington, D.C.: United States Government Printing Office, 1931–44.

Force, Peter, ed. *American Archives.* 9 vols. Washington, D.C.: Clarke and Force, 1837–53.

Ford, Worthington C., ed. *Correspondence and Journals of Samuel Blachley Webb.* 3 vols. New York: privately printed, 1893–94.

——. ed. *Family Letters of Samuel Blachley Webb, 1764–1807.* New York: privately printed, 1912.

——. *General Orders Issued by Major-General Heath, 23 May 1777–3 October 1777.* Brooklyn: Historical Printing Club, 1890.

Franks, David, ed. *The New-York Directory.* New York: Shepard Kollock, 1786.

Futhey, J. Smith. *Historical Discourses Delivered on the Occasion of the One Hundred and Fiftieth Anniversary of the Upper Octorara Presbyterian Church.* Philadelphia: H. B. Ashmead, 1870.

Futhey, J. Smith, and Gilbert Cope. *History of Chester County, Pennsylvania.* Philadelphia: L. H. Everts, 1881.

Gerlach, Don R. *Philip Schuyler and the American Revolution in New York.* Lincoln: University of Nebraska Press, 1964.

Gibbes, Robert W. *Documentary History of the American Revolution.* 3 vols. New York: D. Appleton & Co., 1853–57.

Gibson, James E. *Dr. Bodo Otto and the Medical Background of the American Revolution.* Springfield, Ill.: Charles C. Thomas, 1937.

Gordon, Maurice Bear. *Aesculapius Comes to the Colonies.* Ventnor, N.J.: Ventnor Publishers, Inc., 1949.

Gottschalk, Louis. *Lafayette Joins the American Army.* Chicago: University of Chicago Press, 1937.

Gottschalk, Louis, ed. *The Letters of Lafayette to Washington, 1777–1797.* New York: privately printed by Helen Fahnestock Hubbard, 1944.

Grant, Anne. *Memoirs of an American Lady.* 2 vols. London: Longman et al., 1808.

Graves, Charles B. "Dr. Philip Turner of Norwich, Connecticut." *Annals of Medical History* 10 (1928): 1–24.

Greene, George W. *Life of Nathanael Greene, Major-General in the Army of the Revolution.* 3 vols. New York: G. P. Putnam and Sons (vol. 1); Hurd and Houghton (vols. 2 and 3), 1867–71.

Greene, Nelson. *The Old Mohawk Turnpike Book.* Fort Plain, N.Y., 1924.

Grieffenhagen, George A. "Drug Supplies in the American Revolution." *National Museum Bulletin*, no. 225, paper 16. Washington, D.C., 1961.

Guerra, Francisco. *American Medical Bibliography, 1639–1738.* New York: Lathrop C. Harper, Inc., 1962.

[Halsey, Edward D.] *History of Morris County, New Jersey.* New York: J. Munsell, 1882.

Hamilton, Edward P. *The French and Indian Wars.* Garden City, N.Y.: Doubleday, 1962.

Hand, Edward. "Orderly Book of General Edward Hand." *Pennsylvania Magazine of History and Biography* 41 (1917): 198–223, 257–73, 458–67.

Hatch, Louis C. *The Administration of the American Revolutionary Army.* New York: Longman, Green and Co., 1904.

Hawke, David F. *Benjamin Rush, Revolutionary Gadfly.* Indianapolis: Bobbs-Merrill, 1971.

Heitman, Francis B. *Historical Register of Officers of the Continental Army during the War of the Revolution, April, 1775 to December, 1783.* Washington, D.C.: Rare Book Shop Publishing Co., 1914.

Hill, William H. *Old Fort Edward before 1800.* Ft. Edward, N.Y.: privately printed, 1929.

Houghton, Ida Cochran. *Chronicles of the Cochrans.* 2 vols. Columbus, Ohio: Stoneman Press Co., 1915; F. J. Heen Printing Co., 1935.

Hoyt, Max E. et al. *Index of Revolutionary War Pensions Applications.* Washington, D.C., 1943–.

Humphreys, Frank L. *Life and Times of David Humphreys.* 2 vols. New York: G. P. Putnam's Sons, 1917.

Humphreys, Mary Gay. *Catherine Schuyler.* New York: Charles Scribner's Sons, 1897.

Hunter, Thomas M. "Doctor Samuel Adams, Revolutionary Army Surgeon and Diarist." *United States Armed Forces Journal* 8 (1957): 625–43.

Ives, Mabel Lorenz. *Washington's Morristown Headquarters.* [Montclair, N.J., 1932.]

Jones, Alfred E. "The Loyalists in New Jersey in the Revolution." *Proceedings of the New Jersey Historical Society*, n.s., vol. 12 (1927): 1–55.

Jones, John. *Plain Concise Practical Remarks on the Treatment of Wounds and Fractures. . . .* Philadelphia: Robert Bell, 1776.

Jones, Joseph H. *The Life of Ashbel Green, V.D.M.* New York: R. Carter & Bros., 1849.

Jordan, John W. "The Military Hospital at Bethlehem and Lititz during the Revolution." *Pennsylvania Magazine of History and Biography* 20 (1896): 137–57.

Journals of the Continental Congress, 1774–1789. Edited by Worthington C. Ford, et al. 34 vols. Washington, D.C.: United States Government Printing Office, 1904–37.

Kapp, Friedrich. *The Life of John Kalb.* New York: H. Holt and Co., 1884.

Keith, Charles P. *Chronicles of Pennsylvania from the English Revolution to the Peace of Aix-La-Chapelle, 1688–1748.* 2 vols. Philadelphia: Patterson & White Co., 1917.

Kieffer, John S. "Philadelphia Controversy, 1775–1780." *Bulletin of the History of Medicine* 11 (1942): 148–60.

Kinnan, M. E., ed. *Order Book kept by Peter Kinnan, July 7–Sept. 4, 1776.* Princeton: Princeton University Press, 1931.

Ladenhaim, Jules Calvin. "The 'Doctors' Mob' of 1788." *Journal of the History of Medicine and the Allied Sciences* 5 (1950): 23–43.

Lamb, Martha J. *History of the City of New York.* 2 vols. New York: A. S. Barnes Co., 1877–80.

Lee, Arthur. *Lee Papers.* 4 vols. New York: The New-York Historical Society, 1872–75.

Lee, Richard Henry. *Memoir of the Life of Richard Henry Lee.* 2 vols. Philadelphia: H. C. Carey and I. Lea, 1825.

Livingston, Edwin B. *The Livingstons of Livingston Manor.* New York: The Knickerbocker Press, 1910.

[Lossing, Benson J.] "General Hospitals of the Revolution." *The American Historical Record* 3 (1874): 289–91.

——. *Hours with the Living Men and Women of the Revolution.* New York: Funk and Wagnalls, 1889.

——. *The Life and Times of Philip Schuyler.* 2 vols. New York: Sheldon & Co., 1872–73.

——. *The Pictorial Field-Book of the American Revolution.* 2 vols. New York: Harper and Brothers, 1851–52.

MacFarlan, Douglas. "Locations of Military Hospitals for the Continental Army, 1777–8." *The Picket Post* (Valley Forge) no. 89 (July 1965): 24–25.

McGregor, R. W. David. *History of Freemasonry in New Jersey*, n.p., c. 1937.

MacHenry, James. "Revolutionary Correspondence of Dr. James McHenry." *Pennsylvania Magazine of History and Biography* 29 (1905): 57–58.

McLachlan, James. *Princetonians 1748–1768: A Biographical Dictionary.* Princeton: Princeton University Press, 1976.

McLenahan, Richard L. "The New Jersey Medical History in the Colonial Period." In *Proceedings of the New Jersey Historical Society,* n.s., vol. 10 (1925): 362–74.

[MacWethy, Lou D.] *The Old Palatine Church together with a Description of the Gen. John Cochran House by Milo Nellis.* 3d ed. St. Johnsville, N.Y.: Press of the Enterprise and News, 1930.

Mailler, Marion M. and Janet T. Dempsey. *18th Century Homes in New Windsor.* Vailsgate, N.Y.: National Temple Hill Association, 1968.

Martin, Joseph Plumb. *A Narrative of some of the Adventures, Dangers and Sufferings of a Revolutionary Soldier.* Edited by George F. Scheer. New York: New York Times, 1968.

[Medical Society of New Jersey.] *The Rise, Minutes and Proceedings of the New Jersey Medical Society Established July 23d, 1776.* Newark: Jennings and Hardham, 1875.

Middleton, William S. "Medicine at Valley Forge." *Annals of Medical History,* 3d series, vol. 3 (1941): 461–86.

——. "William Shippen, Jr." *Annals of Medical History,* n.s., vol. 4 (1932): 440–52, 538–49.

Miller, John C. *Origins of the American Revolution.* Boston: Little, Brown, & Co., 1943.

——. *Triumph of Freedom, 1775–1783.* Boston: Little, Brown, & Co., 1948.

Mills, W. Jay. *Historic Houses of New Jersey.* Philadelphia: J. B. Lippincott Co., 1902.

Monro, Donald. *An Account of the Diseases which were most frequent in the British Military Hospitals in Germany.* London: A. Millar, 1764.

Moore, George H. "The Treason of Charles Lee." In *Lee Papers* 4: 335–427.

Morais, Herbert M. "Doctors and the American Revolution." *Schriftenreihe für Geschichte der Naturwissenschaften Technik und Medizin* (1965): 99–120.

Neill, Edward D. "Biographical Sketch of Dr. Jonathan Potts." *New England Historical Genealogical Register* 18 (1864): 21–36.

——. *A Contribution to the Medical History of the American Army during the War for Independence.* St. Paul, Minn.: Macalester College, 1860.

[New Jersey.] *Documents Relating to the Revolutionary History of the State of New Jersey.* Edited by William S. Stryker et al. 5 vols. Trenton: imprint varies, 1901–17.

[New York City.] *Minutes of the Common Council of the City of New York, 1675–1776.* 8 vols. New York: Dodd, Mead & Co., 1905.

Nolan, J. Bennett. *Lafayette in America Day by Day.* Baltimore: Johns Hopkins University Press, 1934.

O'Callaghan, Edmund B., ed. *Calendar of Historical Manuscripts in the Office of the Secretary of State.* 2 vols. Albany, N.Y.: Weed, Parsons, & Co., 1865–66.

——. *The Documentary History of the State of New York.* 4 vols. Albany, N.Y.: Weed, Parsons & Co., 1850–51.

Orth, Samuel P. *Our Foreigners, A Chronicle of Americans in the Making.* New Haven: Yale University Press, 1921.

Owen, William D., ed. *The Medical Department of the United States Army during the Period of the Revolution. The Legislative and Administrative History, 1776–1786.* New York: Paul B. Hoeber, 1920.

Packard, Francis R. *History of Medicine in the United States.* 2 vols. New York: Paul B. Hoeber, 1931.

Peterkin, A. and William Johnston, eds. *Commissioned Officers of the Medical Services of the British Army, 1660–1960.* 2 vols. London: The Wellcome Historical Medical Library, 1968.

Peterson, A. Everett. "John Cochran." In *Dictionary of American Biography* 4 (1930): 251–52.

Phalen, James M. "John Cochran." *Army Medical Bulletin* 52 (April 1940): 14–17.

Pilcher, James E. *The Surgeon Generals of the Army of the United States of America.* Carlisle Pa.: The Association of Military Surgeons, 1905.

Pinkowski, Edward. *Washington's Officers Slept Here.* Philadelphia: Sunshine Press, 1953.

Preston, Richard A. and Leopold Lamontagne. *Royal Fort Frontenac.* Toronto: Champlain Society, 1958.

Radbill, Samuel. "Francis Alison, Jr." *Bulletin of the History of Medicine* 8 (1941): 243–57.

Ray, F. M., ed. *Journal of Dr. Caleb Rea.* Salem, Mass., 1881.

Reed, John F., comp. *A History of the Pennsylvania Campaign and Valley Forge 1777–1778 as Depicted by Original Material of the Author in the Valley Forge National Park Library.* 2 vols., n.p.

Roberts, Octavia. *With Lafayette in America.* Boston: Houghton Mifflin, 1919.

Rogers, Fred B. and A. Reasoner Sayre. *The Healing Art, A History of the Medical Society of New Jersey.* Trenton: Medical Society of New Jersey, 1966.

Ruston, Thomas. *An Essay on Inoculation for the Smallpox.* London: J. Payne, 1767.

Sabine, William H. W., ed. *Historical Memoirs of William Smith.* 2 vols. New York: New York Times, Arno Press, 1969–71.

Saffell, William T. R. *Records of the Revolutionary War.* New York: Pudney and Russell, 1858.

Saffron, Morris H. "Confrontation in New Jersey: The Hospital versus the Line." *Journal of the Medical Society of New Jersey* 73 (1976): 1081–87.

——. "The Tilton Affair." *Journal of the American Medical Association* 236 (1976): 67–72.

Scharf, John T. *History of Delaware, 1609–1888.* 2 vols. Philadelphia: L. J. Richards & Co., 1888.

Schuyler, George W. *Colonial New York: Philip Schuyler and his Family.* 2 vols. New York: Charles Scribner's Sons, 1885.

Schuyler, John. *Institutions of the Society of the Cincinnati, 1783.* New York: Douglas Taylor, 1886.

Sherman, Andrew M. *Historic Morristown, New Jersey: The Story of its First Century.* Morristown: The Howard Publishing Co., 1905.

Sherwood, Sidney. *The University of the State of New York.* Washington, D.C.: United States Government Printing Office, 1900.

Shryock, Richard. *Medical Licensing in America, 1650–1965.* Baltimore: Johns Hopkins University Press, 1967.

Shute, Daniel. "Journal." *New England Historical and Genealogical Register* 84 (1930): 382–89.

Smith, William H., ed. *The St. Clair Papers.* 2 vols. Cincinnati: R. Clarke & Co., 1882.

Sparks, Jared, ed. *Correspondence of the American Revolution, being Letters of Eminent Men to George Washington.* 4 vols. Boston: Little, Brown, & Co., 1853.

——. *Life of Washington.* Boston: Tappan, Whittemore and Mason, 1849; 3 vol. extra-illustrated copy, The New-York Historical Society, 1856.

Steiner, Bernard C. *The Life and Correspondence of James McHenry.* Cleveland: The Burrows Brothers Co., 1907.

Stone, William L. *Life of Joseph Brant (Thayendanegea) Including the Border Wars.* 2 vols. Albany, N.Y.: J. Munsell, 1865.

Stookey, Byron P. *A History of Colonial Medical Education in the Province of New York.* Springfield, Ill.: Charles C. Thomas [1962].

Stryker, William S. *The Battle of Monmouth.* Edited by William Starr Myers. Princeton: Princeton University Press, 1927.

——. ed. *Official Register of the Officers and Men of New Jersey in the Revolutionary War.* Trenton: W. T. Nicholson, 1872.

——. *"The New Jersey Volunteers": Loyalists in the Revolutionary War.* Trenton: Nash, Day and Naar, 1887.

Sullivan, John. *Letters and Papers of Major-General John Sullivan.* Edited by Otis G. Hammond. 3 vols. Concord: New Hampshire Historical Society, 1930–39.

Syrett, Harold C., ed. *The Papers of Alexander Hamilton.* 24 vols. to date. New York: Columbia University Press, 1961–.

Thacher, James. *American Medical Biography: or Memoirs of Eminent Physicians who have flourished in America.* 2 vols. Boston: Richardson and Lord, 1828.

——. *A Military Journal during the American Revolutionary War from 1775 to 1783.* Boston: Richardson and Lord, 1823.

Thane, Elswyth. *Washington's Lady.* New York: Dodd, Mead & Co., 1960.

Thomas, Milton Halsey, ed. "The Memoirs of William Cochran." *The New-York Historical Society Quarterly* 38 (1954): 54–83.

Thoms, Herbert. "Albigence Waldo, Surgeon: His Diary Written at Valley Forge." *Annals of Medical History* 10 (1928): 486–97.

Tilton, James. *Economical Observations on Military Hospitals*. Wilmington: J. Wilson, 1813.

Torres-Reyes, Ricardo. *1779–1780 Encampment (Morristown): A Study of Medical Services*. Washington, D.C.: National Park Service, 1971.

Turner, John Brown, ed. *Journal and Order Book of Captain Robert Kirkwood*. Wilmington: The Historical Society of Delaware, 1910.

Turner, Joseph Brown, ed. "The Records of Londonderry Congregation, now Fagg's Manor, Chester County, Pa." *Journal of the Presbyterian Historical Society* 8 (1915–16): 343–79.

Tuttle, Joseph F. *Annals of Morris County*, n.p., c. 1870.

Van Doren, Carl. *Secret History of the American Revolution*. New York: The Viking Press, 1941.

Waldo, Albigence, "Valley Forge 1777–1778 Diary of Surgeon Albigence Waldo of the Connecticut Line." *Pennsylvania Magazine of History and Biography* 21 (1897): 299–323.

Wall, John P. *The Chronicles of New Brunswick*. New Brunswick, N.J.: Thatcher-Anderson Co., 1931.

Walker, Lewis Burd, ed. *Selections from Letters written by Edward Burd, 1763–1828*. Pottsville, Pa.: Standard Publishing Co., 1899.

Wallace, Paul A. W. "Historic Hope Lodge." *Pennsylvania Magazine of History and Biography* 86 (1962): 115–42.

Warren, Edward. *The Life of John Warren, M.D.* Boston: Noyes, Holmes and Co., 1874.

Washington, George. *The Calendar of the Correspondence of George Washington*. 4 vols. Washington, D.C.: United States Government Printing Office, 1915.

——. *Orderly Book of General Washington kept at Valley Forge, 18 May-11 June, 1778*. Edited by A. P. C. Griffin. Boston: Lamson, Wolffe and Co., 1898.

Webster, Richard. *A History of the Presbyterian Church in America*. Philadelphia: Joseph M. Wilson, 1857.

Weedon, George. *Calendar of the Correspondence of Brigadier-General George Weedon, Hon. Richard Henry Lee, Hon. Arthur Lee, and Major-General Nathanael Greene*. Philadelphia: American Philosophical Society, 1900.

——. *Valley Forge Orderly Book in the Campaign of 1777–1778*. New York: Dodd, Mead & Co., 1902.

Weise, Arthur J. *The History of the City of Albany, New York*. Albany, N.Y.: R. H. Bender, 1884.

Wells, Walter A. "Washington's Predilection for Doctors and Doctoring." *Virginia Medical Monthly* 66 (1939): 65–68.

Whitehead, John. *Washington at Morristown*. Newark: Advertising Printing House, 1899.

Wickes, Stephen. *History of Medicine in New Jersey and of Its Medical Men, from the Settlement of the Province to A.D. 1800*. Newark: M. R. Dennis & Co., 1879.

Wilkinson, James, *Memoirs of My Own Time.* 3 vols. Philadelphia: A Small, 1816.

Wilson, Commissary. *Commissary Wilson's Orderly Book: Expedition of the British and Provincial Army under Major General Jeffrey Amherst against Ticonderoga and Crown Point, 1759.* Albany, N.Y.: J. Munsell, 1857.

Wilson, James Grant, ed. *The Memorial History of the City of New York.* 4 vols. New York: New York History Co., 1892–93.

Wright-St. Clair, Rex E. *Doctors Monro, A Medical Saga.* London: The Wellcome Historical Medical Library, 1964.

BIOGRAPHICAL INDEX

Note on the Index

Biographical data were compiled from innumerable sources, including the Dictionary of National Biography, the Dictionary of American Biography, records of the Daughters of the American Revolution and other patriotic societies, military histories of the various states, abstracts of wills, family genealogies, church records, etc. When authorities differed as to dates, those adopted appeared to be the most reliable. The spelling of a name in the Index may differ from that found in the text of the correspondence. Generally, the state of origin or permanent residence has been added.